Theatre 74

FRONTISPIECE: The new man at the National: Peter Hall

Theatre 74

**Plays
Players
Playwrights
Theatres
Opera
Ballet**

Edited by SHERIDAN MORLEY

HUTCHINSON OF LONDON

Hutchinson & Co. (Publishers) Ltd
3 Fitzroy Square, London W1

London Melbourne Sydney Auckland
Wellington Johannesburg Cape Town
and agencies throughout the world

First published 1974
© Hutchinson & Co. (Publishers) Ltd 1974

Set in Monotype Scotch Roman
Printed in Great Britain by The Anchor Press Ltd
and bound by Wm Brendon & Son Ltd
both of Tiptree, Essex

ISBN 0 09 122290 7

Contents

Illustrations

The numbers below refer to the chapters; the photographs are keyed by letters within each chapter.

Sheridan Morley

Prologue

An uneasy twelvemonth for the British theatre: the imposition of VAT, the petrol shortage, the railway drivers' go-slow, rising wages, rates and insurance costs together with the slump in the economy (coming as it did at a time when the cost of going to a play was, in London at any rate, already becoming prohibitive) all added up to a year in which survival was the main achievement. A glance at the first-night listings in our reference section will indicate that it has been a safe and cautious time in the West End, while of the two leading subsidized companies the National has been in a state of transience and the RSC in one of curious indecision.

In this atmosphere it was perhaps not surprising that Equity should have returned by majority vote to more conservative postures, nor that the long-awaited revival of the home-grown English musical should at last have become a reality . . . in times of austerity the theatre has ever been escapist. Nevertheless, all else was not gloom and despondency: at the Old Vic Peter Hall, who succeeded Olivier in November, dispelled rumours of a merger with the RSC he himself had formed a decade earlier and instead announced an ambitious programme of eight new productions to carry the National company into their three new homes on the South Bank – now due for occupation in April 1975. More significantly, he also announced an extended touring programme at home and abroad and the intention to keep the new National complex open day and night, Sundays included. Earlier, the outgoing Olivier management triumphantly fought off the threat of a sky-scraper hotel on an adjoining South Bank site.

Elsewhere there was also some cause for optimism: new theatres opened in Leicester and Farnham and at New End in Hampstead, whilst on the outer fringes of the West End theatres were reclaimed from a still more ailing film industry in Regent Street and the King's Road, Chelsea. And despite a warning note sounded in the Richards Report (sixteen theatres have been lost to London since 1936) there were signs that other cinemas – such as the Kilburn Empire – would soon return to their rightful function as live theatres. North of the border the Edinburgh Opera House is going ahead despite an estimated cost of £12 million and flagging Festival fortunes, whilst a two-month festival of Scottish theatre came as a sharp reminder that the English have no monopoly of young playwrights.

The Save London Theatres Campaign saved the Shaftesbury from total demolition (it had begun to collapse of its own accord, thereby abruptly ending the run of *Hair*) but sadly not from closure, and although plans to demolish theatres in the Covent Garden and Charing Cross Road areas have mercifully been abandoned for the present, the Criterion remains in some danger. But if the present and the future of the British theatre are at certain financial and architectural risks, its past is now reasonably secure: the British Theatre Museum, due to open shortly in Somerset House, will hopefully provide for theatre historians and students some of the services that film researchers have long been able to take for granted from the BFI. In the regions, new theatres were announced for Hornchurch and Derby, the Blackpool Grand was temporarily saved, and arts centres were scheduled for Plymouth and Aston.

Thames Television announced a new series of grants to young playwrights from all over the country and although the Preservation Bill was left unpassed at the dissolution of the last parliament there was no reason to suppose that the new Minister for the Arts (Hugh Jenkins) would be any less zealous in the theatres' cause than was his Conservative predecessor Norman St John Stevas.

Abroad the RSC, the Actors' Company and the Young Vic had considerable success in America, though with the demise of the World Theatre Seasons and Equity's understandable reluctance to allow Soviet companies to visit Britain until USSR artists were granted more freedom there was less reciprocal touring than of late.

All in all then, a year of mixed verdicts but, as is I hope reflected in the chapters which follow, by no means one of utter despair or retrenchment. In this the fourth annual of its series the intention is once again to provide a kind of international theatrical balance sheet, a picture of the theatre past, present and future as it appears to a widely assorted group of critics, actors, playwrights and directors in each passing year. For this purpose I have taken 'theatre' to include plays, musicals, operas and ballets both conventional and experimental, commercial and subsidized, at home and abroad.

In these nineteen chapters (all but one making their first appearance in print) will again be found comment, criticism, idealism, despair, optimism, fear, ambition, admiration, distaste and nostalgia . . . in short most of the elements that have constituted the theatre in the past twelve months and indeed the past twelve centuries.

For their help in the preparation of this book my thanks must go first as always to the contributors themselves, and equally to the Arts Council of Great Britain for their support; I am additionally grateful to Judith Marten for providing reference material in the fields of opera and ballet. For other information contained in the reference section I owe thanks to *The Stage* and *Plays & Players* as well as to Craig Macdonald at the National Theatre and Peter Harlock at the RSC. For Ian McKellen's Actor's Diary I owe thanks to the arts editor of *The Times* in whose pages it first appeared in a slightly abbreviated form.

For photographs, I am especially grateful to Roy Smith at *Plays & Players* as well as the press officers of the Old Vic, the RSC, the Mermaid, the Actors' Company and innumerable other theatre, ballet and opera companies up and down the land. For archive pictures Ray Mander and Joe Mitchenson have been as always invaluable, and further thanks are due to a sizeable army of theatrical photographers.

Finally, an acknowledgement to Wendy Garcin for her help in typing the reference section and to Harold Harris and the production staff at Hutchinson for the infinite care taken in the publication of these annuals. One last word of annual thanks: to you, whoever and wherever you are, for continuing to support what I and a reassuring number of others believe to be a worthwhile project.

Jottings from Puddle Dock

The founder and artistic director of the Mermaid Theatre recalls its creation and replies to its critics.

The Mermaid was founded in 1951 at our home in Acacia Road, St John's Wood, where we occupied an old boys' school with Assembly Hall attached. There Kirsten Flagstad sang Purcell's *Dido and Aeneas* twice nightly for thirty-six performances, in a triple bill with *Macbeth* performed in a reconstruction of Elizabethan pronunciation and Middleton's comedy *A Trick to Catch the Old One*. This twice nightly pattern was pursued at the Royal Exchange in 1953 and later at Puddle Dock in 1959, along with a shuttle service in our restaurant. Thus you could have dinner and see the show, or see the show and then have dinner. This routine was continued for our first seven years and whatever the frequent roughness and lack of polish I am proud to have done one hundred and fourteen consecutive performances of the *Wakefield Mystery Plays*, and sixty each of *The Witch of Edmonton, The Maid's Tragedy, 'Tis Pity She's a Whore, Eastward Ho!*, three O'Caseys, five Greeks, five GBS, etc. – all on a tiny grant-in aid (£5000 rising to £8000 a year), something which I imagine will never be attempted again.

Although the twice nightly system has much to commend it as a working policy, many actors are naturally unwilling to submit to such a Zatopek-like regimen. But if I could afford to duplicate my leading actors and double up on certain members of staff I would do it again, though with one proviso, you can't cut important plays like Brecht's *Galileo* or *John Gabriel Borkman* to two hours fifteen minutes. But plenty of GBS, O'Casey and nearly all the minor Elizabethans and Jacobeans and most modern plays like *The Bedsitting Room, All In Good Time* and *Alfie* fall well within the twice nightly range. Besides, we only managed to survive by serving two dinners a night.

On the catering front my advice to anyone setting up a theatre even remotely resembling the Mermaid would be, run it yourself. It's a headache; I have to learn much about the art of fiddling and how to set up proper controls. But at its worst Mermaid Catering has never contributed less than £8000 a year to the theatre and at boom periods more like £18000, to supplement subsidy from central government funds and other sources.

At the beginning we were all pretty raw and inexperienced. Our first manager Stephen Croft had to stuff the day's box office takings into his pockets, sometimes £800 or £900 at a time, take them back to his digs and hide them under the mattress before banking them next morning. Then it dawned on us that we ought to buy a safe.

The day we opened, May 29th 1959, the Master of one of the Livery Companies warned me against letting any of our actresses appear in the Square Mile in trousers. 'The City won't stand for that,' he said. But in due course it did, just as it did for the mini skirt, and just as I suppose it will in due course stand for young stockbrokers streaking and for a lady Lord Mayor.

There was angry debate in Common Council over *Lock Up Your Daughters* because, although an exceedingly moral piece, the word 'rape' occurs sixteen times therein. There was also violent objection to the title chosen by John Arden for his Magna Carta play – *Left Handed Liberty*. 'We don't want any of that left nonsense down here,' shouted one committee member. 'It's all very well in Sloane Square but not in the Square Mile.' And when it was discovered that the play contained the line 'Fetch me three strong whores from Billingsgate' a deputation waited on the Lord Mayor urging him to exercise his power of veto over Arden, Miles and Mermaid. But Lord Mayor Sir James Miller, a liberal and resolute Scot, came down on the side of the angels and the three strong whores stayed in. The same week I received an undercover visit from a member of the committee which had objected to the title of

the play, asking if I could persuade Mr Arden to include Simon de
Montfort in the piece as the said Simon was one of his ancestors.
This regardless of the fact that de Montfort doesn't make his
appearance in history until fifty years later.

We have been three times flooded, on one occasion actually
suffering a regurgitation of sewage into the stalls – and had a large
piece carved off our north-west corner to enable articulated lorries
to drive past without smashing through into the coffee bar.

The problem with theatres like the Mermaid and the Royal
Court, Stratford East, Greenwich and the fifty or so civic theatres
trying to earn their living as permanent institutions rather than on
a run-of-the-play investment basis is that you can easily have (and
the Mermaid has had) five or six box office failures in a row,
leaving you £20000 or £30000 or £40000 or £50000 (or in our case
£65000) in the red, with only the hard-pressed Arts Council (who
often have a dozen or so other theatres in a similar pickle) to bail
you out – unless (as in the Mermaid's case) you have a few good
friends like RTZ, Unilever, Ladbrokes and a number of lesser but
no less generous friends to toss you a lifebelt until you can start
swimming again. All this not necessarily on account of bad work
but because some of our best work, like the New York Theatre
Company's *The Brig* and Henry James's *The Other House*, Huntley
Harding's *Licentious Fly* and Terence Feeley's *Bandwagon*, despite
clever production, delightful performances and in many cases
excellent notices, didn't draw at the box office. By the same token
Bill Naughton's *Spring and Port Wine*, chosen as a stop-gap, cast
and rehearsed on the spur of the moment, and as a play far below
the standard of his *All In Good Time* and *Alfie*, made a small
fortune, especially for him.

The West End manager who God knows has problems enough
and whom God bless for his unflagging zeal in finding angels and
providing bread and butter for a regular proportion of Equity's
hungry mouths, has one great advantage. He rarely reads the
notices but goes into the foyer at a quarter to ten the morning
after the first night. If the telephone starts ringing at ten to ten
and there are another thirty calls between then and eleven, he
books a plane to Nice or the Canary Islands and gives himself a
holiday. If the phone only rings once, and that from a lady who has
booked in advance and now wants her money back, he puts the

notice up, drops a line to the angels who have contributed anything up to £200000 of hard cash to capitalize the show and leaves them to lick their wounds, keeping the theatre dark on a skeleton staff until the next attraction turns up. In other words he cuts his losses and gets out, which is something the institutional theatre cannot do. We can offer no inducement to angels. We have to carry our losses from play to play. No chance to ring up the backers and say better luck next time.

In our case the problem was for the first five years complicated by the fact that the warehouse at Puddle Dock (admittedly one of the most seminal theatrical conceptions of the past two hundred years, both physically and in mode of operation) was built by public subscription, personal friends chipping in with fivers and tenners, smaller financial and commercial concerns with fifties and hundreds and one or two of the giants with a thousand or two. But we still opened with a deficit of £55000, which we stupidly paid off out of *Lock Up Your Daughters* revenue instead of stacking it away against the inevitable rainy day and keeping the building fund open.

The consequence was that the £55000 deficit kept reappearing in very pressing terms until the City Corporation and the Arts Council, brought together in one of Arnold Goodman's less publicized but no less felicitous pieces of orchestration, agreed to cough up the capital shortfall pound-for-pound and give us a fresh start.

As to policy we were in a difficulty. George Devine had collared the field of the new drama and as he resoundingly proved was far better equipped for that bit of the crusade than I could ever have been. I simply had a green theatrical thumb, the 'not ignoble ambition' of changing the shape of theatres and their mode of operation. My wife and I had towards the end of the war taken a little revue to the Home Fleet, performing it wherever space could be found above or below decks, on gun sites, in Nissen huts and once on a bare platform lashed between two of HM destroyers *Orwell* and *Opportune*. And it was impossible not to enjoy the freedom and intimacy of such an arrangement. Then I read somewhere that Diderot had defined theatre as 'two planks and a passion'. Lastly I read John Crawford-Adam's book on the Globe Theatre and became infected with the Elizabethan bug. So when in 1951 the opportunity came to build a tiny playhouse in the back garden of our home in St John's Wood and later, in 1953, set up a stage in the central courtyard of the Royal Exchange it was to the classics that we turned, with the concentration very much on methods of staging, especially those which might have been used in the sixteenth and seventeenth centuries: mansions, traps, ropes, pulleys, etc. And when the City leased us the site at Puddle Dock our minds were still locked into the problems of relationship between actor and audience, overflowing into questions of foyer space and catering.

In the event we thought it wise to announce something as all-embracing and flexible as possible, basing it on two general planks: (1) to give a bird's eye view of the world's drama in ten years – or as it may now turn out, thirty or forty years – and (2) to bridge the gap between highbrow and lowbrow by way of under-standability. On the whole I think this policy has been faithfully pursued. Since its opening the Mermaid has presented 136 produc-tions, including six Greek, seven Shakespeare, seven neglected Elizabethan or Jacobean, two Scandinavian, two Russian, six English Classic Revivals, five French, nine Irish, one Italian, fifteen GBS, four German, seven American, five Christmas plays, six musicals and thirty new plays, twelve of which were transferred to West End theatres following their brief scheduled run at Puddle Dock.

I have often been asked why we don't have a permanent company. The answer is simple. For the Mermaid we would require a corps of something like thirty-five under permanent contract, a figure way beyond our means. The only solution was to cast from play to play. Besides, the repertoire system, with the many advantages it undoubtedly has, rules out the transfer of productions to the West End, from which it is possible to derive valuable additional revenue. We could never have stayed afloat without the profit made from *Lock Up Your Daughters, Let's Get a Divorce, Alfie, All In Good Time, The Bedsitting Room, Hadrian VII, Spring and Port Wine* and our other transfers.

Over the whole fifteen-year period since we opened, our gross overall turnover has been nearly £4000000 against total revenue grants from all sources, Arts Council, local authorities and private donations, of just over £296000. In other words a shortfall of 7·4 per cent for the whole period.

Our most important piece of work has been the Molecule Club, which is devoted to infecting the imaginations of young people between the ages of seven and eleven with the wonders of the physical world, the miraculous laws of light, heat, sound, mechanics, magnetism and electricity, etc. We believe these to form a very necessary counter-balance to the literary fantasy which forms the chief part of children's entertainment. It is certainly a field almost untouched in run-of-the-mill primary school education. We all agree that technology has landed us into the fix we now find ourselves in, but it is just as certain that only the application of technology can get us out of it. The children come in school time accompanied by teachers. They pay 30p for admission, the schools pay their fare and the local education authorities do the actual booking.

Thus, in addition to sowing the most exciting ideas in young minds, the Molecule Club has as its second aim teaching children that the living theatre is a thrilling and colourful place, and we hope that some of them will make theatre-going a firm habit in later life.

Twelve years ago, in one of our darkest hours, Frank Hauser gave me a priceless piece of advice: 'Remember that no theatre of our kind has ever failed for want of money, only from lack of momentum.' And sad to say the nearest we ever came to going under was in 1962 when I ventured to present the English première of Mayakovsky's *The Bed Bug*. This was a vast and perhaps foolish undertaking for such a tiny theatre – a cast of thirty with six understudies. But on the whole the dailies gave it a warm and generous welcome and we looked forward to reading the Sundays, one of which as we well knew could make a vast difference at the box office.

Now the end of the play, when Prisipkin, the faithful party worker of the 1920s, is melted out of the block of ice in which he became imprisoned when one of the guests at his dreadful bourgeois wedding knocked an oil lamp over and set the house afire, leaving the local fire brigade to pump the place full of water, is so shocking and in its way so moving that I felt justified in dispensing with curtain calls. Three days later opening the *Sunday Times* I found that Harold Hobson had seized upon this (perhaps a defect in judgement, but nothing to do with the play or its performance) to relegate his notice to the last few lines of his column with the chilling words:

I conclude from the deliberate way in which the management crush the applause at the end of *The Bed Bug* (Mermaid) that Bernard Miles desires in London only the minimum of comment on Mayakovsky's satire. I will respect his wishes, noting only that he thereby deprives himself of a review which would have overwhelmed him with pleasure and pride.

Ten days later in the *Christian Science Monitor*, published in Boston, Mass, which only a few in England read and which has no effect at all on the box office, he wrote: 'The play is presented at the Mermaid with wonderful variety and color . . . I can do no other than record that it is one of the most remarkable theatrical experiences I have ever had.' Thus a senior critic whose praise, admittedly deserved, could have brought an extra thousand pounds a week to the box office dealt a rabbit punch to a tiny and by any token brave little venture, from which it took a couple of years to recover. I shall never cease to wonder why our Harold thought fit to deliver such an unkind cut.

I am also reminded of a BBC critics programme in June 1967, when the delectable Dilys Powell made a Silly Billy of herself with Alexander Walker, John Bowen, Edward Lucie-Smith and a young man named Basil Taylor, discussing the four plays of Euripides I had ventured to bind into a simple composite presentation entitled *The Trojan Wars*. It had been announced on the pre-production leaflet that the aim was to see whether these great but difficult plays stripped down to their bones still carried the kind of dramatic weight they were renowned for. The four gents named above served up such a parody of criticism that my granddaughter ran to fetch me saying 'The Goons are on'. Because I put Clytemnestra into a small and very becoming fur hat one of these brilliant fellows hit on the word 'toque' and everyone giggled. Indeed they giggled again and again. Then they referred to the very biblical word 'slain' as 'fustian' and said they would have preferred 'killed'! I have a transcript of this performance which I hope one day with the BBC's permission to publish in its entirety to show to what a pitiful level criticism can sink.

One has the uneasy feeling that the critics feel themselves to be a tribe of know-alls, the ex-officio Herman Kahns of the dramatic world, that they know exactly how it should have been done and what a pity it was they weren't there to tell us. I suppose that in a period of cultural confusion and the break-up of all recently accepted values criticism is bound to be at a loss for landmarks and warning lights, but what fun it would be if directors and actors could occasionally have space to reply. We accept with pleasure a theatre, and indeed life in general, based upon cut and thrust, but a world which is all cut and no thrust is difficult to endure especially when the most modest group of actors could, given the chance, tie the critics into knots.

At the moment we are in the thick of everyone 'doing his own thing'. This leads to the gimmick and the happening and the suddenly dreamed-up recipe for personal expression (which is in reality about as far from genuine spontaneity as one could possibly get) and this tendency naturally overflows into the arena of criticism. If the artist, writer, actor, composer or whatever, is to be commended for having reached the illusory freedom of doing his own thing and nothing but his own thing, with no concern for tradition or social reference or effect upon others, then why should the critic be compelled to act as a serious mediator between art and audience? Why should not his response to the artist's 'thing' be the doing of his own thing?

There has always been a strong tendency in journalistic criticism to write for effect. The work (in our case the play) inevitably becomes less and less important except as having provided the initial impact that sends the critic off in his own orbit, a sort of launching pad. The need is to prove that the critic has a personality which hits the reader with a good old bang. Who cares about the engineer who built the engine or the mechanic who spun the airscrew when the plane starts curvetting and tracing the critic's own signature in the sky? What does it matter if two esteemed critics say exactly the opposite thing about a given work? Their comments are equally valid and valuable (or valueless?) since each one represents the critic in question and not the work being criticized. Thus in the last resort we get the elevation of the critic himself as the source of sensibility – and it is his originality that must at all costs be vindicated – if necessary, and often it is necessary, on the ruins of the work being analysed or described.

There are many examples in my own limited experience of lack of training and earnestness of purpose amongst the critical fraternity. No less than four senior critics of the national dailies believed that the basic story of *Iphigenia* was that of her miraculous rescue just as her father's knife was raised, and of her immediate transportation to Tauris. It is true that the final scene of *Iphigenia in Aulis* is missing and was supplied by a later hand but I had to point out, had there been no sacrifice there could have been no *Oresteia*!

Hobson took strong exception to the translation of Brecht's *Galileo*, singling out for special censure the phrase in which Galileo describes everything in the universe as being 'on the move'. But that particular piece of the play was not a translation at all, it was written by Charles Laughton who knew well enough that to speak of the tide being 'on the turn', or of the moon being 'on the wane' or of a patient being 'on the mend' is unimpeachable colloquial English.

The total lack of interchange between the stage and its critics is one of the saddest features of the modern situation, since critics have so much to learn from actors and directors and designers – as well as much to teach. Nearly all actors on the modern stage have undergone two or three years' training, often followed by an arduous apprenticeship in the regions. Moreover being inside the play even for a couple of weeks is a very different thing from being outside it. But analysis of the shape of theatres, of the relationship between actor and audience, upon which Tyrone Guthrie wrote and practised so cogently, of sight-lines, of lighting, of questions of gesture, posture, breathing and diction, which are so frequent and so acute in GBS for example, are entirely lacking in present-day criticism. What is badly needed is a system of basic training from which the critical fraternity would I am sure reap handsome benefits in the widening and deepening of their craft. I fully realize the problem of time in a hard-pressed profession but I believe that two hours a week, say between 4.30 p.m. and cocktail time, would be of immense benefit. At one time I would have proposed Tynan as Dean of the Faculty; though somewhat humourless he has a more thorough background knowledge of the world's theatre than any living critic, and writes like an angel. Perhaps Marcus might undertake the job? The syllabus would certainly include the areas I have mentioned above and would add a wide study of the main body of European dramatic and operatic criticism.

For it appears that our native critics come readymade, to put down snap idiosyncratic opinions in the place of mature judgements based upon any set of critical criteria. As Kingsley Martin once told me when I asked him where he found his critics: 'They just turn up and tell me they would like to write. I say, "Well Cuthbert Worsley is off duty for the next week or two. Would you like to cover these?" – handing the acolyte a sheaf of theatre tickets.' And thus a new critic is born; brought up, like Philip Pirrip, 'by hand'.

Another puzzle is why critics always sit in the front seats, especially at the Mermaid. One of the disadvantages of the open stage is that the first two or three rows, occupying the space that the orchestra pit occupies in the picture-frame theatre, are out of focus both visually and aurally, rather like walking round the Victoria and Albert Museum to look at the Raphael cartoons with your face six inches from the wall. Filmgoers know that the front seats are the worst and so do the royal family who, whenever they honour us with their presence, always choose the middle of row J, about a third of the way up the house, where you can take in the spatial tensions and the total shape of things.

There is also the question of the growth and development of a performance. Most actors would agree that the opening night gives only a glimpse of what will be added or chiselled away over the succeeding five or six weeks and it gives me the creeps to think that critics have carried away memories and records of so many incomplete performances. As a music-hall comedian who worked the London Palladium as well as all the other halls in the country, with a fresh routine on every new tour, I would say that during a fortnight of twice-nightly performances, twenty-four performances in all, the number of laughs doubled, partly from greater relaxation and assurance, partly from finding out where they actually were instead of where one thought they would be. Critics who saw *Cowardy Custard*, *Hadrian VII* and *An Inspector Calls* on their first nights (to name only three of our successful productions) have no idea how powerfully they developed in rhythm and vitality and pure density of meaning over the succeeding five or six weeks.

But I would say our chief grudge is that criticism is a one-way street. There is no debate, no interchange, no chance to answer back, even though at the theatre end our livelihoods depend upon it. It could scarcely be denied, even by critics, that immunity from criticism is the very negation of the critical position. But I have found it very difficult to get an answer-back printed.

All the same I think I can best describe the feelings of management and artists towards the critics as one of compassion. Here is a worthy body of men, reliable, punctual, industrious and entirely self-taught, undertaking a bigger work-load than almost any other section of the community, clocking-in night after night and during the last few years lunchtime after lunchtime, wherever an adventurous group of enthusiasts raise the banner of theatre and announce something interesting. Kept short of space, underpaid (I doubt if any one of them takes home much more than £100 a week) and enjoying none of the delights of the creative life, the play reading, the programme planning, the conferences with production manager and designers, the auditions, the battles with agents, the rehearsals, the lighting, the fun and fire of wrestling with the actual material, the delight of taking a script off the page and fighting to turn it into the living mouthpiece of the dramatist. All honour to them therefore for their devotion to duty, which is performed with such dogged persistence.

Finally I hope it may not be thought indelicate if I mention a matter which is particularly wounding to a small and I hope courteous management such as ours. Although they are our guests, the critics rarely say good evening to the host, rarely smile and never say goodbye, but scuttle out, often before the applause has even begun, presumably on the plea that every second counts in getting the notice back to head office. It is of course an intolerable job but as my five-year-old son said when he caught me and my wife having a blazing row over the weighty deficit on our first season at St John's Wood, 'Nobody asked you to do it'; and one is reminded that the royal family's is also a difficult job but that it is carried out with exquisite manners, charm and interest, especially with regard to their hosts. I must in all charity exempt one or two gentlemen from the above and especially Bernard Levin, 'the cheeky chappie of Fleet Street' as we call him here, who always bought me half a pint when he was in critical harness. Perhaps there should be some encouragement to critics in the form of a yearly award. If on the artistic side we offer the Oscar why not for critics the Ottoline, to be worn round the neck at first nights?

I can only add that there is nowhere like the City, and if when I make my final exit from the scene, I were asked to choose an epitaph, I should like to be remembered as the man who with his long-suffering wife and family had the honour of putting the Square Mile back on the theatrical map after its long artistic sleep.

1a (above) The Mermaid site
as it looked in 1958

1b (right) Bernard Miles at
the Mermaid

3d (left) Albert Finney and
son in *Chez Nous*, Globe
Theatre

3e (above) Anna Neagle and
company in *No, No, Nanette*,
Theatre Royal, Drury Lane

3f (right) Angela Lansbury
in *Gypsy*, Piccadilly Theatre

3g (left) Edward Woodward, Leo McKern and Judi Dench in *The Wolf*, Apollo Theatre

3h (below) Kenneth Williams and Jennie Linden in *My Fat Friend*, Globe Theatre

3i (above) Edward Fox and
Leonard Kavanagh in
Knuckle, Comedy Theatre

3j (right) Alastair Sim and
Patricia Routledge in *Dandy
Dick*, Garrick Theatre

3k (above left) Paul Scofield
and Tom Conti in *Savages*,
Comedy Theatre

3l (above right) John Stride,
Vanessa Redgrave and
Jeremy Brett in *Design for
Living*, Phoenix Theatre

3m (left) Ingrid Bergman as
The Constant Wife, Albery
Theatre

Big Business - or Show Business?

A report on the economics of Shaftesbury Avenue (and a welcome for the Theatre Investment Fund) by the Literary Editor of The Times.

Money in the theatre is lost in thousands, made in hundreds, but saved in pennies. – Patrick Ide, managing director of the Theatre Investment Fund.

It is easy to be despondent about the future of London's commercial theatre: early in 1974 West End theatre owners and impresarios had to contend with electricity cuts, railway drivers going slow and a petrol shortage on top of the more permanent problems of 8 per cent VAT and ever rising costs in wages, rates, insurance and the like. Donald Albery, controller of four theatres, the Piccadilly, Wyndhams, Criterion and Albery (where he has his office), told me that for the first time he was really worried about the state of the West End theatre. 'The future of the larger shows and theatres,' he added, 'depends on getting rid of VAT and on how much prices can be put up.' And yet, one hundred yards away in his office on top of the Garrick Theatre, John Hallett, managing director of the Abrahams group (which also includes the Aldwych and the Duchess) could remark: 'We've done very well for four or five years. Taking all our theatres together I suppose we've only been dark for a total of six to eight weeks in all that time.'

On the other side of Charing Cross Road in an antediluvian office block which houses (among others) the Society of West End Theatre Managers, Patrick Ide, as managing director of the new Theatre Investment Fund, was talking with enthusiasm about the

£250 000 he would shortly be injecting into the commercial theatre. Nor did there seem to be any shortage of production plans: H. M. Tennent (under revised management following the death of the firm's mentor, Binkie Beaumont) were readying a musical of *Billy Liar* for Drury Lane, and Bernard Delfont a musical of *The Good Companions* for Her Majesty's (both would cost well over £100 000 to mount); and Paul Raymond, bursting forth from his Soho Revue bar, had just opened the *Royalty Follies*, constructed on a budget (he insists) of £300 000, though it was to close in July. The chances on all three of these shows recouping their investment would seem slim, a chance made slimmer by the depredations of VAT. As Michael White the impresario (*Sleuth, The Beard, Oh Calcutta!*) said: 'VAT is the worst thing. I have shows that would have made a profit but for VAT. On four shows VAT costs me £2000 a week.'

This was the situation early in spring 1974. However black the horizon there are always some theatre people playing the eternal optimist. For me this is one of the unique flavours of the West End theatre that the subsidized Royal Court or Royal Shakespeare or National Theatre never give out. Productions are conceived often from higgledy-piggledy offices in curious corners in theatre eaves (to reach the quarters of John Gale, impresario and current president of the Society of West End Theatre Managers, in the Strand Theatre one aims for the upper circle bar; his actual office is behind the neon sign advertising the theatre's current attraction). Impresarios have none of the subsidized theatre's resources (literary manager, casting director, etc.). They back their judgements, tout for backing from their investors – and cross their fingers. If their judgement is good and their luck holds they make small fortunes. 'You can't become rich just from the theatre these days,' says John Hallett, but occasionally the jackpot is hit (£1000 invested in *No Sex Please We're British* has at the time of writing given a 4000 per cent return). But the odds are slim: Donald Albery reckons 5 to 1 against a show giving any return on its investment; Richard Pilbrow, lighting expert and impresario, suggests 4 to 1.

The forty or so theatres (as well as the cinemas and the two opera houses) are the principle attractions that the West End has to offer those seeking a night out. Theatre and opera, in particular, are the mecca for many foreign tourists. Even on 1st December

1973 when one would have thought the tourists had all gone home for Christmas, the audience at Wyndhams for *Godspell* was 42·7 per cent tourist. In March this year John Gale was telling me that as far as the theatre was concerned, despite all the nation's problems, tourist figures were already up by a third on the previous year.

But what do the tourists come to see? I doubt that they aim for London to view one-set, four-character comedies. Everyone I spoke to agreed that the National Theatre and the Royal Shakespeare at the Aldwych were always high on tourists' lists (there is continuous confusion here: Trevor Nunn, director of the RSC, insists that a lot of European tourists aiming for the National leap into taxis demanding 'Take me to the Olde Viche', and end up at the Aldwych instead). Americans go to American shows in London which may seem surprising, but only a small proportion of American tourists are actually from New York and those that aren't probably wouldn't visit New York to go to the theatre anyway: Broadway's prices are too high.

All these tourists are marvellous for our balance of payments, but the greater their numbers the less Londoners go to the theatre. The cost is a major deterrent (although I'm sure Patrick Ide is right when he says people don't go to the theatre by price, but because they wish to see a particular show). But a night for two at any theatre, with a meal afterwards, transport and babysitting at a minimum of 30p an hour is certainly going to cost £10, and more often nearer £15. In the provinces, however, theatre-going is an increasing habit. Patrick Ide observes that it is the women who in general govern theatre-going; left to themselves few men would go near the theatre.

Whoever the audience variety and quality are important to the West End theatre's survival. While one would hesitate to object to anyone presenting live theatre in London, the turning over by Paul Raymond of the Whitehall and Royalty theatres to shows more attuned to Soho (the *Royalty Follies* and *Pyjama Tops*) simply deprives the proper West End theatre of two useful houses. John Barber, dramatic critic of the *Daily Telegraph*, in two thoughtful articles early in the year, wrote: 'I do not recall a time when dignified theatres displayed so many titillating pictures of undressed girls, or flaunted such catchpenny titles (*Two and Two Make Sex*, *Why Not Stay For Breakfast?*, *Bordello*, in addition to Mr Raymond's

offerings – even his Revue Bar, with its Festival of Erotica, was
being advertised in the newspaper *theatre* lists). Incidentally, while
on the subject of titles, I recall one impresario remarking to me that
The Dirtiest Show in Town needed no enticing front-of-house quota-
tions from the critics; as he suggested, all one needs to do is to
present a comedy called '*I Laughed Till My Ribs Ached*'. It is what
Michael Codron calls 'marketing theatre – the more the marketing
the less good the theatre. Some producers concentrate on the marketing and do very well by it. I'd rather get the product right'.

What worries most people in the business ('and it is a business,
not simply an artistic enterprise', insists Patrick Ide) is that each
rise in production costs, unless matched by a rise in seat prices,
lessens the chance of the investor seeing a return on his money.
Thus, it is reasoned, managements will increasingly try to play
safe, and safe to most commercial minds means a limited range of
offerings from Paul Raymond's follies to thrillers and sexy comedies with a cast of no more than half a dozen and one set. But as
John Gale remarks it is a great mistake to go into a production
'because it is commercial – more often it isn't'. The remark of
impresario Peter Saunders that a West End of *Hamlets* would be as
dull as a West End of *Mousetraps* seems apt here.

In 1952 John Hallett recalls that an impresario was charged
£425 a week for renting the Garrick and this was a straight let with
no percentages. Out of this came the rates (about £50), insurances,
overheads and so on, and the profit was about £200 a week, or as
Hallett adds, a return on capital of about 4 per cent, hardly
magnificent. Today rates are £160 a week and all other costs have
gone up: a head carpenter, for instance, gets over £40 a week
(about £12 10s. in 1952). The minimum charge for the Garrick is
now £620 a week (and this has not altered for six years) but, as I
will show, there is also a complex arrangement based on a percentage of the gross takings: in the Garrick's case the figure is 20 per
cent (although increasingly elsewhere in the West End it has been
upped by theatre owners to 22·5 per cent).

At the Garrick that 20 per cent starts after the gross takings
rise above £3100 (mathematically-minded readers will have
already realized that the Garrick's minimum of £620 is simply 20
per cent of £3100; or, as Hallett puts it, £620 on account of 20
per cent). It may be that a production's weekly running costs are

more than £3100, which could mean that Hallett would start receiving his 20 per cent of the gross even if the takings were over the £3100 mark but under the show's own break-even point. 'Our attitude is that we must contribute more to the theatre than simply being stern bricks-and-mortar, money-grubbing landlords', says Hallett. Thus if the break figure is high Hallett will negotiate with the show's management and come to some arrangement. But, as he says: 'that 20 per cent is what I live on'. After all if Hallett only received a straight £620 he would only make a profit of £90 a week – at a theatre which he reckons would cost £1000000 to rebuild. Thus a theatre management's skill is in choosing a produc-tion which he believes will succeed; the more profitable the show the greater the 20 per cent. But if the theatre is dark Hallett loses £1100 a week, which includes paying the theatre's staff, whose wages are normally paid by the management renting the theatre (and if you think £1100 sounds a lot, remember that the bill to keep the Theatre Royal, Drury Lane, ticking over when dark is over £3000 a week, with heating alone said to amount to over £100 a week in winter).

Costs of putting on a show have risen steadily, even spectacu-larly, over the years. Among musicals, *Oliver* cost £15000 to mount in 1960, *A Funny Thing Happened on the Way to the Forum* £40000 in 1963, *Fiddler on the Roof* £67000 in 1967, *Gone With the Wind* about £150000 in 1972. Among comedies John Gale reckons that *Boeing-Boeing* which cost £5500 to stage in 1962 would be more like £20000 in 1973.

How does this £20000 get spent? A large chunk is the guarantee of four to six weeks' rent and so on that the impresario has to give to the theatre management. A play, after all, may run only 10 days, but that further four weeks' rent allows a theatre management to cover itself financially while signing up a substitute attraction. Then there are sets to be designed and built, rehearsals, press relations, photographs, advertising, printing. It all mounts up. But before an impresario starts seeing a return on this investment he has to service his running costs. We have already seen the kind of sums an impresario must expect to hand over to the theatre management (Michael White reckons in round figures that one must now think in terms of £2000, and that includes theatre staff, lighting and heating). In addition there are the casts' salaries, royalty payments to the author and usually the director. The impresario takes his management fee and there are further substantial charges for everything from hire charges for set decorations to accountancy.

John Hallett has a good rule of thumb for impresarios; the break figure should be half one's reasonable expected take. But it does not follow if one's break figure is £4000 and one can reasonably expect to take £8000 at the box office that one's profit will be £4000 – because so many people, from the theatre management and the leading actors to the author and the director, will be on a percentage, possibly adding up to 35 per cent to 40 per cent of the receipts. For the small-cast, one-set play the economics and the chances of a return given a reasonable first night reception are still good. Anthony Shaffer's play *Sleuth* with its deceptively small cast has allowed its impresario, Michael White, to support 'a lot of odd ball ventures'. But more costly productions such as musicals may be going the way of the dinosaur. Michael White presented the musical version of *The Two Gentlemen of Verona* at the Phoenix Theatre and it took between £9000 and £10000 a week, but still lost £60000 when its run ended after eight months. Another Michael White interest, *The Rocky Horror Show*, which is far cheaper than most musicals today, opened in July 1973 at the Classic, King's Road. By March 1974, despite tremendous business, it still hadn't recouped its initial investment, and Michael White was saying that prices would have to go up: the top priced stalls from £2·20 to £2·50. Has there, in fact, been a musical presented in the last two years that has actually made a profit? *Grease* failed to recoup; *Pippin*'s loss, like that of *No, No, Nanette*, was in six figures. It is not just the initial costs that are high, but musicals tend to have big casts as well as an orchestra so the weekly bill is vast compared with the one-set comedy. As Donald Albery says the odds now are that however successful a musical is today, it will still show a very poor return on the capital invested.

The gamble is so great that one does wonder why managements still take the risk. One impresario I asked replied – anonymously – 'because I'm a sucker; I love them; I'm nuts'. The economics are staggering. If a musical costs £150000 to stage and has running costs of £12000 a week, the chances of averaging a net profit of £2000 a week are slim, even in the biggest London theatres, and that would still mean 75 weeks before the initial investment was recovered. It is musicals such as *Oliver, My Fair Lady* and *Godspell* that have that sort of run.

If the West End theatre is to have any future, Donald Albery, for one, believes that first VAT must go. There is puzzlement, for instance, that books are exempt. Politicians refrained from saddling books with VAT on the basis that it would be a tax on knowledge, but many books are entertainment, so why, it is argued, should they be exempted when plays are not? Donald Albery believes that VAT more than any other single cause is responsible for the demise of the big show. VAT is penal because it is charged on every ticket. Thus if a theatre takes £8000 a week, 8 per cent goes to the Chancellor of the Exchequer rather than to the production. As John Gale noted, the theatre has been ill-served by successive governments. It took 40 years to get rid of the Entertainments Tax (originally a temporary measure from the First World War); Selective Employment Tax was introduced by a Labour government in the sixties, but was ultimately removed.

Since the fifties property has been the investment to put your money in for maximum appreciation, but one should have avoided the West End's theatres. On a purely mercenary basis theatres are a disaster area. Consider: most London theatres are used for about 25 hours a week; they take up a great deal of space, but the return per square foot is minute because so much of the auditorium is empty space. Put an office block on the site and your return would multiply staggeringly overnight.

The West End's theatres are, to a certain extent, protected. In some cases the actual buildings have had preservation orders placed on them. In fact if you own a theatre and are allowed to pull it down, Greater London Council regulations state that whatever you put in its place must include a theatre. Thus when the Stoll in Kingsway was demolished in the fifties, the office block that took its place contained a theatre (the Royalty) in the basement. The old Winter Garden in Drury Lane is slightly different; the New London Theatre is the principal occupier of the site, but the complex also includes shops and offices. The Scala in Charlotte Street is different again, having a small auditorium built into a new block; John Hallett, who controls its destinies, readily expects it to be used more as a cinema than a theatre. As he recalls: 'The old Scala was a great shame. It was big – 1200 seats and could take a lot of money – but on the wrong site. Apart from *Peter Pan* annually at Christmas we were forced in the main to let it to amateur operatic companies. I would be making thirty-six contracts a year, whereas in our other theatres I suppose I average two a year'. Meanwhile the future of another theatre, the Shaftesbury (formerly the Princes), and closed as a result of a fall of plaster from the ceiling, remains the subject of interested speculation.

Many London theatres are controlled by leaseholders and this in some cases is further cause for concern. Donald Albery has no security of tenure at the Criterion (which his family has controlled for years) because of the on-off-on-off-on Piccadilly redevelopment schemes. When he spent £45000 on modernization in 1971 it was an act of faith based on the theory that whatever happened was bound to be many years off. A great deal of money has been spent on restoring Wyndhams, even though the lease on this and on the Albery (they back onto each other) have only 3.5 and 5.5 years respectively to run. He reckons he needs the security of a new lease with a minimum of 28 years before it is worth spending more large sums on further improvements such as air conditioning.

The Abrahams theatres are in a far stronger position because the family owns the freeholds (with the exception of the Garrick which is on long lease from the GLC). The Aldwych was modernized two years ago; £85000 is being spent on the Duchess Theatre with the Fortune and Garrick to follow. There are in fact few other theatres actually run by their freeholders: the Phoenix, the Vaudeville and Piccadilly among them, and in all cases they have spent considerable sums on modernization and refurbishment. But the return on the investment is not good: John Hallett says that the Abrahams family have yet to see seven per cent for their money, even in the very good recent years.

It is not for the want of trying. Take the front of house – barmaids have to be paid an evening's wages for perhaps half an hour's work before curtain up and in the interval. As GLC regulations insist that theatres employ one usherette for every 100 seats that means, for example, eight usherettes at the Garrick. Then there are the cloakrooms which have to be manned, although they are barely used in summer. To spread the load the Abrahams group bought control of a catering company which also looks after much of the front of house side of many other theatres apart from their own. But the profit here is still small, about £20000 last year, or about 3 per cent on a turnover of £700000 a year.

Programmes are another bugbear. For years every theatre or group produced its own with varying results: Hallett recalls that theirs were eight pages for 6d. and 'a bit tatty'. Then along came *Playbill*, which was based on the American pattern of a magazine covering enough theatres to guarantee a circulation of a size to tempt the major advertisers. At first theatres received it free (on the theory that the publishers lived off the advertising revenue), but it didn't work; theatres were asked to pay 2d, then 3d a copy – and the publishers folded. *Playbill*'s successor, again with some editorial common to all subscribing theatres, is another Abrahams company. The problems are considerable, mainly because print runs are comparatively short, but Hallett reckons that perhaps in five years they will see their investment back.

If theatres are struggling to make ends meet, ought not the government take action? At the beginning of this article I mentioned the attraction the theatre is for tourists. But it goes deeper than that, as every theatre person will tell you. Says Donald Albery:

The theatre provides the reason for people to come to London; the hotels, restaurants and the like get the spin-off. If all the theatres were replaced by offices London would lose its cultural heart, many restaurants and shops would go out of business, tourists would come in much smaller numbers. In the end this would mean there would be fewer restaurants, fewer shops and paradoxically landlords would no longer be able to get the highest rents in the world and inflated rents for their offices as hardly anyone would voluntarily want to work there. Theatres are the loss-leaders of the West End and a small price to pay for the advantages they give.

Michael White reinforces this view: 'Theatres are a vital part of the economy of central London.'

Of all the ingredients that make up the West End theatre it is, I believe, the impresarios who matter most, or as Patrick Ide put it: 'The flair of the impresarios is what the theatre lives on.' The pressures of recent times have brought considerable changes. Michael Codron, when we spoke early in the spring, was involved in fewer new productions than for many years; familiar management

names such as Harold Fielding, Bill Freedman, Toby Rowland and
Donald Albery were quiescent. Why? Says Albery: 'Many experienced managements have dropped out because the odds of
making a profit on a big show like a musical are declining. Their
place is being taken by less experienced people. Now when experts
drop out there is usually a good reason. The writing is on the wall
for the big theatres and the big shows.'

Albery, never a producer who much liked presenting one-set,
small-cast plays, says that the odds are stacked so hugely against
even the more elaborate straight plays such as Barry England's
Conduct Unbecoming and *The Prime of Miss Jean Brodie* (which he
presented) that he has opted out of production, remaining a
theatre manager and administrator. All his spare time is now
occupied in fighting proposals which if passed would seriously
endanger no less than three out of four of his theatres. There is
common agreement that the dearth of new impresarios is worrying.
Where would the West End theatre be today without the flair of
Michael Codron, who introduced Harold Pinter, Joe Orton, John
Mortimer and David Hare along with many others to the West
End? But Codron has been in management for nearly 20 years.
Others who have succeeded since then include Michael White,
Eddie Kulukundis, John Gale and recently Ray Cooney. But not
one of these could be described as young. John Barber commented:
'Too many wise, tired, wealthy mandarins sit at the top, too few
zealots are banging at their doors.'

Michael White started as a producer in 1961 with capital of
£1000, but reckons a budding producer needs £20000 to get off the
ground in the West End today. This is not production money, but
simply for offices, staff, buying scripts and so on. John Gale became
a producer when he was thirty after 10 years as an actor. He had
no private means. 'My first success, a revival of *Candida*, was
capitalized at £2000. Dirk Bogarde put up £1000 and there was
£500 from another investor. I had to raise £500.' *Boeing-Boeing*,
which firmly established Gale in the West End, cost £6000. A film
company put up £2000, but Gale had to raise £4000, 'which was a
sweat'. As he says now: 'It's a forbidding prospect for a young
producer to have to raise £20000 today.'

John Hallett takes a harder attitude – and possibly the most
realistic. 'Anyone who starts in this business and hasn't got financial

backing other than his own, shouldn't try. You need one, two, three firm investors to act as sounding boards to see you through your first two years or so. You've got to have financial backing; the man who is fretting over the last £2000 of his own money is most likely to make bad judgements.'

Only in rare cases today are theatre owners also in management, thus they rely on impresarios for attractions to fill their theatres. But although as Michael White says, 'there aren't enough producers who would do anything other than light comedies', there are always more shows in production than West End theatres to take them. It is difficult to see what can be done to help the new producer; John Gale insists that knowledge and experience of the theatre is vital before one jumps into the West End maelstrom (Michael Codron, for example, gained his early grounding working for Jack Hylton). There are exceptions such as Eddie Kulukundis, wealthy scion of a Greek ship-owning family, whose enthusiasm carried him forward to begin with, although at considerable personal cost to himself.

John Gale sees the current revival in touring as an invaluable training ground; he cites the case of Jeremy Kingston's play *Signs of the Times* which he presented in the West End at the Vaudeville, but which toured this spring under Bill Kenright's management. Kenright is a new name, briefly in the West End early this year with *The Collector*, a dramatization of John Fowles's novel. To help Kenright with the *Signs of the Times* tour, Gale told me that he handed over the set at a purely nominal rent.

John Hallett looks to the Theatre Investment Fund for help. They could, he feels, watch over and guide budding impresarios and if one in four made the grade it would have been money well spent. Patrick Ide, as managing director of the TIF, agrees. When we spoke the fund was still under starter's orders. Helping young impresarios is high among his priorities, but as a start the TIF will be a minority investor (sums from £500 to £5000) in as many productions as possible in order to get experience. The fund's purpose, broadly speaking, being to encourage and assist managements in the production of new plays and revivals in London and on tour.

The TIF has been launched with a float of £250000 from two sources – £100000 as a once and for all dowry from the Arts Council,

and £150000 from a small cast of private investors assembled by
Lord Goodman. There is the view that £250000 is next to useless;
certainly there were members of the Society of West End Theatre
Managers who had hoped for £1000000; and again the fund has
been an elephantine time in gestation with the value of money
declining all the time. But as Ide says: 'Money solves few problems
in the theatre.' Donald Albery, whose idea the TIF was, views it as
a kind of 'theatrical National Film Finance Corporation, that would
be an indirect way of helping the commercial theatre'. Spreading
the £250000 around in small doses would do more good than if
handed over in one lump to one company where much of the
subsidy would go on administration and things other than production.

Not everyone is for it; Michael White feels the Arts Council
would have been better to spend the money on taking over two
West End theatres and offering them at a peppercorn rent with all
staff costs paid (thereby halving the cost of putting on a £20000
production immediately) to producers to try out plays on a maximum of a month's rental; the successes would then transfer into a
fully commercial theatre.

Again the successful producers have their backers and need not
seek the TIF's assistance, thus depriving the TIF of one source of
possibly lucrative profits to put back into the fund. But Ide sees it
as part of his job to convert the doubters. And ultimately, if the
fund is successful, he sees it benefiting all producers; it could,
perhaps, launch a co-operative 'Let's go to the theatre' advertising
campaign, in the manner of brewers selling the delights of the public
house rather than specific brews.

In the matter of plays, the TIF might become a commissioning
angel as there does seem to be a shortage of new serious work.
Michael Codron's only imminent production in February was
David Hare's *Knuckle*, yet he recalls finding a play a month to put
on at the Arts a decade ago. 'Are there new writers whom I'm
unable to recognize because I've become staid? I mentioned
recently to Peggy Ramsey, the agent, that there appeared to be less
material, less interesting new writers than in my Arts days. We had
the cream of what was going, but would it be possible to run the
Arts on that system today? I thought not; Peggy Ramsey dis-
agreed. The situation has changed: the place of the Arts has been

taken by the Bush, the King's Head, by Hampstead, Greenwich and the provinces.'

Patrick Ide has plans to encourage the touring theatre, which in recent years has seen a remarkable recovery from the doldrums of the sixties. Tours are shorter these days, which suits actors sated by television who welcome the opportunity of giving 10 to 12 weeks to live theatre. Their names are sufficient to allow them choice of plays, which in turn means that many successes of the past are in for a new innings. But the revival industry is haphazard to the extreme. There are few managements who appear to have any coherent idea of what should be revived, what plays are worth a second look. Shaw, Wilde, Coward . . . but who else? Too many managers are followers of fashion. Priestley's *An Inspector Calls* was revived at the Mermaid and promptly the National Theatre announced *Eden End* and Bernard Delfont a musical of *The Good Companions*; another example – the Royal Court's production of Middleton's *The Changeling* led to a clutch of *Changelings* around the country. One hopes that the TIF influence will be felt here, because well-chosen revivals would provide a much-needed additional flavour to the West End.

The TIF is not in business as a subsidy agent. Ide hopes his investments will at least break even, at best show a small profit. Looking further into the future he foresees the day when local councils in London, airlines, hotel operators, restaurateurs and the like will invest in the TIF on the basis that the continuance of a flourishing West End theatre is in all their interests. Far-fetched? Not at all; there is even a chance of a dividend. All in all the TIF is a shaft of light in a stormy sky. Welcome!

The West End: 1973-4

The drama critic and arts editor of The Financial Times *surveys the year in the commercial theatre.*

The more progressive elements in the theatre are not as a rule well represented in the West End houses; yet the West End houses soldier on, making money for their owners and lessees, if not always for their guardian angels, and giving work to actors, stagehands, electricians, carpenters, public relations consultants and the rest. I have felt for a long time that insufficient credit was given among the intelligentsia to the middle-brow, middle-class theatre, so it is in that area that I begin; and begin, what's more, with a name that is always the second (Agatha Christie's being the first) thrown by contemptuous critics at unadventurous managements.

If Terence Rattigan's *In Praise of Love* had hit a market less disturbed by the after-effects of *Look Back in Anger* (itself now as old-fashioned as *French Without Tears*) and *The Birthday Party*, it would have been a great success. Rattigan's previous double bills, *Playbill* in 1948 and *Separate Tables* in 1954, both did well. *In Praise of Love* is as good as either of them. The short farcical piece *Before Dawn* made what I suppose is a tactical error; it assumed that audiences would be familiar with the story of *Tosca*, and so they would have been in the West End in 1954. For Toscaphiles, the play was delightful. But the longer, more serious piece, *After Lydia*, seems to me the best writing Rattigan has given us since *The Browning Version*; it happens to be about the kind of people I know (and like) and it hits them and their problems off perfectly.

In Praise of Love, graced by John Dexter's production and two splendid performances by Donald Sinden, stumbled through a short run at the Duchess. O tempora, o mores . . .

Other eminent writers had better fortune. A revival of Maugham's *The Constant Wife* at the Albery (the new name for the New Theatre) seems at the time of writing to be going on for ever. This is no doubt partly due to the presence in it of Ingrid Bergman; the 'star system', however much disliked by the artistic directors of subsidized companies, is still with us, its only fault being that managements are reluctant to boost new stars. Miss Bergman is a star, anyway. So is Glenda Jackson, who attracted audiences to John Mortimer's latest instalment of quasi-autobiography, *Collaborators*. That it was she rather than Mr Mortimer who lured them is evident from the fact that when she and John Wood were replaced by Diane Cilento and Peter McEnery (who ought to be a star by now) the houses shrank at once.

Since I have strayed into the subject of stars, we may as well look at what happened to some more of them. Before I leave Glenda Jackson, it must go on record that she contrived to sell out a whole three-week season of Genet's *The Maids* at Greenwich – not a play normally likely to appeal to the coach-trade. Claire Bloom's Blanche in *A Streetcar Named Desire* opened to well earned superlatives. Keith Michell could do nothing with yet another bit about the Brownings, nor Kenneth More do much with a well conceived, ill-executed farce, *Signs of the Times*. Alec Guinness gave a quite remarkable comic performance in Alan Bennett's *Habeas Corpus*. Vanessa Redgrave is, as I write, still illuminating Coward's *Design for Living*. Albert Finney holds his own with an exceptionally good cast in Peter Nichols's *Chez Nous*. However, back to the plays.

We were talking about eminent writers. Coward is represented by two of his less sparkling pieces, *Design for Living*, played in too realistic a style and so muting the talents of Miss Redgrave, John Stride and Jeremy Brett; and *Relative Values*, a dreary bit of snobbery that had a short run at the Westminster, temporarily released from its obligations to MRA. Tennessee Williams, besides *Streetcar*, offered *Small Craft Warnings*, a recent, not very distinguished, piece imported from the adventurous Hampstead Theatre Club to the West End with two specially memorable performances, by Elaine Stritch and Frances de la Tour. Chekhov and Ibsen came no nearer than the suburbs; at Greenwich there were fine productions of *The Seagull* and *Ghosts* under Jonathan Miller. Shakespeare, that super-eminent writer, fared less well under Dr Miller with an abridged, apolitical *Hamlet*, and even less well at the Bankside Globe, still only an open-air framework, with a beta-minus production of *Twelfth Night* and a gamma-minus one of *Antony and Cleopatra* too dreadful to describe. For the Swan of Avon this year, you had to go the Old Vic or the Aldwych.

For Wilde, you had to go to Euston, where the Dolphin company put on as sparkling a presentation of *The Importance of Being Earnest* as I've seen for a long time, brisk and real instead of being languid and decadent, and beautifully designed by Bernard Culshaw in the manner of Beardsley. It was specially welcome because the Dolphins had just given us a very tedious piece by Adrian Mitchell about people on a bus and one of the worst *Macbeths* in living memory. No sooner had Peter James, the director, given us this earnest of his true ability than it was announced that he was going off in the autumn to run the theatre in Sheffield.

Three new writers commended themselves to me. Charles Laurence indeed commended himself to everyone with his first West End play *My Fat Friend*, whose promising run was only brought to an end by the indisposition of Kenneth Williams in the lead. Mr Laurence then turned out *Snap!*, originally said to have been called *Clap*, and about that very subject. My own view of *Snap!* was more friendly than most; it seemed to me that it was being condemned for matters that would readily have been forgiven in Etherege or Wycherley. Not, of course, that it is as good as Etherege or Wycherley, but Maggie Smith, God bless her, played it as if she believed it was, and so added an extra layer of enjoyment. Next, Colin Welland, with an interesting play, *Say Goodnight to Grandma*. One remembers Mr Welland driving a squad car in *Z Cars* in the days that set it up as the best ever television series, which I suppose it still is; one remembers him next with clever plays for the same medium like *Banglestein's Boys* and *A Roomful of Holes*. Whether or not *Say Goodnight to Grandma* began life as a television play I don't know, but on the stage it certainly filled its two-hour-plus slot without rattling, and it revealed a capacity rare in today's playwrights, the ability to write a long, developing scene. Characters and situations were both worthwhile, and Patrick Dromgoole's production reached a finely grisly climax.

Thirdly, Eric Chappell. Who? Eric Chappell. He wrote a little comedy called *The Banana Box* about the private lives of students in a provincial university that I followed from Leicester to Hampstead to Shaftesbury Avenue because I so admired the truth of the materials on which the author built up his situations. Perhaps I was optimistic in believing that a play about lovelorn students could still attract West End audiences (remember *French Without Tears*?), but I am steady in my admiration for Mr Chappell's writing.

Comedy from better established writers is specially well represented in the '73–4 period by two plays that have the look of farces but turn out on inspection to be full of contemporary social comment. Alan Bennett's *Habeas Corpus* is a farce about farce; like most farces since Molière, it is about sexual intrigue; it includes falling trousers and jokes about tits; it presents a celibate clergyman and a pompous official in striped pants; but it looks at them all from one pace back. The attitude is not 'Wouldn't it be funny if Alec Guinness's trousers came down?' but 'Wouldn't it be funny if in order to be funny I made Alec Guinness's trousers come down?' – so all depths of brow are satisfied from the simple to the sophisticated, for down they come all right.

Alan Ayckbourn has undoubtedly become our best writer of light comedy and *Absurd Person Singular*, in spite of its dreadful title, is a farcical comedy on a very high level. It is in three acts wherein the fortunes of three married couples on three successive Christmas Eves are presented as a series of ridiculous blunders, but in which there is much sharp inspection of the mores of suburban married life. The middle act is really quite extraordinary; throughout its progress one character, played heartrendingly by Anna Calder-Marshall, is determinedly trying to commit suicide. Yet, as Hamlet mendaciously told the King, there is no offence in the world; they do but poison in jest (and gas themselves in jest, and electrocute themselves in jest). This is a masterpiece of comic writing that reinforces my long held belief that you can joke about absolutely anything if you do it with enough skill. The production, strongly cast and beautifully directed, was a joy, and as I write it has just entered on a second lease of life with a new cast but remaining at the Criterion. Remaining? The Westminster City

Council is determined that the Criterion shall be sacrificed so that they can replan Piccadilly Circus.

A third farcical comedy of above average merit is Pinero's splendid veteran *Dandy Dick*, which transferred triumphantly from Sir John Clements's final season at Chichester to play at the Garrick, with Alastair Sim suffering happily at its core. And an unexpected triumph came in from Oxford – another farewell, Frank Hauser's last production at the Playhouse – in the shape of Molnar's *The Wolf*.

The Wolf, ably adapted by Frank Hauser, is an object-lesson to comedy writers. Molnar, like Feydeau, builds up a complex structure in his first act, and then plays astonishing tricks with it in his second before clearing everything away in his third. What appears to be a simple case of jealousy between Leo McKern and Judi Dench blossoms into gorgeous fantasy when Edward Woodward as the suspected intruder appears constantly at a diplomatic ball in every role from ambassador to waiter. Like *Absurd Person Singular*, *The Wolf* has also begun a second round, not only with a new company but at a new theatre as well, the New London in the wilds of Drury Lane. There are more treasures in Molnar waiting for the adaptor's hand – *The Swan*, *The Guardsman*, but please not *Liliom*.

While I am still teetering on the edge of low comedy, I may as well finish off my observations on the year's clutch of real farces. I must declare that I have very rigid views about farce. Plays in which the characters self-evidently have no existence outside the stage, who spring into existence at curtain-up and are packed away in a trunk at curtain-down, who are created like puppets with no purpose except to people farcical situations, are not for me.

So I can have nothing kind to say about *Two and Two Make Sex*, in which Richard Harris and Leslie Darbon have described the whole action in their awful title, and in which that polished comedian Patrick Cargill is reduced to a series of formulae. I can do little but record the existence of *Why Not Stay for Breakfast?*, which also took two people to write, and one of them Ray Cooney, no less, who also directed it, bad cess to him. (The other was Gene Stone.) This one contains one situation and Derek Nimmo, another polished comedian drowning in drivel. *Signs of the Times* by fellow-critic Jeremy Kingston, which I mentioned earlier on, struck me as having begun life as a sophisticated comedy and having then been battered into a farce by producer-director Allan Davis. At least the characters were assumed to have followed some kind of activity away from the stage, and the conception of a horoscope in *The Times* is potentially a fruitful one, even if it only bore sour fruit in this instance. And once more, a lovely actor, Kenneth More, was at the heart of things, doing his best to keep the ship floating.

We also saw two examples of that genre, fashionable when I was a lad but now seldom encountered, the comedy thriller, but we did not see them long. *Dead Easy* was a dreadful piece in which Irene Handl played Irene Handl, a part in which she is unequalled, for five or six performances; and *Gomes*, which gave your actual Roy Dotrice the part of a retired butler scaring his rich employer to death with adventures in the supernatural, ran for about the same time. But stay – was *Gomes* really meant to be a comedy? If not, what was that spectral nun doing coming downstairs in the electric invalid chair? It certainly was no comedy for its backers; clearly it was an expensive production, and report says that thousands of pounds were spent during its gestation period on manifestations of ESP that never ultimately appeared. But there's a silver lining to every cloud: Roy Dotrice was provoked into giving us another season of *Brief Lives*, his superb evocation of John Aubrey in old age. And now for something completely different.

It is a bad year in which the Royal Court can't chalk up two or three productions of exceptional value, and they have more than fulfilled their quota in the year under review. Christopher Hampton's *Savages* opened in April, a play at once bitter and sympathetic in which contemporary brands of civilization are tested against one another by showing them against the background of the Brazilians' treatment of their fast-dying Indian population: government authoritarianism, urban guerrilla protest, Christian indoctrination, artistic appreciation, all existing side by side with the Indian problem, none doing anything to help. The play contained a stunning performance by Paul Scofield; when I saw it after its transfer to the Comedy there was a party of French visitors behind me who broke into spontaneous bravos each time he spoke one of the Indian legends with which the play is punctuated.

Savages was followed by *The Sea*, Edward Bond's first new play of the year. (His second was *Bingo*, which was seen only at Exeter.) *The Sea* introduces a fresh side of Bond, less concerned

with cruelty and horror, more with the subtleties of human relationships; indeed it is positively romantic, a step in the right direction. *The Sea* contained fine playing by Coral Browne as a grande
dame and Ian Holm as a mad draper's assistant.

There were two new plays by David Storey instead of the usual
single annual offering. The first of them, *Cromwell*, was cast in a
new mould for Storey – a historical tale with mystical overtones,
written partly in verse. Alas, it amounted to very little. It was
followed by *The Farm*, however, in which the author reverted to
his old form and was once more given the advantage of production
by the faithful Lindsay Anderson. *The Farm* moved on to the May
Fair for a short run.

Peter Gill did not have such success with his production of
D. H. Lawrence's *The Merry Go Round* as he had earlier with the
three short plays that brought Lawrence back into the theatrical
map. *The Merry Go Round* is set in the same kind of world as *A
Collier's Friday Night*, but it is a comedy evidently modelled on the
commercial comedies fashionable in its day – 1913 – but transferred
to this new milieu. Peter Gill got the milieu dead right, as always,
but in the process the comedy dropped out.

The Rocky Horror Show was judged by the *Evening Standard*
panel of critics as the best new musical of the year. Well, what was
the competition? Normally one looks for quality in the American
imports, and certainly there was quality a-plenty in *Gypsy*, which
finally crossed the Atlantic to the Piccadilly after a decade and a
half, with Angela Lansbury acting like a real actress in the lead and
singing boisterously through her transmitting apparatus. Hardly a
new musical, however. America provided no less than four other
offerings. The musical version of *Two Gentlemen of Verona*, fundamentally a pleasant little jeu d'esprit, seemed to have been too long
on the road. 'It grew and developed as it went along,' said a programme note at the Phoenix, and that is exactly how it looked, full
of silly gags and business that emphasized the juvenility of the
conception. At least it gave parts to two talented players, B. J.
Arnau and Derek Griffiths, but as it provided nothing worthwhile
for Mr Griffiths to do that compliment must be cut in half.

Grease at Mr Delfont's sumptuous new New London Theatre
was to bring back the magic of the early rock days of the fifties, but
a good deal of determination was needed to put on that febrile

mood. Of course if you were sixteen in the mid-fifties you are a company director or a shop-steward or a mother of three by now, and the temptation to dance in the aisles or slash the upholstery is easily resisted. *Pippin* at Her Majesty's was easily resisted, too, a pathetic (and under-cast) mishandling of a historical figure decked out with some unhistorical facts and a colourful staging by Bob Fosse that it didn't deserve.

At Drury Lane there was a mock twenties production of *No, No, Nanette* that had not much to recommend it but those wonderful songs of Vincent Youmans and a more acceptable brand of nostalgia, being devised for grown people. Strictly speaking, I suppose one should include *The King and I* as an American import too, but the show that went to the Adelphi and occupied it a good deal longer than its management expected was a home-grown production that originally saw life on the touring circuit. Peter Wyngarde and Sally Anne Howes gave sympathetic performances in the lead parts, the costumes were colourful and pretty, and Richard Rodgers's music displayed its lasting qualities to good purpose.

The home-grown products struck no sparks. What is it about the average British musical that is so bloodless? Mostly, I think, the choice of libretto is to blame; it seems always to be based on some work well known and well loved in another form. What can songs and dances add to *Trelawny of the Wells* or *Tom Brown's Schooldays*? What, in the event, did they add to Arnold Bennett's *The Card*? Here was a musical with a well-turned book by Keith Waterhouse and Willis Hall, and a cast that included such likeable people as Jim Dale and Millicent Martin. Why, O why didn't Val May just leave it as a straight play? The songs were quite unmemorable, the lyrics clearly designed to fit the music. To turn a familiar work into a valid musical, you need lyrics that can look the book in the face, as we had in *My Fair Lady* or *Applause*. Whatever the reason (and another factor is that the British do not at the moment possess musical performers with that elusive thing 'star quality'), *The Card* didn't occupy the Queen's long.

Away from the West End, Greenwich gave us a pretty *Zorba* with Alfred Marks in it, which I thought critically under-rated on the whole; and at the Round House there was a perfectly disastrous bit of bad pornography, *Decameron 73*, which no doubt intended to jump on the *Oh Calcutta!* wagon but failed even to get within sight of the bus stop.

The last musical of the year under consideration was a modest revival of the Gershwin–Wodehouse–Bolton success of 1927, *Oh, Kay!* With six in the chorus, five in the band and Amanda Barrie as the only 'name', it was a good try. If I seem to have forgotten *Cockie*, Peter Saunder's misbegotten tribute to the memory of C. B. Cochran, and *Kingdom Coming*, a do-good rock show at the Round House, it's because forgetting them is the kindest thing to do. If I have said nothing of *The Danny La Rue Show*, it's because one can only report that, like Mount Everest, it's there, and those who like Mr La Rue as much as I do will already have seen this, his last performance in drag. If I do not mention *Monty Python* at Drury Lane it's because I believe it belongs on the television screen. I don't count *The Royalty Follies* as theatre either, really.

The early months of 1974 showed on the whole a sharp upgrade in the quality of London theatre. Peter Nichols provided a fine new comedy, *Chez Nous*, in which, as is his wont, he touched on an unspeakable subject and spoke about it, so demonstrating that it was not unspeakable at all. In this case, the subject was the seduction of a very young girl, and it was used as the basis of a beautifully made romantic comedy spoilt only by the extraordinary intrusion of an American couple whose only contribution is an anecdote of singular tiresomeness. (Surely Peter Nichols isn't trying to persuade us that dirtying your underclothes is really touching and romantic?) *Chez Nous* was faultlessly cast, with Denholm Elliott and Albert Finney in the two main men's roles and Geraldine McEwan and Pat Heywood in the women's. There was a pleasant ceremony after the play had run for a few weeks; Miss Heywood's name was promoted, at the insistence of her co-leads, to the same eminence in the neon sign as theirs. Too bad that the 'energy crisis' kept the neons from shining.

A week after the opening of *Chez Nous* we had a revival of Anouilh's *Waltz of the Toreadors*, providing a long awaited opportunity of seeing Trevor Howard on the state again. The occasion was less glad than one had hoped at the first night, for Mr. Howard had a touch of throat trouble that kept him from throwing himself totally into the part of the amorous old General Saint-Pé; but it is a play that I was very pleased to renew acquaintance with, even though in my mind I unaccountably found myself confusing it with *Eurydice.*

Another week, and another return: Rex Harrison, in Pirandello's *Henry IV* of all things. He played the name part in this extremely complex drama with the skill that is so much more evident when he does not have to radiate any kind of charm. This Henry, of Germany, not of England, and anyway only existing in a madman's illusion, is a middle-aged Italian aristocrat who lost his wits twenty years before the play begins but has subsequently recovered them without telling anyone – a Pirandellian theme if ever there was one. The production was something of a concerto for Rex Harrison, the supporting characters being on the whole less than ideally cast, but the play gave a stimulating evening.

Then in mid March a superb revival of *A Streetcar Named Desire*, directed by an American, Edwin Sherin, and containing not only a memorable performance by Claire Bloom as Blanche but admirable playing by Martin Shaw as Stanley Kowalski, Joss Ackland as the respectable neighbour Mitch and Morag Hood as sister Stella. It was grand to see the Tennessee Williams idiosyncrasies in the first flush of their youth again.

A praiseworthy attempt at creating a new stage star out of a film star, a metamorphosis by no means automatic, was made by Michael Codron when he presented Edward Fox in David Hare's play *Knuckle*, a satirical drama in which a story à la Mickey Spillane was transferred to Guildford, of all places, with the evident object of showing up all big businessmen, and business itself, as despicable. I have no particular love for businessmen, but I am an amateur of satire, and though my colleagues could write that *Knuckle* was 'utterly and dizzyingly enjoyable' it seemed to me to have missed its target.

Finally a quick look round outer London. The Hampstead Theatre Club, under the energetic directorship of Michael Rudman, has been augmenting its own finds with imports from further north: *Play Strindberg*, by Dürrenmatt, was a happy visitor from Newcastle, with likeable playing from Yvonne Mitchell and Freddie Jones, and *Black and White Minstrels* by C. P. Taylor (surely actionable under the Trade Descriptions Act?) was a hilarious, splendidly acted comedy from the Traverse. A welcome find was

George Kelly's 1924 comedy, *The Show-Off*, which gave a bravura comedy part to Al Mancini. Skipping from north to south, Greenwich continued the fine tradition set up there by Robin Phillips before he went for a four-year exile to Canada. Mr. Phillips gave us *Three Sisters* and *Rosmersholm* and the pretty musical of *Zorba* and then emigrated; in the spring Jonathan Miller entered with his season of 'family romances' comprising *Ghosts*, *The Seagull* and *Hamlet* of which I have already spoken. There was also *The Maids*, by no means a good production, but a successful one at least.

To the west, the Actors Company, fresh from their successes in New York, put on a season of all their repertoire, which is a formidable one – *The Wood Demon*, *The Way of the World*, *King Lear*, *'Tis Pity She's a Whore*, an English version of Feydeau's *Le Dindon* called *Ruling the Roost*. They had a deserved success there too. But to the east, only sorrow. Joan Littlewood's Theatre Royal, Stratford, ran into money trouble and closed down in March when its final production, *Gentlemen Prefer Anything*, finished. But that is another story.

The National Theatre: Olivier's Final Year

The drama critic of the Guardian *reviews the Old and Young Vic companies at home and away.*

In 1944 James Agate wrote:

One of my more horrid nightmares is about a National Theatre. I envisage a gaunt, hideous building, half barracks, half public baths, stuck down in a part of London remote from restaurants and unfriendly of approach. The director is an amateur who once produced a masque at Slough. The company is dud. The audience is made up of young men in corduroy trousers and the widows of veterinary surgeons. The repertory consists of Shakespeare's *Twelfth Night*, some of the later plays of Priestley and Shaw's *Jitta's Atonement*. Nothing atones to me for the jitters this nightmare affords.

The jaundiced vision of a brilliant reactionary critic? Maybe. But Agate had a habit of hitting nails firmly on their heads; for he went on to say that 'in my view any truly national theatre must be peripatetic'. Somewhat optimistically, he argued that a travelling National Theatre would make a profit in the big cities. 'But,' he added, 'a man is not necessarily smaller-minded because he lives in a smaller town. Let places the size of, say, Huntingdon, be visited, so that there is a worthwhile theatre within the occasional reach of everybody. And let the State, pocketing profits and making losses good, keep this travelling theatre on an even financial keel.'

Why resurrect this now? Because the most exciting experience afforded by the National Theatre in the year under review was watching Jonathan Miller's production of *Measure for Measure* playing to a packed, eager and attentive house in Horsham, Sussex. The production boasted no stars, no TV names, no opulent multiple settings. The audience, quite simply, had come to hear an unfamiliar play and they reacted with a rapt stillness to Shakespeare's complex, ironic fable. This, I suddenly realized, is what a National Theatre is all about: not playing to the theatre saturated audiences of central London but making good drama available to everyone around the country. As Miller himself said, it's as absurd to have a National Theatre situated on the South Bank as it would be to have a National Health Service centred on Guy's Hospital.

One may be accused of base ingratitude for knocking a project that people have been campaigning for since 1848. But my point is that the definition of a National Theatre should change with the times. And it seems to me sadly ironic that at a moment when the theatre is becoming much more rootless, flexible and impermanent and when it is becoming literally impossible to gauge the kind of theatrical experience people will want in 25 years' time that we should be erecting a 10 million pound metropolitan monument on the South Bank. As Agate again said, with uncanny foresight, 'I feel that this is not the time and London is not the place for a pleasure-dome as stately as Sydney would decree.' Though I should in fairness point out he was referring to Sydney Carroll and not to the Australian opera-centre.

But, while questioning the path the National Theatre is taking, I will admit that the final year of Laurence Olivier's directorship yielded a number of first-rate productions. Indeed it was odd that Olivier, allegedly a tradition conscious actor-manager, bowed out with a blistering performance as a Glaswegian Trotskyite in a play about the possibility of revolution in Britain, Trevor Griffiths's *The Party*. Meanwhile Peter Hall, the allegedly bold young innovator, bowed in with a gaudily spectacular and vacuously decorative production of *The Tempest* that Beerbohm Tree would not have been (and probably wasn't) ashamed of. A visitor from Mars might well have assumed that the direction of the National Theatre was passing from the hands of a volatile radical to an academic conservative.

Enlightened radicalism was, in fact, the keynote of Olivier's final season; and even if it didn't always come off, it was at least exhilarating. I was amazed, for instance, how few people appreciated the extent to which Michael Blakemore's production of *The Cherry Orchard* broke with theatrical tradition. For instead of the usual elegiac lament for the replacement of a dithery aristocratic family by a bumptious arriviste we got an assertion of the inevitability of a historical process; instead of English mortgage melodrama we got the play Chekhov actually wrote. And, implicitly, it asked the one question no one usually dares put: why shouldn't the cherry orchard be chopped down and the Ranevsky estate sold?

The key to the play lies in Lopakhin, who purchases the estate. Play him as an upstart peasant with mud on his boots and you instantly load the dice. But Chekhov said in a letter to Stanislavsky in 1903: 'True Lopakhin is a merchant but he's a decent person in the full sense of the word and his bearing must be that of a completely dignified and intelligent man . . . When choosing an actor for this part it must not be forgotten that Lopakhin was loved by Varya, a serious and religious girl. She wouldn't love some wretched money-grubbing peasant.' And the great success of this production was Denis Quilley's merchant: dapper, self-possessed, efficient and filled with a sense of limitless possibilities. He's the only actor I've heard who's given real weight and value to the lines – 'The Lord God has given us vast forests, immense fields, wide horizons; surely we ought to be giants, living in such a country as this . . .'

If Lopakhin was not vulgarized, the family were not sentimentalized. I remember being moved to tears by Peggy Ashcroft and John Gielgud as Ranevsky and Gaev in Michel St Denis's production at the Aldwych in 1961. Yet, in a way, their very dignity, style and grace minimized the characters' irresponsibility and moral decay. Constance Cummings and Michael Hordern may not have achieved the same rhapsodic poetry but they left you in no doubt as to Ranevsky's and Gaev's frivolity and absorption in domestic minutiae: I shall long remember the moment for instance when Lopakhin urged on them the necessity of leasing the cherry orchard and its land for villas while they were busy popping eyes and pulling faces in imitation of their old aunt in Yaroslavl. And Hordern's slightly furtive physical gestures – like stroking Anya's beautiful blonde hair as she swept past – suggested a man for whom the family had become a sexual substitute.

Where Blakemore raised hackles and hell, of course, was in his ending: as the family departed the revolve whirled round to reveal the old manservant, Firs, locked in his room, which resembled an old broom-cupboard, and left apparently to die. I thought this perfectly legitimate, pinpointing, as it did, the unthinking cruelty of the family and the monstrous gulf between the classes in pre-Revolutionary Russia. In that sense it was perfectly in line with his vision of the play as an account of a historically inevitable process, and it's only because we've always used Chekhov in England to symbolize a mood of vague Tory nostalgia for the disappearance of old values that there was such an outcry at Blakemore's conclusion. A more sentimental production would have got a much better response.

Peter Shaffer's *Equus* was another example of Olivier's (and Tynan's?) determination that the National Theatre's tenth season should be as radical as possible. For if Peter Shaffer had gone to a commercial manager and told him that he had written a play about a 17-year-old boy who blinded six horses with a metal spike, that the boy had become passionately attached to one horse, finding in it a combination of sexual and religious satisfaction, and that the play's message was that by rooting out people's abnormalities you destroy a part of their humanity, one can imagine the afore-mentioned manager staring pretty glumly at his paté de campagne and filet de bœuf bordelaise. But I think the play more than earned its place on the National's stage, and John Dexter's production and Alec McCowen's performance as the psychiatrist made up for their earlier misreading of Molière's *The Misanthrope*.

Like Shaffer's earlier plays, *The Royal Hunt of the Sun* and *The Battle of Shrivings*, *Equus* was built around a conflict between reason and instinct, Apollo and Dionysus. And the message was quite plain: reason by itself is never enough. Martin Dysart, Shaffer's psychiatrist seeking to understand and cure the horse-blinding hero, was left envying the boy's passion and worship. 'Without worship you shrink,' he said. 'It's as brutal as that.' And the implication was that by curing the boy and sending him back into what passes for normal society, he was robbing him of some-thing vital. 'Passion, you see, can be destroyed by a doctor. It cannot be created.'

Intellectually, the play's thesis is questionable. It's all very well to say there must be a quality of worship in life for it to be meaning-ful. But I should have thought it rather mattered what one worshipped. A man who worships gold, power or the infliction of physical pain seems to me in no way to be envied: conversely a life devoted to reason need not be devoid of either physical or intellectual passion (vide Bertrand Russell). But, for all that, the play provided a dazzling theatrical experience, combining a detective story excitement with astonishing visual impact. Dexter is a great theatrical animator and by placing a section of the audience on stage behind the actors he created the effect of people staring down into an operating theatre or a miniature bull-ring. Moreover the representation of horses by actors – which could have had acutely embarrassing pantomime overtones – worked in the simplest way: upright, brown-jerseyed actors, wearing skeletal equine heads through which their own features were clearly visible, became horses through a simple twitch of the body or restless pawing of the ground. Alec McCowen (like the RSC's John Wood) is also one of those players who can genuinely act mind, and his performance as the psychiatrist was an exemplary study of desiccated cerebration. Indeed I thought it unfair that Peter Firth, who played the horse-blinding boy, ran off with so many of the notices: though he was perfectly convincing as a turbulent, introverted adolescent, I suspect this was astute Dexterous casting rather than great acting. Looking back on *Equus* I don't think it was the best play of 1973, but none left a stronger visual imprint.

The National's latter-day radicalism, however, came a disastrous cropper with their next production: an adaptation by Wole Soyinka of *The Bacchae* by Euripides. Presumably it was intended as a classical counterpart to *Equus*: a further example of the dangers of a life of cerebration and of the need for liberated ecstasy. But Soyinka's adaptation gravely vulgarized Euripides's masterpiece by turning it into a simple-minded plea for doing your own thing. Indeed as the bacchantes drank from Pentheus's severed head – which at the last became a fountain of wine – unsuspecting customers might have been excused for thinking Euripides's play was an apology for capital punishment. And instead of a nourishing debate between the need for order in society and for personal liberation, we got a trivial tract full of lines like 'Oh yes a handsome profile – quite an asset in your mode of life' (and this to Dionysus).

Admittedly *The Bacchae* is not an easy play to stage today.

Indeed after watching a number of staid muscular bacchantes whirling like dervishes in a celebrated Oxford Playhouse production some years back, I remember a friend of mine remarking: 'It's not everyday you get the chance to see twelve lesbians on the same stage.' And, even when totally modernized, as in a rock music version at Watford a couple of seasons ago, something of the play's primal force still seems to be lost. (Actually the best production I have seen was given by the Tower Theatre Company in a converted Presbyterian church in Edinburgh in the early sixties: I remember ceaseless drumbeats, clear speech and a pervading sense of ritual.) But anything would have been better than Roland Joffe's mish-mash with rump-brandishing fillies from the National's stable rushing about the stage as if they were high on aspirin rather than ecstasy; with Martin Shaw as Dionysus projecting a bisexual aloofness as if he were the touring version of Robert Stephens's Atahuallpa; and with Constance Cummings's Agave making a wild eyed entrance down a stalls ramp suggesting something inexplicably nasty had been going on in the coffee-bar.

The only people to emerge with any credit were Julian Curry whose Tiresias had a flinty, balding splendour, and John Shrapnel whose hefty close-cropped Pentheus momentarily suggested some power-hungry Pentagon redneck literally screaming for order. But for the rest this sorry travesty suggested not so much enlightened radicalism as a perverse and wilful misunderstanding of what the *The Bacchae* is actually about.

Fortunately the National recovered its nerve with Franco Zeffirelli's production of Eduardo De Filippo's glorious and moving Neapolitan comedy, *Saturday, Sunday, Monday*. I was astonished and appalled at the way so many of my colleagues dismissed it as merely an Italian *Coronation Street* or Neapolitan *Waggoner's Walk*. For soap-opera deals only in surface emotions and manufactured crises: Eduardo's comedy is about genuine despair. It may seem to be about a trivial husband–wife quarrel in the course of a bustling family weekend: in fact it's about the ambivalent nature of family life which, under its strangulating cosiness, allows people to with-draw into a mute and self-torturing hatred.

Indeed the play presents one image I shall never forget. It is Sunday lunchtime in the Priore family's marble-tiled Naples apartment. Rosa, the mistress of the house, has prepared a ragout with sacramental fervour. Everyone is dressed in weekend finery from the upstairs accountant in a check sports-jacket to the sedate banker who has turned into a show-off amateur Pulcinella. All is festivity, gaiety and exuberant, trivial chatter. But downstage, apart from the rest, sits Peppino who is convinced his wife, Rosa, is having an affaire with the accountant. And as he silently broods, his heart quietly cracking, while the family enjoys its monumental Sabbath lunch, we know we are in the presence of a real Chekhovian dramatist who can mingle laughter and tears in equal proportions.

The play is, in fact, genuine popular theatre. But whereas we think of that as something broad-bottomed and extravagant, Eduardo's comedy is based on thrift, care and subtlety. His long-range technique, for instance, enables incidents to gather force as the evening goes on: Rosa's loving preparation of a ragout at curtain-rise not only shows that cooking is for her an assertion of female dignity but also helps to fuel her husband's Othello-like jealousy. And the stage is packed with lovingly observed minor characters from the sluttish maid with the bandaged leg and visible underwear (a brilliant cameo from Anna Carteret) to grandfather Antonio, a mad-hatter who reshapes every visitor's titfer into something like a distended pudding-basin. Olivier was magnificent in this role: sly, capering and devilish with a sense of mischief offsetting his drooping walrus moustache and sagging frame. At one superb moment, he politely relieved a visitor of his hat, ostentatiously planted it on a chair and then, secreting it under his coat, exited with the reproachful gaze of a wounded doe.

John Osborne dismissed the whole show as 'airport culture'. But I thought Zeffirelli's production, unlike his awful National *Much Ado About Nothing*, really did persuade you that you were watching an Italian family at play. And Frank Finlay as Peppino beautifully adopted Eduardo's own acting technique (seen at the Aldwych in *Napoli Milionaria*) of providing a still centre in a whirlpool of activity: dapper, grave and trim like a middle-class Keaton, his very quietness made his eventual eruption of emotion seem like a thunderbolt from the heavens. And Joan Plowright's Rosa was not blowzy and matronly but neat and tender and filled with devotional piety in her attitude to food. Martin Esslin got it right when he evoked the name of *Hobson's Choice*; and just as that regional masterpiece (also with Finlay and Plowright) was one of the

National's earliest triumphs, so Eduardo's sad, heartaching comedy brought Olivier's ten-year reign close to its memorable close.

That came, however, with Trevor Griffiths's *The Party*, greeted with those howls of derision English critics always reserve for a rumbustious major talent (Mr Griffiths can console himself with the thought that Whiting, Pinter, Osborne, Arden and, latterly, David Hare have all been subjected to the same rough handling while Coward and Rattigan are still treated with sycophantic and overblown admiration). I think the reason why *The Party* was so generally detested was not merely that it dared to discuss the possibility of revolution in an English (as opposed to American or French) context, but also that it offered the audience three alternative approaches to social change and then left them to decide which was preferable. The English attitude to political theatre seems to be that if we must suffer it at all, at least the damned fellow can give us a simple, clear-cut message to wrap up and take home afterwards. And that Griffiths refused to do.

He also broke another golden rule of modern British theatre: that any speech lasting more than three minutes is a sign of self-indulgent verbosity. In fact Griffiths's play, set in a TV producer's home during May 1968, contained two long 20-minute speeches which in their intellectual sinew and polemical force rivalled anything heard on the British stage since *Saint Joan*. One argued that the new centres of the world revolutionary struggle were not London, Paris, Turin but China, Cuba, Vietnam, the Third World in fact. The second, delivered by Laurence Olivier as a Glaswegian Trotskyite, argued that only through the organization of disciplined revolutionary parties will change ever occur. Both these lines were then held up to critical examination by a drunken left-wing playwright who contended that revolution was a spontaneous growth that occurred only when 'masses of people decide to take on the state and ruling class'.

The arguments themselves were the kind you might hear on any university campus, encounter in any literate political group or read in any intelligent magazine. The exhilaration came from hearing these topics discussed on the English stage where politics is invariably reduced to slogans. Moreover there was a genuine dialectical excitement about hearing a rock solid argument established and then countered by the next speaker. But, above all, the play caught with unerring accuracy the divisiveness, internal jealousy and sheer insecurity of the British left: in particular, of the intellectual left which is summed up by the Trotskyite in a classic phrase. 'You enjoy biting the hand that feeds you but you'll never bite it off.'

John Dexter's production had its flaws (in particular a sexy opening with a naked couple writhing on a bed under a tilted mirror: a scene later cut) and Denis Quilley seemed spectacularly miscast as an LSE lecturer. Indeed Mr Quilley's heavy editorializing about his character (like the gentleman in Daisy Ashford, he was 'very sneery') undermined the whole of the first long speech. But Olivier gave a thrilling performance as the Glaswegian, Tagg, phrasing his long speech with the subtlety of a piece of music and rising to a formidable brick-red crescendo of anger that made the very ground shake. I doubt whether Olivier knows that many Glaswegian Trotskyites, but through sheer acting genius he got under the skin of this one. Nor should one underestimate his buccaneering audacity in choosing this play as the final throw of his ten defiant fever-chart years as head of the National Theatre.

His successor, Peter Hall, bowed in quickly with a production of *The Tempest* using an almost entirely new company (only Denis Quilley survived). And I can only record, with the deepest melancholy, that it was the worst production of this play I have ever seen and one of the three or four worst Shakespearean productions I have encountered in the professional theatre. For it was based on a piece of fatuous historical misunderstanding: namely that *The Tempest* is a masque, a form of private theatrical entertainment that flourished in Renaissance Italy and seventeenth century England. Well, I have news for Mr Hall. *The Tempest* is not a masque. It is a play. And it is actually about specific things such as the triumph of charity over revenge, about the colonial instinct in man and about political usurpation. You would never have guessed this, however, from Mr Hall's production which swamped the stage in effects of breath-bereaving vulgarity: Juno's descent from the skies on a garishly painted rainbow at which even Paul Raymond might have blanched, pantomime trees glistening with coloured lights suggesting less Prospero's magic isle than the sea-front at Margate and a dance by 'the sunburnt sicklemen of August weary' evoking a number three tour of *Oklahoma* on its last legs in West Hartlepool.

The tragedy is that Sir John Gielgud – a great Prospero in Peter Brook's 1957 Stratford production – was here upstaged by the scenery and forced to give a low-key, muted performance that was a mere shadow of its former self. Arthur Lowe and Julian Orchard came off quite well as the comics chiefly I suspect because they were able to advance to the edge of the stage and ignore John Bury's self-raising set. But the rest of the company looked as if they were trapped in some awful nightmare from which there was no escape, at least until the end of the season. It was a dire start to Mr Hall's term of office, and suggested that the enlightened radicalism of Olivier and Tynan had given way to the mindless spectacle of Flo Ziegfeld.

In fact, if one wanted to see Shakespeare properly done one had to turn to the National Theatre's mobile production, directed by Jonathan Miller, of *Measure for Measure*. Here all was clarity, urgency and directness. Setting the play in a repressive 1940-ish bureaucracy, Miller leaned heavily on the Freudian echoes of the Viennese background. Thus Angelo became a dangerously repressed and nervy figure who, declaring his passion to Isabella ('Now do I give my sensual race the rein'), was able to do no more than place a tentative hand on her thigh. Isabella herself was not the usual cloistered novitiate but a busy worker-priestess with a briefcase full of papers and no truck with sex. And the Duke was no haloed God substitute but a rapacious senior civil servant. Indeed I shan't easily forget the ending with Isabella backing away from the Duke's proposal in appalled horror as if she has discovered yet another Angelo.

Where some directors are like interior decorators giving a play a false gloss and sheen, Miller is like an X-ray specialist who exposes the structure and sinew of the work in question. And his *Measure for Measure* worked both as an exciting piece of narrative, as an analysis of the dangers of repressing the libido and as a demonstration of company discipline. Julian Curry's precise, bird-like Angelo, Gillian Barge's attenuated Isabella and Alan Mac-Naughtan's silvery, insinuating Duke were all strong performances; but they were backed by a wealth of excellent support. And to sit and hear a local audience listening to the play as if it was springing on them for the first time was to realize that the National Theatre's true task is to take drama out to the people and not to play to the pampered, culture bloated, self-satisfied mailing-list buffs of central London.

As always, I found the atmosphere at the Young Vic infinitely healthier and more democratic than that at the Old Vic. Frank Dunlop's playhouse is one of the great triumphs of modern times, and should in fact serve as a prototype for anyone building a new theatre anywhere in Britain. During the year Dunlop once again established a sane balance between revivals of standard modern classics (*Rosencrantz and Guildenstern Are Dead, The Caretaker* and *Roots*), Shakespeare (*Much Ado About Nothing*) and the occasional surprise revival (Rattigan's *French Without Tears*). Stoppard's *Rosencrantz*, in Bernard Goss's production, actually came over better at the Young Vic than it did in the sumptuous National Theatre original: swifter, cleaner, sharper and funnier with Nicky Henson and Andrew Robertson establishing a genuine music-hall rapport as the attendant lords finding themselves on the fringe of great events. I didn't care much for the Pinter revival which seemed to be happening behind an invisible gauze, and *Roots*, I thought, was marred by one or two vulgar, reppy performances, although Tamara Ustinov's Beatie was extremely touching in her bright eyed puppy-like eagerness.

However, *Much Ado About Nothing* was given a brilliant Risorgimento production by Frank Dunlop that had one of the most credible Beatrice and Benedicks I have seen in Denise Coffey and Andrew Robertson, and even Rattigan's lightweight *French Without Tears* earned its stage-time in another mellow, beautifully set (by Carl Toms) Dunlop production. Like B. A. Young in *Theatre 73*, I get constant refreshment out of going to the Young Vic: the shining youthful faces, the generally high company standards, the catholic choice of play, the blast of pop music as you go in, even the acrid coffee in paper cups in the bar all help to make it a cheerful, informal, endlessly stimulating place in which to watch a play. I gather that under the new dispensation the Young Vic will become more or less detached from the National Theatre organization. But all I can say is that I hope Peter Hall pops down there occasionally to see how it is possible to give a theatrical building a sense of expectant life. If he can capture that feeling in his South Bank cultural fortress, he will be extremely lucky.

The New Man at the National

Peter Hall talks of his plans with the arts reporter of the Evening
Standard *and offers a facility for the British theatre as a whole.*

Clouds sometimes swirl around Peter Hall's apartment at the top
of a Barbican tower and you get an uneasy feeling you are in
Valhalla. That is, if you can get to the tower without being killed.
The approach road is still not properly made up and there are no
pavements offering refuge from the busy traffic.

Mr Hall likes new things and is obviously happy living in this
bright ultra-modern home with walls of glass. There are modern
paintings everywhere and the latest in lighting and furnishing in
the large open lounge. But there is also a harpsichord and in his
study with its shiny black walls you'll find an upright piano and
on one wall the Royal Horticultural Society's colour chart. There
are also, of course, volumes of *Spotlight* and several books on the
Mozart operas. If you glance out of the window you look down on
St Paul's and can see across to the new National Theatre on the
South Bank. If you look straight down you can see the foundations
of the new RSC Barbican theatre.

He maintains he's at his lowest between 5 and 7 p.m. As it
happens we met at 6 p.m. for a drink and a talk about the new
National Theatre. There was not the slightest sign of the energy
flagging. He had been up at 6.30 a.m. and working at his desk at
7 before having breakfast with his two children at 8.30. This is his
regular routine. One can understand why. He is concerned with so
many different things involved in the opening of the new National
Theatre on the South Bank.

Within a few minutes he had talked about the logistics of the productions going into the new theatre, the seat pricing policy, contracts for actors, the catering facilities for the public, visits by foreign companies, how to secure the maximum use of the magnificent workshops, facilities for TV films, and so on. There is also his work casting productions and seeing new productions in London and the regions. And directing.

There is a striking buoyancy about him. The direct brown eyes fix you, smiling. He seems sure-footed, despite all the work involved. His short beard is turning grey, otherwise he looks a young forty-three. The gear is contemporary: shirt open at the neck, green trousers, leather jacket. He smokes small cigars as he talks.

At one point his small son came into the room with a cello bigger than he was and asked his father to tune it. Then a little later came the sound from the next room of Vera Lynn singing 'We'll Meet Again'. This turned out to be part of the film track of Hall's film of *Akenfield*, the sequence being a village hall dance in 1943. The room next door, filled full of equipment, is used for cutting and editing films.

The Hall career is already well known. The Suffolk stationmaster's son who won a scholarship to Cambridge where he directed his first play. At twenty-four he was director of the Arts Theatre in London when it was a much more important theatre than it is now. At twenty-nine he was given complete control of the Stratford Memorial Theatre and he built up, between 1959 and 1968, the RSC into one of the best classical companies in the world. Since then there have been operas and films, with varying success. Since he began directing he has been responsible for more than eighty major productions – four a year on average.

'My generation of directors was so lucky,' he says. 'There was a big vacuum after the war. I suppose we're now the establishment.' He laughs as he talks about the Cambridge Mafia, 'all the people who were at Cambridge around the same time: John Barton, Peter Wood, Toby Robertson, Jonathan Miller, Julian Slade, David Jones, Tony Church, Michael Birkett, Michael Bakewell, Freddy Raphael . . .' Hall is undoubtedly The Godfather. Cambridge is the most important factor in understanding him. It was there that his brilliance became plain but it was also the foundation of the confidence and attitudes that have never left him and the key for the successful escape from his early environment.

He talks easily about his young days if you ask. 'Most of my family were farm labourers and odd-job men. Yes, my grandfather was a rat catcher.' A smile. 'I grew up on a little railway station at Barnham, near Thetford. The line is closed now, of course. We lived in a two-up and two-down little house on the station with a waterpump outside and oil lamps. I'd pump the water out in the mornings. There were four trains a day.'

He was an only child and his parents were ambitious for him. He and they knew the only escape route was through education. He won a scholarship to the Perse school in Cambridge and became head boy. Then he won a scholarship to the university. 'If I'd been born 20 years earlier I would not have got to the university and I'd be God knows what.' He sees a great deal of his parents. Is there a divide of interests between them now? 'It is a bit difficult. One is judging them – or are they judging me?' One aspect of being an only child still affects him. 'As a director I can associate in some measure to any form of human relationship except brother and sister. I'm very anxious about that. I'm fascinated by it looking from the outside and watching my own children.'

At this point he did not know the actual date the National Theatre company would occupy the new building on the South Bank and its three theatres. Either February or a month or so later:

But the organization is ready and the minute we're told the date of occupation we're ready. This is the result of two years' work. We have and are continuing to build up a bank of productions. We've also planned the work for the actors so they know when they are coming to us and when they are free of us. We want extreme flexibility.

I want particularly to reduce the time lag between when an author writes a play and sees it put on. This will happen in the Cottesloe, the small theatre. A writer can't write another play until the one he has finished has been performed – consummated. Shakespeare wrote thirty-three plays because he was driven to that productivity. Today there is such a time lapse.

The main theatre, the Olivier, will be used for the National Theatre's repertoire of between four and seven productions but the Lyttelton will be used not only by the National but by visiting companies and for seasons round a theme. For example I would like to see seasons of a particular dramatist's work or a designer's or a certain period of European drama.

We're trying to work out a sensible rhythm for the actors' lives so they will have a commitment to us and a freedom from us. Three different forms of contract are being offered, each is calculated around a basic eight-month span.

I want the seat price policy to be acceptable in community terms. I want the people who can and want to pay more but I don't want to keep out those who can't. It will not be an expensive theatre.

I want the catering to be available for people who want to pop in for a drink and a snack. We don't want institutional airport catering. This is still a problem we're wrestling over. There are seven bars, a restaurant, and two self-service buffets. These and the terraces will be open to the public all day every day. Tickets will only be necessary to get into the auditoriums.

I want the whole place to be a unique riverside centre for the public. There will be a great variety of offerings constantly on show, including Sundays.

As well as the productions in the main auditoria there will be lunch-time, late-night and other performances on the terraces and in the foyers.

I also want to see the absolutely magnificent workshops available for the whole of the London theatre. I want them to be used to the maximum in every way possible.

Hall said he was already at work on his shopping list of regional and foreign companies he is inviting to perform on the South Bank. Particularly regional companies. 'This has got to be a facility for the British theatre as a whole, not just a home for the National Theatre company which represents the tastes of its director and his associates.'

He had also planned a big step-up in touring by the National Theatre company not only in this country but abroad.

He returns to the subject of actors and the big responsibility of the theatre to look after talent – 'to have the right people in the right places at the right time'. He went on: 'One knows a lot of talent starts to shrivel if there is not the right opportunity for it. This is a very tough profession. Everyone who has talent is sooner or later recognized but in a small number of cases it is too late.'

He also plans to nourish associations with European dramatists. 'I have an unpleasant feeling that unless we find some actual purpose in life in this country we will decline into a second rate sensibility. The theatre is important to prevent this and we must nourish our knowledge of Europe. I feel a European. You can't work in the theatre and opera, and travel without feeling this.'

Finally, turning to his own career, what about a statement he once made that 'a man's present contains not only his past but his future?' He replied:

One's life and career is an already written scenario. It may be extremely sentimental and fatalistic to say it but if I'm absolutely honest one half of me did believe I would run the RSC and the other half believed it was impossible. I sort of half knew in my bones the National might come into my life. And I'm pretty sure I'll end up living in Suffolk as an old man or at Cambridge. One likes to think one will be having something to do with the university at the end.

Regrets at reaching the age of forty-three?

My main reaction is that of awareness of the passing years, and one must intensify even more what one does. There is so much I still want to do. I want to direct Ibsen and Chekhov, the Greek tragedies, *Tamberlaine* (desperately), Shaw, most of the Mozart operas at Glyndebourne and *The Ring*, one day. I've nearly done *The Ring* three times. I've studied it so much it comes out of my ears. I love making films. There's so much I'd like to do and haven't done. I've only made one film that is absolutely me, *The Homecoming*.

But most of all I like running something. And what more could one ask at forty-three than being director of the National Theatre when the British theatre is bursting with talent?

Three Theatres in One

*. . . and a fourth 'whose backcloth is London'. An architectural look at
the new South Bank complex.*

Denys Lasdun's National Theatre building, due to open early in
1975, is not one theatre, but three. Indeed, in a sense it is four
theatres – possibly in fine weather even five. Before any of the
august aldermen who sought so hard to trim the scale of capital
spending on the project succumb to apoplexy, let me explain. The
building, whose cluster of white concrete towers rises from the
riverside just downstream of Waterloo Bridge, contains two large
theatres as big as or bigger than the present Old Vic, and one much
smaller studio or experimental theatre. But Lasdun says: 'There is
a fourth theatre, whose backcloth is London'. The stage is the river,
on one of whose sharpest bends his building has a key position. And
what is going on on that stage, he says, 'is a conversation between
St Paul's, Somerset House, Waterloo Bridge – and the theatre'. A
powerful and glittering cast, indeed, with everyone waiting to see
how the newcomer will perform.

How will it perform? National Theatre people appear convinced that it will work superbly. The National's general manager,
Anthony Easterbrook, notes: 'Architects always say that in
designing a theatre, you must start with the stage–audience relationship. In practice, they rarely seem to. But Lasdun certainly
has done it.' The word 'perform' as applied to a theatre building
can be said to pose four different questions. How does it perform
for the people who work in it, whether actors or technicians or

administrators? How does it perform for the audience when watching and listening? How does it perform in its public places outside the auditoriums, as a place to arrive in and spend time in, to eat or drink in or simply kill time in? And finally, how does it perform visually as a building in the town and, in this case, river, scene? Let us look initially at the third of those aspects – what the new National will be like for the theatre-goer arriving there for the first time in 1975, and how it strikes him as he approaches it.

The theatregoer coming by car first becomes aware of his destination when, if coming from the north, he is crossing Waterloo Bridge: a cluster of white towers (two fly-towers and four tops of lift-shafts), and below them a number of apparently separate horizontal spaces alive with people. From the south he sees the shape of the building clearly as he reaches the Waterloo Road–York Road roundabout – the distant view that Lasdun thinks the best.

In either case the driver must double back onto the Belvedere Road–Upper Ground axis that passes below the bridge. The access road to the entrance runs one-way along the east side of the building. The driver can dip down into the car park before he reaches it, however, and he and his passengers take a lift to the foyer. Or, if for instance he has an elderly or infirm passenger, he may drive on round the north (river) side of the building and set them down there, under cover. That alighting point, which will also take coaches and VIP cars, is, the architect believes, 'probably the largest covered setting down place of any building in London'. Your car driver then goes on round to use a second ramp down to the underground car park from the west side of the building. Either way, on a wet night the arrival should be remarkably dry and painless.

But what of the majority who (either from poverty or by choice) arrive carless, on foot or by public transport. From bus stops on Waterloo Bridge there are direct stairways down to the theatre. From the Waterloo Station direction, the GLC's upper level walkway system, soon to be roofed over, provides one link straight to a terrace on the west side of the theatre. A new pedestrian underpass beneath Upper Ground links with the low-level footway system from the centre of the Waterloo roundabout. There is a choice of routes round the theatre from the south – open for fine weather, in the protection of overhanging arcades in bad weather.

But all routes lead to the main entrance – which is really three entrances, one above another. The bottom one is below ground at car park level, the next at ground level, the third, with an exciting flight of steps rising up to it, at first floor, walkway, level. The story of that flight of steps, set in an L-shaped corner of the building and its focal point as seen both from the bridge and the riverside, is worth the telling. Lasdun originally designed two flights of steps, one on each side of the present location. Olivier saw the plans and demurred. Dramatically it was a mistake, he said, to dilute attention by splitting the point of entrance. Lasdun accepted the argument and redesigned that part of the building with one dramatic staircase.

The story spotlights the way in which this building is the result, again in Lasdun's words, of 'a confrontation between the art of drama and the art of architecture'. It also illustrates an important feature of Lasdun's commission. The client for the building was the South Bank Theatre Board, representing the providers of the money. But it was the users, the National Theatre, who within financial limits wrote Lasdun's brief and conducted the day-to-day dialogue with the architect. (Far too many buildings suffer from having the architect's brief written by a client who is not the user and does not sufficiently understand his needs.)

But on into the building, pausing only to notice, in the key and most accessible position next to the staircase, the main booking office – approachable on fine days without even entering the building, and with the possibility in rain or if there are long queues, for ticket buyers to be led round inside the building past a refreshment counter while they wait. For this is a cardinal point about the new National. Its foyers and bars and terraces and buffets are conceived as public space, which people are free to enter and use whether they are going to a performance or not. 'The building will be alive,' says Lasdun. 'We are determined that it should not be a dead building,' says Easterbrook. 'We shall only look at tickets when people try to enter the auditoriums.'

So then (a nod being as a good as a wink) on, in! And the first thing that perhaps we notice is that the beautifully laid blue-brick paving runs on into the building, giving us time to walk the rain off our feet. Then carpet (likely to be a neutral earth colour that will not date) takes over. The next thing we notice is that the walls

are bare white concrete of an unusually pure mix, with no adorn-
ment or decoration. It is almost puritan in its economy: concrete,
carpets, lights – and people. 'You are the decoration,' explains
Lasdun. And for those who habitually use 'concrete' as an architectural term of abuse, he would add that there is concrete and concrete. The effect he has sought to produce is given by the quality of
the concrete, the texture of the concrete, and the very careful,
skilful lighting of the concrete. The only exception is the handrail.
'Where your hand is likely to go, or where you have to touch or are
very near to something, you are protected by a beautiful dark
brown wood.' The ceilings are a coffer-like 'diagrid' in a fine
marbled concrete.

The next thing we notice is that this part of the building is a big
and dramatic public space – a huge drawing room; like the Piazza
San Marco in Venice, says Lasdun – but not one that reveals itself
at once. We discover it gradually, as we turn corners or climb stairs,
pass through doorways or look through a window or over a parapet.
It starts, and in all save two places remains, human scale, with
ceilings 8 ft–9 ft high. The two main foyers, one for the 899 seat
Lyttelton Theatre, one for the 1165 seat Olivier Theatre, the one
higher and to one side of the other, are the exceptions.

Entering the foyer to the lower Lyttelton Theatre, for instance,
we have suddenly an impression of tall, white floodlit columns, and
glimpses on into other more intimate places, half hidden by wall
angles or staircases. The columns are something like 30 ft tall, but
the shape of the space, and the contrast with lower ceilings elsewhere, makes it seem higher and almost temple-like. And we notice
something else. The columns, rectangular in cross-section, are
sometimes at right angles to each other, sometimes on the diagonal.
The significance of this does not appear at first. It is that the two
auditoria are at 45 degrees to each other, meeting at the foyer area.
The plan of this part of the foyer is rather like that familiar geometrical concept 'the squares on the other two sides' of an isosceles
triangle. In place of the square on the hypotneuse is the open air
focus, with ticket office, to bridge and river. And the more one
looks, the more the incredible purity of design grows on one. There
is no angle to be found, no wall, no pillar, no staircase parapet, that
is not either at 90 or at 45 degrees to all other verticals.

Each of the two main theatres has, in effect, three foyers: a stalls foyer, a circle foyer and a buffet, each at a different level and each with an entirely different character. Whereas the stalls foyer of the Lyttelton Theatre is spacious with views out through an unusual concave 'reverse bay window' of vast proportions, the dress circle foyer is dark and intimate with only glimpses out above and below a terrace hung on the side of the building. Higher up again and to one side, the buffet is like a diamond-shaped platform with breast-high ramparts on most sides, and the buffet counter projecting, peninsula-like, from a diagonal wall. Increasingly one realizes that this public part of the building, arranged round the outside of the L represented by the two auditoria, is not so much a solid as a series of platforms suspended at different levels and in different vertical relationships to one another. The fact that Lasdun brilliantly refrains from the obvious and does not join walls vertically but often just stops short of doing so, enhances this sense of lightness and of unfolding vistas and levels. His stairway walls are broken at the turn to give views out into foyers or bars. His main restaurant, hung midway between ground and first floor, has two large dramatic windows at right angles to each other: one frames Somerset House; the other looks out on the columns and spaces of the Lyttelton stalls foyer.

As the warning sounds for curtain-up, we move towards the auditoriums, and sense an immediate change of atmosphere. The ceiling heights of the approach corridors become lower; the walls are clad in hessian. These 'hush tunnels' are deliberately designed to put us in a quieter, more expectant mood. And so into one or other of the auditoriums: the Lyttelton, pointing south-west from the focus of foyers, a theatre with proscenium arch; the Olivier, pointing south-east with an open stage after the fashion of the Globe, the arena of Verona or the theatre at Epidorus.

Why two main auditoriums? Architect and theatre people answer as one. One auditorium combining the two roles and qualities was just not possible. 'You can't turn a duck into a swan,' says Lasdun dismissively. 'It would have been false economy,' says Easterbrook, 'tying directors and actors down to an uncomfortable compromise for ever after.' They fought the false economics of politicians and accountants manfully and won.

Lyttelton (557 stalls, 342 circle) is, however, not plain English conventional proscenium arch. The proscenium arch is a false one

and can be moved or removed. The stage is in five sections, each of
which is a lift that can rise, fall or rake. The front three sections can
drop to form a good size orchestra pit. The fire curtain has an upper
and a lower half, one rising, the other dropping – and the lower
section forms a front wall to the orchestra pit. The main stage
(excluding this front strip) is roughly 40 ft by 40 ft. It is matched
by equivalent areas to one side and back, almost 30 ft high, from
which scenery can be moved on tracks. Above the main stage an
80 ft high fly-tower can carry the taller sets. Seats are mounted
on bench-type supports, beneath which (one to every one or two
seats) are the air conditioning outlets. Few British theatres or halls
have really silent air conditioning. (The Queen Elizabeth Hall is one
exception, though Easterbrook points out that it is if anything
more important to have silent air conditioning for a Pinter play,
where the pauses can be of great dramatic significance, than for a
Beethoven quartet.) By spreading rather than concentrating outlets, the equipment here avoids any noticeable hiss or draught.

At the back of the stalls in the Lyttelton, as in the Olivier, is a
row of glass-screened control rooms for director, stage manager,
lighting and sound personnel. Windows can be slid down for natural
sound. At the back of the circle are more boxes fitted with front
projection apparatus and simultaneous translation. Both auditoriums are designed for maximum contact and rapport between
actors and audience. Contrast the Old Vic, which has a transverse
aisle running across the stalls in front of row O. That transverse
aisle is a dead spot for actors on stage. In the Lyttelton it does not
exist. Nor is there any centre aisle. The actor looks at and speaks
to audience, not dead space. And the auditorium goes more than
one row further back than the equivalent of the Old Vic's row O.
The Lyttelton should be a more intimate theatre than the Old Vic,
thinks Easterbrook.

The Olivier auditorium is, in plan, two squares with over-
lapping corners forming a third square. One square is the theatre's
huge and well equipped backstage area, the second, with its far
corner cut off, is the audience, seats spread out in a fan shape. The
smaller common area has set in it a 40 ft diameter circle, and that is
the stage. And what a stage! It consists of a drum going down
45 ft, in which are built two independent, semicircular lifts with a
sliding lid to cover one or other of them. Each lift can take a set

40 ft wide, 20 ft deep and 25 ft high, weighing up to 9·5 tons. The stage can revolve silently, and its two separate lifts can rise and fall as it does so. The lifts can go up or down in 27 seconds and one revolution of the stage can take any time between 12 seconds and 2·5 hours. Actors can enter or leave the lift at midway points (there are safety devices to prevent their being chewed up in the revolve) and above the stage in the fly-tower is a grid with more than ninety hoists. The lighting is similarly wide and flexible in its range. It is therefore no surprise to learn that a concrete box high in the backstage area houses a computer to programme it all. But the most important point about the Olivier auditorium is, none the less, that it has met directors' and actors' demands for a 'theatre in one room' in which the actor on the stage has his audience fanning out in front of him over an angle of 90 degrees, instead of acting 'into a tunnel'.

Which brings us to the workshop behind the stage, the bulk of the iceberg of which we normally only see the tip. This may be taken in two parts. Actors' accommodation, and production unit. This latter, a combination of factory and cathedral, is housed in a distinct though linked building to the south, lower and faced in white flint brick. Its most surprising aspect is its roadways. The scenery entrance can take two 40 ft lorries side by side and from this point wide roadways 25 ft high – as big as an ordinary semi-detached house – run in two directions linking metalwork, carpentry and paint shops to the stages of the two theatres. There are also scenery docks, a fireproof store for as yet untreated timber, and two major rehearsal rooms each of which can take full size scenery. This area also accommodates armourers and property departments. Props. workshops are in small units, to avoid the difficulties and conflicts of, say, two people in the same room, one sculpting, the other engaged in delicate work on some parchment document.

Dressing room spaces for 135 are arranged round an open court-yard in the centre of the building on four floors. Most actors have dressing spaces grouped in half-dozens, with sitting out area, showers and lavatories and wardrobes in common. The dressing cubical itself, curtained off but with lockable cupboards and drawers, is however more spacious and well equipped than even stars have in most theatres. By a loudspeaker above his make-up

mirror, the actor can select sound from any auditorium and control
its volume. The lockable drawer is, points out Easterbrook, deep
enough to take a gin bottle. Stars have dressing rooms either with
their own sitting room, shower and toilet facilities or grouped in
pairs, sharing these facilities. The actors, like other theatre staff,
have the use of the 100 seat staff restuarant next to the public
restaurant but with even better views, looking towards St Paul's. In
arranging it thus, Lasdun was giving effect to Olivier's demand that
theatre people, who spent most time in the building, should enjoy
the very best position. Above the dressing rooms and set back from
the courtyard behind a terrace, are laundry, wardrobe and costume
departments with drying rooms for cloth and space for hanging 100
metres of dyed cloth.

Close to the stages are the green-room and VIP reception rooms
with their own washrooms and direct access both to the dressing
room block and to the front stalls of their respective theatres. In
the main foyer is a 'communications point' with phone and plug-in
point for microphone so that the house manager can make public
announcements. At each entry point to the auditoria are phones so
that staff can quickly check with the office any query on tickets.

On the eastern corner of the main building, with its own
entrance, is the Cottesloe (or Studio) Theatre, which the architect
managed early on to embed so deeply in his design as to defeat the
most determined efforts of economy-minded politicians to remove
it. The National Theatre places great store by it. Inside, during
construction, it looked just like a very large, bare squash court – indeed building workers regularly played fottball in it. It has a
separate entrance because it was felt that some of its younger
devotees might not care to be associated with the dinner-jacket and
tiara goings-on of gala nights in the main theatres. The National's
managers believe that experiment is the life-blood of living theatre,
but the studio theatre is meant for top quality experiment, and
that is why its space and equipment are generous. It must tempt
your Halls, Brooks and Oliviers to use it.

And finally the riverside, with its diagonals of blue brick paving
echoing the coffer-like 'diagrid' ceilings of the foyers, its sunken
road, grass bank up to the riverside walk, and double row of trees
to be provided by the GLC. All this integrates with the terraces,
on one of which is an attractive roof garden and space, in fine

weather, for small dramatic events – that possible fifth theatre!
All this, says Lasdun, must 'be alive with people. There's not much
point in having a space [like this riverside one between theatre,
bridge and river] unless you activate it.' He hopes to see not only
railway timetable-like displays, announcing what the theatre has to
offer, along the arcades at ground level, but all manner of activities
from newspaper and flower selling to cabaret and art exhibitions.
'Peter Hall intends to have the place humming.' The National
Theatre will interconnect with other activities at the Festival and
Queen Elizabeth Halls, Hayward Gallery and National Film
Theatre and should, in Lasdun's expectation, 'have a profound
effect on the whole South Bank.' The public parts of the building
will be open all day and every day, its buffets, bars and foyers
tempting people in with food and drink, events and happenings. He
has, he says, tried to design the interiors as a one-class place. 'People
should feel equally comfortable in jeans or evening dress.' And
they should be moved to join in. Lasdun believes and hopes the
building has the qualities to stimulate that. As a favourable omen,
he cites the day of the topping-out ceremony. Plenty of beer for
the workforce is, of course, traditional on these occasions. Even
so, it was a surprise when in that upper foyer, bricklayers and
plasterers' labourers 'suddenly began dancing and singing'. If the
building sometimes stimulates regular theatregoers to do that then,
one feels, Denys Lasdun will be well satisfied.

Royal Shakespeare Company

The drama critic of the New Statesman *reports on the RSC at* Stratford, the Aldwych and the Place.

The Royal Shakespeare Company's main function is, of course, to give us Shakespeare, and in 1973 it seemed to be very nearly its only one. The custom of tempering the Stratford season with a play by one of the lesser Elizabethans or Jacobeans continued, alas, to be observed only in the breach. Those marvellous productions of *The Revenger's Tragedy* and *Women Beware Women* are now only a dwindling memory. At the Aldwych, the previous year's offerings remained in the repertoire until a long and formidable World Theatre Season, after which Shakespeare was performed until Christmas. If there hadn't been a short experimental season at the 250 seat Place in the late autumn, there would have been no new plays at all from the RSC in 1973: nothing but Bardomania from *The Island of the Mighty* in 1972 to *Sherlock Holmes* in 1974.

But, in my view, the concentration was fully justified. On the one hand, it's true that the company plays Shakespeare the better for being intermittently immersed in other work. Would John Wood have been so effective as Brutus if he hadn't tackled Richard Rowan in *Exiles* or the weary, introverted Yakov in Gorki's *Enemies*? Would he, later still, have made so unexpectedly complex a Holmes if he hadn't been Brutus? The RSC's system has been, roughly speaking, to have the Stratford and Aldwych companies swap places each year, so that the actor who is Lear one year may find himself playing Pinter's Caretaker the next. Largely as a result, Shakespeare has been performed with more psychological realism, his poetry spoken with a more exacting sense of its meaning, and more attention has been given to the text of modern plays, greater dramatic resonance achieved.

On the other hand, it was a genuinely exceptional year. The RSC usually brings south one or two of the previous season's Stratford offerings – but how could it do so when those offerings had been planned and executed as one long production, organic and indivisible? 1972 had been the year of the Roman plays, and now London had to be given a chance to see what many critics, myself included, had hailed as a notable achievement. And so everything else was squeezed out while *Coriolanus, Julius Caesar, Antony and Cleopatra* and *Titus Andronicus* were squeezed in – a tricky undertaking, with so large a cast involved. Indeed, the soothsayer had actually to enter through the Aldwych auditorium, shouting 'beware the Ides of March' from the point where I and several of my fellow reviewers customarily sit: which lent a certain wry ambiguity to Caesar's reply, 'Who is it in the press that calls on me?' 'It is the *Daily Telegraph*', muttered my neighbour beneath his breath.

Especially in *Julius Caesar*, much of the imperial spectacle was lost en route from the vaulty Stratford stage (which reminded some of a vast, white, very clean bathroom) to the relative coal bunker of the Aldwych. The banners, the brazen emblems, the marching and counter-marching soldiery had a more arbitrary, less carefully drilled look. But the performers mostly weathered the trip with success, and the main newcomer to the cast was little short of superb. I mean Nicol Williamson, who had taken on the title-role in *Coriolanus* from the gifted but flimsy Ian Hogg.

Mr Williamson hasn't the sort of charisma traditionally associated with noblemen in British productions of Shakespeare, and his Coriolanus was neither heroic, nor romantic, nor even attractive. No advertising agency would have hired him to promote deodorant, though a well meaning friend might have sent him some. No computer dating bureau would have accepted anyone so raw and sweaty onto its list, as it certainly would have Olivier or Burton or even Ian Hogg when they took the part. He had none of that public school fastidiousness, that narcissism, others have found in

Coriolanus. Rather, he was a tough-minded puritan, uncompromising in his socio-political convictions, and tending towards
fanaticism, a John Knox of Ancient Rome. In his mouth, the
mildest remark could become massively sarcastic, a blend of growl,
sneer and spit. Even his mother – a very wolfish Margaret Tyzack –
seemed to exasperate him with her constant attentions. Happiness
for him, one felt, was single-handed conquest on the battlefield,
unencumbered by relatives or admirers or the lumpen proletariat
of Rome.

But Mr Williamson wasn't only capable of authority, anger
and high contempt: he didn't only spend the evening stalking the
Italian braes in search of heretics to decapitate. His most remarkable
efforts were reserved for the moment when his mother persuaded
him not to destroy Rome. Mr Williamson stood there, his face red
and anguished, holding the audience rapt for a longer pause than I
can recall having endured before in a theatre. After what seemed
minutes, he suddenly put out his hand; and then, after what
seemed yet more minutes, he spoke. 'Mother, mother, what have
you done?' came with a pucker and a sob, painful to see, and we
realized that the mailed fist held, of all things, a baby's rattle.

The production around this performance had not, however,
travelled well from Stratford to London. On the first night, at
least, it seemed sloppy and sleepy, with messengers wandering on
stage to report cataclysmic events in voices that implied they were
really referring to some fleeting contretemps with the tea-lady in
the green-room. Trevor Nunn, the director of the RSC, was responsible for this, as he was for the other three Roman plays, all of
which survived the journey better. Indeed, *Titus Andronicus* had
actually improved – partly because Colin Blakely, in the title role,
was far less verbally affected than before, and partly because Mr
Nunn seemed at last to be directing the play as it was rather than
the play as he wished it to be.

He explained the purpose of the season himself in last year's
edition of this series, so I won't reopen the argument, at least in any
detail. It seems to me sensible and rewarding to present the three
mature plays together, since they have more in common than the
coincidence of being set in Rome. In which others does Shakespeare take so concentrated an interest in politics? Where else does
he so carefully chart the terrain in which public and private motives

collide? Moreover, the three plays work towards a logical and topical conclusion, the triumph of the organization man (one might say, the Eurocrat) at the end of *Antony and Cleopatra*. But *Titus* is an apprentice work, crude and stupid beside them, with verse that bumps and hobbles along, on wooden crutches. At Stratford Mr Nunn, helped by waxen grapes, tried to suggest that it was, in fact, a sensuous and luxurious portrayal of the fall of Ancient Rome; in London, he dropped this pretence, which made its inclusion in the season even more bewildering, but the production itself more straightforward and vigorous. And Mr Blakely – though still inclined to tell his mutilated daughter that she 'hust noo heands' – brought a grizzled, earnest honesty to his part, precluding all possibility of laughter.

Nunn's two most successful productions were, however, *Julius Caesar* and *Antony and Cleopatra*. True, the latter lacked a pretty important element, some would say the most important element. One could not be absolutely sure that Janet Suzman's Cleopatra was genuinely in love with Richard Johnson's genial, fruity Antony. If one was to enjoy the performace, it was necessary to accept the possibility that Cleopatra's wiles exceeded her passion. This was, you felt, the Shaw Cleopatra caught in the process of becoming the Shakespeare Cleopatra, and perhaps even achieving that status in a noble, indeed regal death. She was a skittish, wayward girl, but also formidably intelligent, the mistress of her emotions and not their victim; one who committed suicide, not for lost love, but to preserve her independence and integrity and, as such, a pristine propagandist for what we now call women's liberation.

I admired this performance, for all its self-imposed limitations. But if I were to choose one player from the Roman cycle for special celebration, it would have to be the Brutus and Saturninus, John Wood. Mr Wood is, I believe, the most intellectually exciting actor in Britain. He hasn't enormous physical presence – indeed, it was impossible to resist comparing him in his toga with Wee Willie Winkie in his nightgown, all knobbly elbows, scrawny skin and ectomorphic chest. He hasn't the emotional power of an Anthony Hopkins, let alone an Olivier. But for subtlety, for irony, for self-mockery, for introversion, for neurosis, for double or treble meanings, he is the very man. Indeed, one might describe him as *Seven Types of Ambiguity* made flesh. As such, he's the most thoroughly modern actor we have, the one who most completely expresses the convoluted, self-doubting spirit of our age.

At Stratford, his Saturninus was narcissistic, hysterical and conceivably even certifiable, slithering across the floor (as he did) to sink his teeth into a sycophant's calf, and his Brutus was a marvel. He showed us self-esteem, priggishness, condescension, self-absorption, intellectual dexterity, not to say complexity. Here was someone at his happiest when he could sit alone and contemplate the fascinating absurdity of a world where one dear friend could assassinate another. The problem of Roman liberty became a sort of de Bono brain-teaser, designed for his special enjoyment, and solved by the spinsterish jab he eventually gave to the throat of Caesar (who said, as well he might, 'Et tu, Brute?' and died of absolute bewilderment). His tragic flaw was to overrate the importance of thought and the power of reason, as he himself seemed to realize at the end of the play, when he put a dreadful sarcasm into the claim that Brutus 'bears too great a mind' to go captive to Rome. This was a man who could boast of and scoff at his own virtues in a single breath.

When it reached London, this extraordinary performance was much more muted (as, less regrettably, was Mr Wood's Saturninus). Mr Nunn had evidently decided that, because of it, the emphasis of the production was too exclusively on the gyrations of the liberal conscience and too little on the business of power politics. So Mr Wood tried to efface himself, and other characters were given more attention. At Stratford, Brutus had treated the furious Cassius in the tent scene with weary exasperation and a poorly disguised contempt that even outlived their supposed reconciliation; in London, much of the primness had gone from his voice, the mocking smile from his face – he was warmer, friendlier, and *was* reconciled. If anything, Patrick Stewart's Cassius (incoherently battering the table with blunt instruments and flinging military papers about) was allowed to dominate the confrontation. More justice was perhaps done to the play, but at the cost of some disappointment to connoisseurs of bravura acting.

Perhaps because so many had to be in London for the Roman season, the company at Stratford lacked depth in 1973. Several of the smaller parts – and some not so small – were less well played than usual. Altogether, it was a weaker than average season,

offering duller than average plays in worse than average productions. It was the early Shakespeare we mainly saw and, when he
wasn't with us, we got the Shakespeare of the middle comedies.
Indeed, the most mature works at Stratford in 1973 were *The
Taming of the Shrew* and *As You Like It*, neither of which could
exactly be described as a searing study of the human condition.
And both were handled in a way, very characteristic of modern
Shakespeare production, that implied that their directors believed
them, not just immature, but feeble and dull.

That's to say, both were relentlessly galvanized into a life rather
different from the one Shakespeare actually gave them. Instead of
trying to extract anything humane (or even human) from the
famous scene in which Katherine is systematically denied food by
Petruchio's servants, Clifford Williams mounted a sort of flying
circus, an amiable riot in which Katherine herself was all but
invisible behind the papier maché hams, custard pies, apples and
tomatoes that were being flung about her by leaping acrobats.
Finally, a carrot descended near her on a tiny parachute, clinching
proof (if any were needed) that the comedy in this production
would come more from 'business' than from character. We missed
the humour of Katherine's compliant words to the aged male
traveller – 'young budding virgin, fair, fresh and sweet' – since he,
she and Petruchio were all inexplicably balancing on a suspended
plank, and the joke had become whether or not one of them would
fall off. Thus did adult wit deteriorate into nursery knockabout.
Thus is Shakespeare often cheapened nowadays for audiences
presumed to be too frivolous and stupid to want anything but a
little childish fun.

Alan Bates, a cheeky Paduan coster, fitted easily enough into
this capering context, but Susan Fleetwood's Katherine deserved
better. She gave us not just a character but a developing character:
interest, amusement and respect when she couldn't instantly
squash her uppish wooer; tears of wounded hope, not rage, when
he seemed about to jilt her; the occasional flirtatious glance when
he began to tame her, implying that, for all her protestations, she
fundamentally consented; and, finally, the sort of solid, warm
affection that Miss Fleetwood, above almost all actresses, is able to
project. It was a pity Mr Williams didn't throw away his Bumper
Fun Book, and allow this intelligent and subtle performance to

dictate the character of this production and, rather similarly, a pity that Buzz Goodbody didn't make more of her great good fortune in having Eileen Atkins as her Rosalind in *As You Like It*.

Miss Atkins was sharp and witty, and tried to be something more: every now and then her face would break into barely concealed sexual longing, and you felt she might do something indecorous and embarrassing, like seize Orlando by the biceps and kiss him. There was also an ambitious and interesting Jacques from Richard Pasco: not the usual romantic, gentlemanly melancholic, but an unkempt, glazed creature in a white suit, a run-down dandy who appeared to have stumbled, not altogether soberly, out of the pages of Dostoievsky. His text was evidently Duke Senior's denunciation of the character:

> Most mischievous foul fin, in chiding sin.
> For thou thyself hast been a libertine,
> As sensual as the brutish sting itself;
> And all the embossed sores and headed evils
> That thou with license of free foot hast caught,
> Wouldst thou disgorge into the general world.

Mr Pasco did, for once, sound and look like someone who was apt to disgorge embossed sores. Blinking through his specs at the light, half staggering and half loping across the stage to seize the Duke by the lapel and scrabble at his chest, twitching and sneering as he stammered over the word 'p-pleasure', he presented a bizarre and even disturbing picture. This was, you felt, a man half crazed with old desires and old guilts, and blaming the world for it.

It was a bold reassessment, worth the trip to Stratford in itself. And yet what one mainly remembered was, once more, stage effect that had little to do either with character or with Shakespeare. Pop music reverberated through the aluminium glades, hey-ding-a-ding to the sound of skiffle on a tea-chest; Touchstone, in cap and checks, became a sort of manic tic-tac man, wandered in from a nearby racecourse, and the characters in general, from Rosalind's unisex denims to the lords' velvet jackets, seemed to have emerged from some wildly variegated modern boutique; Sir Oliver Martext left Touchstone (now in a top hat) and Audrey (in dungarees and bridal veil) wheeling a pram and with 'just married' around his neck; and so it went on. The programme suggested that Miss

Goodbody thought the play was about women's place in society or some such: her production showed little but a desire to frisk through the evening as painlessly as possible. A sort of factitious urban glee had been introduced into the pastoral atmosphere, and little that was subtle or gentle or mellow could survive it. Extract Pasco and perhaps Miss Atkins, and *As You Like It* had fallen victim to its director's desperation to amuse.

After this, David Jones's *Love's Labour's Lost* seemed refreshingly muted: it was a happy, unpretentious production tucked into an all green set, like a grass tent, and offering good, warm performances from Bernard Lloyd as the king and Ian Richardson as Berowne. One couldn't quickly forget the latter's comic fury and disbelief after hearing his voice gasp and choke out of emotional control, 'I, forsooth, in *love*!', or his exquisitely timed panic when this love became common knowledge. The unexpected delivery of his secret love-letter produced a double-take in a thousand. But *Love's Labour's Lost*, for all its vernal charm, is a pretty flimsy piece of work, and, however well directed, insufficient in itself to rescue the Stratford season from the triviality it seemed at times to be so assiduously pursuing. Solidity had to come, if from anywhere, from the one history and the one tragedy on view: *Richard II* and *Romeo and Juliet*. Let me record at once that many, perhaps most, critics liked the first of these productions and disliked the second. I propose to put the opposite view.

Both the main parts in *Richard* were, I must admit, very well performed. Indeed, if the comparison means anything, they were better performed than the main parts in *Romeo and Juliet*. Moreover, Ian Richardson and Richard Pasco showed their versatility by swapping Richard and Bolingbroke on alternate nights, a task beyond Timothy Dalton and Estelle Kohler even in an age of unisex trousers. Of the two, Richardson, being a rather subtler and more introverted actor, was probably the more impressive, even as Bolingbroke, whom he played as a demure Elizabethan courtier spoiled by power and finally disgusted by it (he greeted the ex-king's corpse with a great, guilty howl). His Richard was prim, disdainful, cool, ironic, malicious and fastidious, a nastier and more dangerous fellow than Pasco's sturdy, not very sensitive optimist. In the death cell he seemed to have achieved a mellow wisdom, a serenity, where Pasco was merely resilient and cheerful. Pasco's

Bolingbroke, too, was more extroverted, an energetic and reasonably honest nobleman hardened and finally coarsened by
experience.

I wish I could say that John Barton's production gave me as
much pleasure as the performances at its centre. But it was not to
be. The evening's distinguishing characteristic was emphasis and
exaggeration. The text, one would imagine, makes it clear enough
that the action of the play occurs in a soi-disant Christian society,
which constantly asks itself if mortals can depose the ruler God has
anointed. But mere clarity was not enough for Barton. His production positively teemed with crosses and cowls, some of them
covering unexpected heads. The gardeners, Richard's murderers and
those conspiring against Bolingbroke all appeared dressed as
friars, standing in geometrical patterns and moving in unison, as if
they were re-enacting some medieval liturgy, not acting out an
Elizabethan play. Indeed, whether they wore cowls or gowns or
dresses or anything else, all the supporting characters appeared to
have been reduced to an attendant chorus of incanting acolytes,
doomed forever to glide around the stage in ponderously sym-
metrical rituals.

Nor did Mr Barton's editorializing tendency end with the
monks and friars and solemn processions. The play is full of feeling
for 'this blessed plot, this earth, this realm, this England'; so he
actually put a pot of native sod at the very front of the stage, for
Carlisle to finger meaningfully on his line about 'cursed earth' and
for the Queen to run through her fingers when she spoke about
'rebellious earth'. Because Richard fancifully describes himself as
a 'mockery king of snows', a facsimile snowman was plumped on
stage and made to melt during the description of his ride towards
abdication. And so it went on. Northumberland appeared on stilts
with claws for feet, just to show us how powerful and vicious the
character is and, presumably for similar reasons, Sir Pierce of
Exton came in for the kill, not only on stilts, but sporting a
vaguely Eastern headdress, a droopy moustache and a large cross-
bow, like some misplaced Samurai. What Shakespeare left implicit
was relentlessly italicized. Indeed, one sometimes felt that we were
not seeing Shakespeare's play at all, but a long lecture about it,
with illustrations.

But, so far from imposing his own editorial voice on the play,

Terry Hands looked at *Romeo and Juliet* with a fresh eye, un-clouded by theatrical custom, and showed us a Shakespeare whose existence in such a context we had hardly suspected. Out went the sweet swan of Avon, gracefully inclining his neck in homage to the lovers, and in came someone whom one could recognize as the future author of *Troilus and Cressida* and *Lear*. This was, I think, a very important production, but not one that can have appealed either to the romantics or to the traditionalists. Mr Hands's two main texts, it seemed, were Juliet's declaration that she found the con-tract with Romeo 'too rash, too unadvised, too sudden', and Friar Lawrence's famous line about violent delights having violent ends. What he did was bring out the rashness and violence of the lovers' liaison and relate it, as directly as he could, to the rashness and violence of Verona, with its fiery Tybalts and feuding clans. Thus he showed that a play whose denouement has usually seemed to depend on chance could, in fact, be played as an Aristotelian tragedy. Chance, in the form of Brother John failing to get a letter through to Romeo, was only the superficial cause of disaster: the first and main cause was human frailty. Mr Hands's lovers were killed because of a tragic flaw in society and in themselves; that impetuousness, that innate wildness, more animal than human, which leads Tybalt to attack Romeo, Mercutio to join the fray, Romeo to take revenge, Capulet to force Paris on Juliet, Romeo and Juliet themselves to love in an instant and marry in two, and the two of them to commit suicide in the tomb.

Little of the effect came from gratuitous stage business, of the kind introduced by a Barton or Williams or Goodbody. Nearly all came from the efforts of the actors to explore their characters without either preconceptions or disrespect to the text. It's true that Bernard Lloyd's Mercutio did carry about with him a large doll, which he proceeded to dismember in the speech about Rosa-lind's high forehead, fine feet and quivering thigh. But this was his idea of a joke, a wayward obscenity to amuse his mocking, sex obsessed crowd. It was in character. So, at any rate, one felt at the time, especially when one contemplated the Mercutio Mr Lloyd actually gave us: no amiable Inns of Court wit, but the violent product of a violent society – quick to anger, eager to fight, a brawler, a drinker and a misogynist as well. He made no distinction between love and sex: both disgusted him equally:

This drivelling love is like a great natural, that runs lolling up and down to hide his bauble in a hole.

Or, in the reading suggested by Dover-Wilson and accepted by Hands:

> O, Romeo, that she were, O, that she were
> An open arse, thou a poperin pear.

And none of the disdain and cynicism in the Queen Mab speech was missed:

> O'er ladies' lips, who straight on kisses dream,
> Which oft the angry Mab with blisters plagues,
> Because their breaths with sweetmeats tainted are:

Here, we realized, was an embryo example of that sexual horror Shakespeare was to express so forcefully in *Hamlet, Measure for Measure, Troilus and Cressida*, and *The Winter's Tale*. Mercutio, for all his youth and apparent glee, was the true ancestor of the mad Leontes.

In my view, this was a perfectly possible reading of the text. But it was widely disliked, as, for some of the same reasons, were the Romeo of Timothy Dalton and the Juliet of Estelle Kohler. She should not have flaunted her sexuality so unabashedly at her father's feast, nor yelled at her mother so rudely when marriage with Paris was suggested, nor thrown herself at Romeo quite so recklessly: 'heroines' don't do such things. Again, he shouldn't have screeched, moaned, hacked and dug away at Tybalt's body: 'heroes' aren't like that. But if one accepted Mr Hands's interpretation – as I did – then one obviously had to expect excess and even hysteria from the lovers. Anything else would have been sentimental and absurd, especially in that *Clockwork Orange* of a Verona. What seemed to me objectionable about these performances was not their intensity, but their relative lack of technical expertise. Neither of them, and certainly not Mr Dalton, had the range to make their emotions consistently interesting as well as white-hot, nor quite enough assurance to be altogether credible in their extremer moments. It was a pity: one would have liked to see the production justify itself in all respects. As it was, it had to be rated a bold and intelligent attempt, a fascinating half success. But, given the present state of Shakespeare production, that is high praise in itself.

It was with some relief, then, that we left Shakespeare at Stratford and Shakespeare at the Aldwych, and went off to see the RSC's clutch of new or newish plays at the Place. Could it repeat the success of the experimental season it had mounted there in the company's annus mirabilis, 1971? Then we'd been offered *Occupations*, by a new author called Trevor Griffiths, and Robin Phillips's riveting, if misconceived, production of *Miss Julie* – what now? Well, there were no stunning surprises, no theatrical revelations, and sometimes not even much success. I failed altogether to respond to John Wiles's *Lesson of Blood and Roses*, and cannot regret having missed *Sylvia Plath*. 'It tells us virtually nothing new about the poet,' wrote my stand-in at the *New Statesman*, Russell Davies, 'but offers first a faintly bland mixture of biographical matter and rhythmically chanted poems, and then a performance of the Plath play *Three Women*, a desperate, wordy struggle between mind and flesh in the maternity ward.' Not the sort of review, one feels, that gets wrenched out of context and proudly emblazoned across the theatre foyer.

On the other hand, it was good to get a second chance to see one of the few plays in which the South African playwright, Athol Fugard, shows us poor whites instead of blacks or coloured: *Hello and Goodbye*, originally staged at the King's Head Theatre earlier in the year. Ben Kingsley and Janet Suzman played the only two characters, both there and at the Place, and each gave an appropriately restive, haggard performance: he, still shakily in thrall to the Bible-thumping paterfamilias (now dead in the bedroom) and she scarcely less so, for all her slummy bravado. Human lives rarely come as warped as this, even in Fugard; but the two performers brought considerable credibility to the situation. They also reminded us of Fugard's back-against-the-wall faith in the value of the human failure and in his ability to soldier on in a hostile and callous world. It made a disturbing evening, and yet not exactly a pessimistic one.

But the season's serious success was undoubtedly *Cries from Casement*, by David Rudkin, who had been absent from the legitimate theatre since the RSC had presented his *Afore Night Come* over 10 years before. One left the theatre hoping that he wouldn't

take another such sabbatical. Not that there were no qualifications
to be made. *Cries from Casement* had originally been a radio play,
and it still seemed somewhat wordy. Worse, the visual invention in
Terry Hands's production was often feeble or irrelevant or both. It
would have been better to have cut much of the long, obtrusive
and surely superfluous historical resumé rather than to have it
recited by men in oilskins, roaring, rushing, and hurling about what
appeared to be flour, like tipsy lifeboatmen inexplicably transported to a Mother's Pride factory. 'The potato famine,' someone
cried; and what appeared to be Grace Darling crashed to the bakery
floor.

Again, Rudkin's thinking often seemed tendentious, to put it
mildly. One quite accepted his argument that a sexual outsider,
like Casement, was likely to have a special sympathy for the rejected and oppressed. But what of the notion that there was something emotionally analogous between the man's two strongest
desires – to be overwhelmed by alien male flesh and to bury himself,
both literally and figuratively, in his native land? That his homo-
sexuality was a form of patriotism, and vice versa? As one contemplated this mystical mumbo-jumbo, one was forced to wonder
whether Mr Rudkin was suffering from an acute confusion of terms
– that he was equating one thing with the other because both
happened to be called 'sod'. And yet there was much to admire and
remember: intelligence and sensitivity, a genuine and unpretentious
passion for the subject, a marvellous feeling for language, another
solid performance from the admirable Colin Blakely. Indeed,
Mr Blakely was a rock in the seething flux of apparently demented
seafarers, firm and solid, whether he was wryly switching personae
from surrogate Englishman to lusty Irishman, or calmly reporting
his own trial and death, or (finally) haranguing future generations
about the need to unite Ulster with Eire and find a national
identity. He was funny and moving, and conceivably even inspiring.

He was also funny (if not moving or inspiring) in Philip Magdalany's *Section Nine*. This was the last of the five offerings at the
Place, and I must admit that I enjoyed it far more than some of
my grimmer fellow critics. 'A dirty joke,' harrumphed one, as if to
end any further discussion about the play. But dirty jokes are
surely perfectly justifiable if they are imaginative and surprising
and amusing, if they attempt to put down moral pomposity or

sexual pretension, and if they suggest an unashamed and unscato-
logical enjoyment of the body. These tests, so it seemed to me, were
all passed by Mr Magdalany's joke about the scientist who turns
homosexual and disappears with the formulae for the apocalypse
bomb tatooed on his penis, thus forcing the patriotic sleuths of the
CIA to become hustlers and seducers. It all seemed pretty harmless.
Indeed, a good deal of positively useful fun was had at the expense
of antiseptic American bureaucracy and red blooded American
machismo – the last massively represented, in a hilarious scene in
some Turkish baths, by Mr Blakely with gun, military medals and
elaborate female wig. The play later transferred from the Place to
the Aldwych, but without quite the public success some of us had
prophesied, presumably because the Aldwych was too large a
theatre for its very intimate amusements.

And so in came 1974, to bring a little modern drama to the
RSC's London home. I propose to say nothing of *Duck Song*,
except that it was by David Mercer and that, as his admirers
know, he is capable of writing both coolly, wittily and cuttingly (as
he did in *After Haggerty*), and self-indulgently, incoherently and
tediously. As most people agreed, this was the product of his
second self, and silence seems the most charitable critical response.
I prefer to end this survey on an optimistic note, and that means
ending with Frank Dunlop's revival of that old thunderer, William
Gillette's *Sherlock Holmes*.

Oh yes, it was melodramatic and absurd and confusing, a
mixture of *A Scandal in Bohemia*, *The Final Problem* and God
knows what else. It was full of lines like Moriarty's 'notify the
lascar that I may require the gaschamber in Stepney tonight'. But
it clearly touched something in the audience, which reacted with
unsophisticated and unpatronizing glee, just like the children at
Treasure Island, *Peter Pan* and the other seasonal regurgitations.
This was, one felt, a Christmas pantomime for adults – reassuring
them with a world in which whites were whites, blacks blacks, and
British skill and imperturbability, encapsulated by Holmes himself, could solve every problem at the puff of a pipe or scrape of a
violin string. I am, I protest, as rigorously opposed as anyone else
to what's nowadays denounced as escapism, at any rate when, as
has sometimes happened, it threatens to engulf great stretches of
the British theatre. But it would be a very dour puritan who denied

the RSC, of all companies, a holiday from its customary seriousness – or its audiences a brief respite from the England of the early part of 1974.

Dunlop's production stayed clear of the extremes both of melodrama and of burlesque: Nicholas Selby, Barbara Leigh-Hunt, Philip Locke, Mary Rutherford, Trevor Peacock and Tim Pigot-Smith all played as if they believed, at least to some extent, in the literal reality of their parts. And who should turn up as Sherlock Holmes himself but that Gordian knot of the acting profession, the ever intricate John Wood? He was cool, authoritative and ironic, his humour sometimes wearily tolerant and sometimes ferociously scornful. He also summoned up a gentle self-mockery, guiding us unprotesting and more or less straightfaced through the ludicrous ending, in which Holmes rejects his 'old love' (cocaine) for 'home! life! love!' (Miss Rutherford). But, being John Wood, he achieved more than that. 'Crime is commonplace,' he had to declare, 'existence commonplace'; and he hawked up those c's with a contempt that seemed to embrace everything, including his own intelligence. Holmes suddenly became Hamlet, wryly lamenting an 'unprofitable world' or, perhaps more precisely, an extension of Mr Wood's own Brutus, driven by circumstance towards disillusion and even existential despair. With so many gifted and dependable players in its ranks, the future of the RSC cannot be bad. With leading actors like Richardson, Pasco and (above all) Wood, experts at making much out of little, it must be bright.

4A–F PRODUCTIONS AT THE NATIONAL

4a   Joan Plowright and Laurence Olivier in *Saturday, Sunday, Monday*

4b   (above left) Gillian Barge and Michael Hordern in *The Cherry Orchard*

4c   (far left) Alec McCowen and Peter Firth in *Equus*

4d   (left) John Shrapnel and Martin Shaw in *The Bacchae*

4e   (above) Gillian Barge, Ronald Pickup, Gawn Grainger, Laurence Olivier and Rachel Davies in *The Party*

4f   (right) John Gielgud and Michael Feast in *The Tempest*

6A–F THE NEW NATIONAL COMPLEX

6a (top) The new National: exterior view

6b (bottom) The new National: seen from the river (model)

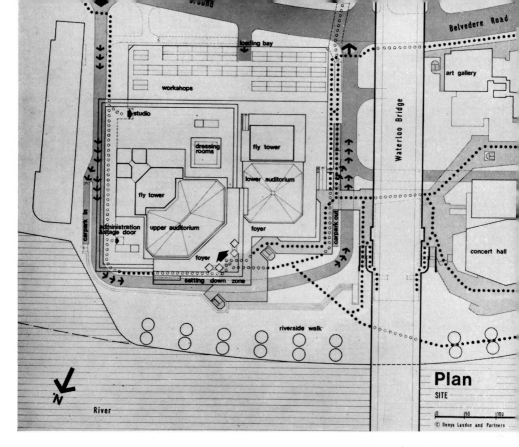

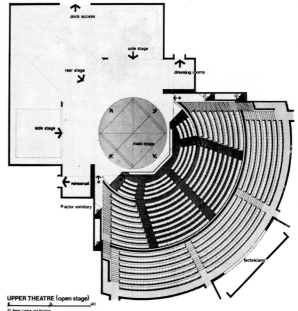

6c (above) The new
National: ground plan

6d (right) The new National:
the Olivier

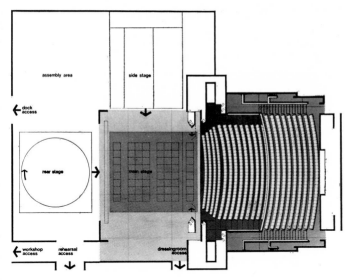

LOWER THEATRE (proscenium stage)

© Denys Lasdun and Partners

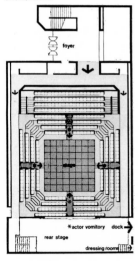

foyer

stage

*actor vomitory   dock ➡

rear stage

dressing rooms

arena stage

proscenium stage

transverse stage

arena stage

thrust stage

STUDIO THEATRE

© Denys Lasdun and Partners

7c (above left) Susan
Fleetwood and Alan Bates
in *The Taming of the Shrew*

7d (above right) Timothy
Dalton and Estelle Kohler
as *Romeo and Juliet*

7e (left) Eileen Atkins and
David Suchet in *As You Like It*

Use all Gently - for God's Sake

Shakespeare is not as Shakespeare's done. An unrepentant onslaught on today's producers by the founder of the New Renaissance Movement.

The last time I saw *Hamlet* – and in the interests of not being poisoned when I go up to London, I'm not mentioning any names – the actor playing Horatio gave a most realistic performance at the end of the play, when Fortinbras clumps about the stage, looking reprovingly at all the dead bodies. Horatio, played by A. Non, spoke his lines about how these dead bodies came to be dead with great conviction. It was as though he, A. Non, after two years in RADA, and a further sentence in the provinces, had suddenly got involved in a murder case, and a lot of the people who made up his social set were suddenly dead all around him. He stuttered; he sounded unbelieving; he was shocked: it was clearly not at all the sort of thing he, a young modern actor, was used to. I don't know what effect he had on everybody else, but he brought to a crisis point in me that ghastly nausea which overtakes me when I watch modern productions of Shakespeare. I longed for it to end, and the nightmare once more to be over.

I must admit I prefer Shakespeare on the page to on the stage. On the page he works his magic; scenes coalesce and converge in relentless troops of dramatic power; lightning flashes, humour, glory, pathos; I am moved by his shining humanity, his seraphic common sense, his wisdom; I am ravished by the rich, rare worlds he conjures up of Rome, Egypt, Italy and old England. But when I go and see it acted out on stage, it is all suddenly turned into flat, trendy, plodding contemporariness. And the only wonder I come to feel on walking out of the theatre is that of marvelling at how dull Shakespeare can be made to be. The transformation is almost unbelievable.

The style of modern Shakespearean acting is of course merely an expression of the tastes of our age. In the arts at the moment we believe that to be contemporary is the thing: never mind if Shakespeare was trying to evoke an ancient world of Imperial splendour and Roman stoicism, if we can show that it's like the Greek colonels or the Nazis, who happen to be trendy at the moment, then we have made the play contemporary, and therefore good. We also have a great tradition, now well over a hundred years old, of realism. The minute analysis and representation of the mundane world is often the aim of literature today. We are also extremely shy of anything heroic, and also of anything deeply emotional. The heroic and the emotional are only really exploited in commercial or popular art, like war comics, or women's magazines. It is therefore only natural that the classical acting of the moment should not be classical at all, but topical, realistic, unheroic and non-emotional.

To me the acceptable style of Shakespearean acting died the death when Glen Byam Shaw gave up the Shakespeare Memorial Theatre and Peter Hall took over. It was a most significant change, which mirrors all the progress of the arts in this century. I remember with great enthusiasm the productions under Glen Byam Shaw. Shakespeare was produced as a theatrical entertainer. Each play was allowed to be different, to have its own sort of set, and its own star, and the productions were full of colour, drama, and starquality. It was like going to the opera: a rare, rich, classy, exciting sort of evening. Peter Hall introduced the ensemble style of production and acting. The cast was a social unit. He also introduced the academic-reading production. The play had a contempoarry message. He also introduced the leather and tin type of setting. The scenery was functional and not distracting. An immense lethargic dullness descended over the bard. Shakespeare was taken back to school, he was re-educated: he was forbidden to be big, glamorous and theatrical, and made raw, relevant, sombre and concerned. To me this is completely to warp the essential nature of Shakespeare's plays as they were originally intended. In fact there could hardly be minds less like that of Bertolt Brecht, whose type of theatre was the inspiration of the whole enterprise, than the apprentices and bourgeois of London, who went to the Globe, and Queen Elizabeth I and James I of England, who watched Shakespeare at home.

But let me get back to A. Non and his performance as Horatio, for in this little cameo we can study a microcosm of the big changes in production style and artistic fashion. The performance, though very realistic and a good bit of acting, was basically disastrous for two main reasons. Firstly it was not in character. It is highly unlikely that Horatio, a Renaissance scholar, a courtier, and a stoic, who is more of an antique Roman than a Dane, would behave like A. Non, young modern actor, and ex-student of RADA. Had Horatio gone to RADA himself, and led the sheltered life of the modern theatre, no doubt he might have been baffled, perplexed, lost for words, and stunned, when a large royal family suddenly collapsed screaming all around him. But as he was a scholarly, stoical courtier, he reacts in the resigned, noble, mature way that Shakespeare's lines suggest. I realize that the words resigned, noble and mature certainly do not embody very popular or fashionable concepts, but the actor must surely try and act what is in the text, rather than what he wishes were in the text.

The second reason why this performance was plain wrong lies in the nature of the dialogue being spoken. I don't know if you have ever looked at Shakespeare's texts closely, but you must have noticed that, although the words often begin in a neat line down the left hand margin, they do not always end in a neat line down the right hand margin. This is because the lines of dialogue are written in a form called verse. Strange to say, but every line of Shakespeare written in this way is meant to have a special kind of rhythm based on the fact that it will almost invariably be made up of ten or eleven syllables, and that these syllables will be arranged in groups of two, called feet, which are predominantly of the rhythm */, as in the word *delay* or the word *embrace*. It is therefore quite likely that Shakespeare did not intend his dialogue to be spoken as if it were the spontaneous utterance of a character at all. But this is such a wild assertion, I feel I must *delay* a little in order to *embrace* my argument.

Since the time of Stanislavsky, it has been assumed that it is a good thing to become the character you portray, and to speak the lines as if they were his actual conversation. This is the basis of the realistic theatre. The set represents a room or a scene just as if it were real, and the characters walk about in the set just as if they were real people. When they enter through the stage windows, in order to arrange the flowers in a vase down left, it is merely to give the impression they are not an actor walking onto a stage, but a person with some legitimate business in their own drawing room. This convention does very well for most modern plays, and indeed even the endless vapidity of the dialogue in *The Caretaker*, for instance, which was claimed to be something new, is merely an even more dogged attempt to be realistic, and so fall in with the fashions of the last hundred years. But Shakespeare is not part of our convention. He wrote around the year 1600, which surprising as it may seem to his modern producers, was in fact nearly 400 years ago.

The plays of Shakespeare then, and the plays of Racine and Molière, and the Greek tragedians, in fact all great plays, have another convention. They do not attempt to show audiences anything more or less than a performance. When an actor comes on stage, he is not meant to be Hamlet walking into his study to fetch a book, but an actor representing Hamlet walking onto a stage. The actor may be gorgeously and fantastically dressed (in the case of Hamlet, not so); the stage may be gorgeously and fantastically decorated (in the case of *Hamlet*, it would be swathed in the customary black hangings of tragedy); but it was still a stage, and he an actor. What he spoke on the stage was a carefully written speech. In modern terms – and to be contemporary is everything – the performance was somewhere between a church service, a political convention, a poetry reading, and a play. To give it its closest parallel it was an opera, whose music was verse and whose arias rhetoric. There was nothing about it that attempted the Fourth Wall realism, in the shadow of which we find our dishonourable graves.

A. Non's technique then of realistic delivery is wrong on this count, since it ignores the nature of the medium. Had he rolled off the speeches with the intent of moving the audience with an eloquent delivery, had he given them a Churchillian ring, big-hearted, generous, suffused with deep feeling, he would have been playing it more as Shakespeare wanted. And we know what Shakespeare wants because he tells us in *Hamlet*.

In Act three, Scene two in Hamlet's speech to the players, it seems to me that Shakespeare has gone out of his way to leave a testament on acting. Indeed in other places in this his longest and most intricate play, he has also hinted at what he regards as true theatre and true playcraft. 'Speak the speech, I pray you,' says Hamlet, and goes into a long lecture, telling the players how to do their own job: a precedent, if nothing else, for articles like this. Firstly he says speak the speech fluently and quickly. Do not mouth it with monotonous, extreme gestures. Even when you act a passionate speech, maintain a certain balance and smoothness. It's no good screaming the house down. Next, he tempers this by warning against tameness. Use your discretion is his main advice. Without being extreme, let the gestures come from the words of the text, and try to give a true representation of human qualities, and of the temper of the time.

I realize that in this last piece of advice Hamlet, and probably Shakespeare, is urging his players to be contemporary, which is just what I have been claiming they should not be. It could be argued that what was contemporary to Shakespeare is ancient to us, and there is some truth in this. But I don't think in any case we can interpret this last remark in the light of Stanislavsky. What Shakespeare had in mind when he speaks of a realistic reflection of the age could not have been the sort of acting which in our time is the medium of films and television series. Indeed had he been alive today, Hamlet's advice to the players might have been slanted against all forms of realism.

We can, however, draw more definite conclusions from the rest of the speech. Hamlet insists that the action comes from the word. He does not claim that the action should spring from the situation of the scene. In productions of Shakespeare, which are moulded from improvisation sessions, the situation of the scene is often taken as the starting point for the acting. A. Non thinks himself into the situation of seeing a dead royal family. From his instinctive reactions he builds up his performance. This is clearly against Shakespeare's advice. Hamlet's remark indicates that an actor ought to build up his performance from the speech itself. If the speech is mature, noble and resigned: that is how he should act it, never mind what he feels, or even what he thinks Horatio would feel: he must follow what Shakespeare makes Horatio feel, as is embodied in the poetic temper of the speech.

Hamlet says don't rant. The speech should always be delivered in a coherent, temperate manner: even in a passion there should be a certain smoothness. To the Elizabethans acting was a type of oratory. B. L. Joseph in his book on *Elizabethan Acting* draws numerous parallels between the two, and shows that actors moved their audiences just as orators did. When you think about it, oratory is more directly interested in moving an audience than realistic acting, for a realistic actor builds up his performance in himself, while an orator builds up his as a piece of audience manipulation. Hitler and Churchill were more powerful actors in their time, on this score than, say, Gerald du Maurier. Hamlet's advice here seems to me to insist on a certain detachment from the performance, which would be more suitable to what we regard as oratory than to what we now regard as acting.

Hamlet says speak the speech trippingly, in other words swiftly and nimbly. In many Shakespeare productions, this advice is wholly ignored. Indeed in the most trendy and fashionable productions, such as Brook's *Midsummer Night's Dream*, a lot of effort has obviously gone into making the speeches sound like dollops of slowly hardening concrete. At the end of this beautifully tasteful production, Oberon and Puck used a most interesting delivery for the last speeches of the play. These speeches, which Shakespeare took pains to make suitably magic and ritualistic by composing them in octosyllabic couplets, were delivered not as if by orators of distinction and sensibility, nor as if by an imp and a king of the fairies, but as if by two embarrassed school prefects at the end of a charity concert for an old folk's home. It was a remarkable piece of acting. The pair of them looked down bashfully at their fingernails, coughed, stuttered, paused for thought, and were overcome with realistic shyness and pride, but it was all slighly less appropriate to the play than if the Treorchy Male Voice Choir had come on and sung Christmas carols. In fact, now I think about it, far less appropriate.

The advice to speak trippingly seems to me to be the most important single exhortation which might be made to modern producers of Shakespeare. When the plays are 3000 lines long, and the pace and momentum are beautifully modulated by the greatest craftsman the theatre has ever known, in the speeches themselves, there is no place at all for realistic Pinteresque pauses. The actors may get a great kick out of pretending to grope for the word Shakespeare put down in black and white, but for the audience it is just sheer boredom to have the natural flow of the play interferred with. I am myself peculiarly allergic to this sort of thing. When I hear an actor, relentlessly dead from the neck downwards to any feeling for pace, rhythm, tone or feeling, recite one of Shakespeare's masterpieces of expression in wildly inappropriate fits and lulls, I feel positively sick. To have a concrete ear, leaden imagination, and undeveloped emotions is unfortunate, but to take up Shakespearean acting, and to be urged publicly to exhibit your short-comings, is rather like cutting up the bard's corpse and beating his admirers with the dismembered limbs.

The best bit of Shakespearean acting I have ever seen, in the sense that it might most profitably stand as a model to others, though I do not claim it was the greatest performance I have ever seen, happened in a fairly tatty production of *The Merchant of Venice*, which staggered round the provinces and flumped into London for a while thereafter. This was Ralph Richardson's Shylock. I had read in those learned, arty, critics' books that Richardson was not really a Shakespearean actor at all, so I did not expect much. It was not a spectacular evening, and I don't think the old boy was trying very hard. In fact he had a temperance that may give it smoothness to a T. But the point about it was it was so deliciously easy to watch. You didn't have to feel embarrassed. You weren't watching a realistic portrayal of what it is like to be victimized by wicked bourgeois society. You didn't have to be concerned, or shocked out of your complacency, or disturbed, or any other of those pseudo-artistic experiences which fashion finds so precious. You just sat back and enjoyed it. Richardson walked through the part nobly and eloquently. He struck the most expressive and striking attitudes. His speeches seemed to make a kind of music, and indeed the whole performance was free and flowed and had a musical, infective, effective and affecting structure. When he tossed down his knife at the end of the trial, he did it with such a wealth of contempt. It was as if he were saying: you crew of raw, half-finished, trivial trendies, I despise your cliquishness, your shallowness and pride. No modern style of acting could get across that withering nobility, for the modern style of acting is of the camp Shylock despised. How well his words might fit the modern theatre!

But what is it then that Richardson had, that modern acting doesn't have, and that I believe Shakespeare wanted? One first thing we must realize is that Shakespeare was a gent. The way his characters speak is incorrigibly courtly and courteous. This is perhaps what makes even his comics seem genteel, when you compare them, say, with those of Molière. The Renaissance, under the influence of Castiglione, were mad about behaving in a gracious way. The Shakespearean actor then must try to act with nobility. A style derived from old-fashioned kitchen-sink dramas, or that continual heartburn style, of which Inspector Barlow is possibly the originator, certainly a master, suits very badly indeed with Shakespeare's princes and courtiers.

Secondly, the actor should forget all about Stanislavsky. He should have some concern now and then for those blobs out front, all of whom have paid one or several quid to have something done to them. He should renounce the self-indulgence of writing the play all over again to fit his own limited imagination, and seek to perform with sufficient expertise and sufficient feeling to move his audience. He himself should appreciate the poetry in which nearly all Shakespeare is written, and then his acting might be forceful enough to inspire others.

Finally, he should remember the traditions of the medium. At the moment I think all the arts have got so girlishly excited about doing their own little new thing, that the real power of the arts, which has so often been tapped in the past, is completely forgotten. When we read how Kean's delivery of certain lines were so pathetic the audience wept copiously, and how his delivery of other lines was so frightening that pregnant ladies had miscarriages, we realize, stumbling bored stiff from yet another Shakespeare production, that something is lacking which used to be there. And now I mention Kean, there is a concluding moral to be drawn, which I will unashamedly expound.

The cult of realism has many advantages, but it certainly limits the power of a work of art. Tolstoy, who is realistic, cannot rival the power to move of Homer, who is epic, or Shakespeare, who is dramatic. The thin film of unreality adds a great deal of magic. The last time I was really stirred by a true feeling of tragedy was at a performance of Stravinsky's *Oedipus Rex*. At the end the messenger entered to narrate the blinding of the king. He sang his Latin text with smoothly moving and yet passionate gestures. Somehow this stylized presentation of lamentation was absolutely thrilling: the unreal, ritualistic, magical essence of drama was revealed. And the mention of Kean also reminds me of a slightly lesser thrill received in Alan Badel's performance in the play of that name – yet another marvellous discovery of Frank Hauser. When Badel came on in the last scene as Kean playing Othello, I found his intentionally unnatural, booming-voiced performance far more affecting, for that short moment, than his own real performance of Othello, which I saw earlier. Clearly the old fashioned, semi-chanting style of delivery has a great deal of primitive magic in it, which the actor has only got to stoop to use. I set up a company myself once to act in this way. We performed *Macbeth* out of doors on the opposite bank to the Shakespeare Memorial Theatre, claiming we were more true to the bard. I can't comment on my own productions, but I will say this: if you adopt this old style, you get rid of all that embarrassment in an audience, which often breaks out in laughter at the tragic bits. When you act in this style it is all so much more relaxed: you never feel the actor is slightly uncomfortable, and the ghosts and witches can run mad as they like.

My advice is then: backwards at the double! We've spent years now pretending that Shakespeare is Harold Pinter or John Osborne. Thank God, he's not: he is William Shakespeare. The cult of anything contemporary or novel is OK now and then, but a very bad general policy. It is clear enough what happens when you follow it through: you end up with a kind of glib, journalistic, flash-in-the-pan approach to art, and the power, the magic, the humanity of the medium is forgotten. Only shallow things are going to be relevant today as opposed to yesterday, the really deep things are here all the time.

Modern Shakespearean actors should be like modern musicians. They should be skilful, adroit, sensitive, and knowledgeable. You don't hear a pianist breaking up the flow of the Moonlight Sonata with a pause he thinks is deeply meaningful. You don't find opera singers who can't keep time, or ballet dancers who halt the progress of the orchestra with a sudden clever Dick piece of business. Shakespeare could easily be as thrilling and moving as opera, if only he were performed with similar understanding. But alas, we are in a trough of such relentless bad taste, that I suppose we shall have more review-skit *Merchant of Venices*, more truncated *Hamlets*, more indoctrinated *Coriolani*, and for those whose contemporary minds, trivialized almost to the point of disappearance, can't cope with the imaginative effort of seeing fairies as Shakespeare drew them, special circus productions of *The Dream*, with namby-pamby sideshows for the tiny tots. With producers like this, it's surprising that actors can cope at all. I offer them my condolences, as well as my advice. I now sit back to await King Lear in a toy car and Noddy hat.

An Actor's Diary

*During the Actors' Company's triumphant season in New York at the
beginning of 1974, Ian McKellen kept this diary, which is preceded by
a description of the company and its aims.*

The Actors' Company

There is an increasing disaffection in the British theatre (and,
indeed, in society generally) for that kind of dominating head of a
large enterprise who accumulates authority to himself and merely
employs his staff rather than co-operates with them. Small groups
of young British actors have set up democratic ensembles; but the
Actors' Company seems to be the first group of established actors
who draw collectively on decades of experience and take control of
those basic decisions which affect their work. Decisions about what
plays to do, where to perform them, for how long, how they should
be budgeted and cast and directed. The actors thereby become
their own artistic director. Put simply, the workers are in control.

It was hoped that the Actors' Company, meeting regularly to
plan their first season in 1972, would soon establish a unique
rapport of confidence and interdependence that would inform their
work on stage as well as backstage. To that end a few basic principles were agreed on: equal pay and billing for all, a sharing of
leading as well as smaller parts – a company of equals. Finance
came from the touring department of the Arts Council of Great
Britain (DALTA) via the Cambridge Theatre Company who acted
as benevolent manager for the 12 week tour. Overwhelming critical
acclaim was followed by a direct grant from DALTA for a second
tour in 1973. The Actors' Company became a limited company and

appointed a full-time administrator. Now an executive committee of current members advises on and approves day-to-day decisions. Overall artistic policy and final responsibility remain with all the actors.

So in its first two years, the Actors' Company has become an efficient yet experimenting organization capable of instigating imaginative programmes and carrying them out. There is the spirit of a family, of a genuine ensemble. As members join and leave, policies may change. Financial support from the Arts Council or elsewhere will always be necessary. In the meantime, the example of the Actors' Company is as potent as its achievement.

On 24th January 1974 the Actors' Company left London to take part in a season of British Theatre at The Brooklyn Academy of Music in New York.

14 JANUARY: Final preparations of our new production of *King Lear* in energy-starved rehearsal rooms. As Edgar, I try playing the storm scenes unclothed. Poor Tom's very cold. Last fittings of costumes and first look at the scenery during its trial mounting. Alan Barlow has fashioned 40 miles of rough, thick string that can be lit to represent masonry, forests, sky and rain. The company had requested just such a simple visual style to allow a fast-moving, uncluttered presentation. String Lear.

23rd: A free day to pack: but half of us take District Line to meet front-of-house staff at the Wimbledon Theatre whither we'll return after New York. Box office ladies thrilled to be photographed with our John Woodvine of ITV's *New Scotland Yard*. Wimbledon likes its stars – we can hear a packed matinée roaring at Basil Brush's pantomime. Will they return in the spring to see our Chekhov, Congreve, Feydeau, Ford and Shakespeare? The company insists on equal billing of actors. Our star is the Company.

24th: 12.30 p.m. flight from Gatwick – free from British Caledonian. Our sets, though, have gone on by sea. Formalities at Kennedy waived by customs man who has booked for *Lear*. Most are to stay at the Chelsea Hotel where Dylan Thomas died, some with friends. My host is an American actor who trained 12 years ago at RADA. We compare lots and I'm introduced to the near-impossibility of working in New York Theatre. TV commercials and serials, radio and underpaid off-off-Broadway shows are main sources of income.

Broadway itself is a dream turned nightmare – empty theatres, old fashioned musicals, interminable runs or immediate closures – all governed by Clive Barnes, Limey drama critic of the *New York Times*.

25th: 10.30 a.m. to Sardi's, still-flourishing theatre restaurant, near Times Square. Guests of the Drama Desk – i.e. NY theatre critics – some know the company from 1973 Edinburgh Festival. Barnes not there. Coffee and Danish pastries. We explain the company's democracy (equal pay and equal votes at regular policy meetings); our finance (mainly from DALTA – touring department of Arts Council); our aims (overall high standards by sharing out the leading and the supporting parts). There is nothing similar in New York (or London for that matter). Properly subsidized theatre is foreign to America; perhaps because there was never an aristocracy whose arts patronage (as in Europe) could now be adopted by the state.

2 p.m. *Lear* rehearsals resumed.

7.30 p.m. with Sheila Reid to the Winter Gardens – Broadway's great vaudeville theatre – Actors' Benefit performance by Liza Minnelli. She is wonderfully energetic, unsentimental; toward the end of $2\frac{1}{2}$ hours, aggressively so. She croons 'Mammy' lovingly and we all think of her mother. But Miss Minnelli's forte is fortissimo. Soon her voice is torrential and then climactically it stops. The 40 piece orchestra behind her stops and through the calculated silence, from the mezzanine circle, screams: 'We love you, Liza!' At which Liza puts elegant hand on hip, mumbles 'Oh really!' and, falling to her knees in true Jolson, Garland style, pounds out like Niagara, 'I'd walk a million miles for one of your smiles, my maaaaaamm-meeeee!' 'Love me if you must,' is the message, 'but admire me too – for myself.' Then another happening. On stage trundles Broadway's other superstar, Clive Barnes, to profess admiration and love (in correct order). He presents a memento of the charity occasion and is kissed. May I live to see, after a similar do at the Palladium, Harold Hobson as lovingly embraced by Shirley Bassey.

27th: Morning, adjusting *Knots* to a new stage – almost like touring at home.

Evening to a Sunday night opening (most theatres here take Monday as the Sabbath) of *Lorelei* – a reworking of Carol Channing's greatest success – with the original star on stage and Anita

Loos, the original author, in the stalls. We watch, from our box, the audience as much as the stage – all white, all middle-aged, all cheering – necrophiliacs at a wake.

Others in the company more dutifully attend the RSC's closing performance of *Richard II* at the Brooklyn Academy of Music – our theatre for the coming four weeks. So called to avoid the vulgar associations which 'Theater' held for the genteel Brooklyn of 80 years ago, BAM has two adjacent auditoria – the larger Opera House, where we'll do three of our plays, and the Music Hall for *Knots*. They share a large foyer, the whole encased in a newly cleaned, floodlit, white-brick fortress challenging the barren, unglamorous, run-down downtown of Brooklyn. It's only a mile across to Manhattan and 20 minutes by cab up the frost-havocked avenues to Times Square. (Is BAM New York's Wimbledon Theatre?) We've been warned that America's pioneering spirit stops at Brooklyn Bridge so we shall need all publicity, luck and Clive Barnes to urge an emigration south. But the weather is Spring and shirt-sleeves and we're not depressed. At sea, though, there are storms and the *Lear* sets and costumes are delayed by them.

28th: Dress rehearsal for *Wood Demon* – David Giles has done some tidying redirection and as we've already done the play fifty times in 1973, there's nothing untoward now. Friendly and efficient local stage staff – with overtime, they earn probably twice the actors on Equity minimum of 300 dollars a week. Robert Eddison and I share the stage-level dressing room where Caruso reputedly died. Our dresser is Mexican Indian and provides fresh apple-juice and anglophilia against the overheating. There is, though, no hot water to wash away greasepaint.

29th: Nearly 2000 at *Wood Demon* opening, laugh from the first scene blowing the gloom off Chekhov.

30th: 1.15 a.m. at 72nd Street news-stand we read Clive Barnes: 'It was all very Chekhov and all beautifully acted. This play is one of those rarities that does not deserve to be so rare, and the company is a joy to welcome.'

10.30 a.m. Rehearse *Lear*. The sets, etc., are nearer port but far from being at BAM in time for full technical, lighting and dress rehearsals. Should we cancel the opening? Bookings are heavy.

2.30 p.m. Company meeting encourages the director David

William to our nearly unanimous decision to open on schedule, with or without the sets.

8 p.m. *Knots* opens – an hour's music-hall adaptation by one of us, Edward Petherbridge, of R. D. Laing's tangles, disjunctions, impasses – apt, considering String Lear. The Music Hall holds 750 – a bit uncomfortable after the intimacy of our Christmas season at the Shaw Theatre, Euston Road. Another friendly audience.

31st: Newspapers praise the company's good humour and versatility – Juan Moreno's juggling and tap, Caroline Blakiston's organ-playing, Paola Dionisotti's cartwheels! – but undervalue the text's complexities. Is New York less sophisticated than its reputation? Certainly it is excited (cheers at the end) and generous.

Yesterday a party by a local conservation society and invitations to individual homes. Everyone insists that British stage acting is the best in the world. Overwhelming lady goes on and on about my brilliant *Richard II* last week – I'm Ian, I'm English, so I must be the RSC's Richardson! Today is Friday. *Lear* opens Saturday: sets now due Sunday. So the stage is hung with curtains, the space between lit as theatrically as possible and the cast parade in their own clothes. Robert Eddison, as the king, borrows a long, white, suede coat taking comfort from false hair and beard which the wigmaster brought over as hand-luggage. Lear's daughters wear evening dresses; his knights a uniform of windcheaters. There are swords – so I can kill Matthew Long all right as Edmund. We hold an undress rehearsal.

2 FEBRUARY: Before the first night (our third in five days!) Margery Mason (who has assisted the director) apologises to the audience and challenges them to enjoy the crisis and the words – think when we speak of horses, that you see them. . . .

The final run-through of any play (without the encumbrances of sets, costumes, make-up) often seems superior to subsequent performances in intensity and clarity: but we can underestimate how much audiences depend on illusion and spectacle. Tonight we try and compensate for their lack – voices soar and imaginations work. Most of the company have been together through two seasons – that helps in a crisis. A standing ovation at curtain-fall. Some of us rush to the traditional first night restaurant, Sardi's, for indigestible canelloni.

3rd: 12.15 p.m. En route for a 1.30 p.m. matinée, I'm trapped on the Brooklyn subway which breaks down between stations. All the carriages, inside and out, are covered with engaging graffiti so I settle down to decipher. No obscenity, no politics, no cartoons, just repetitive scribblings, in coloured felt-tip, of Puerto Rican names and abbreviated addresses, e.g. TICO 118 (his street). Tico, like Liza, is shouting his individuality. I'm pretty near shouting, too, with half an hour to curtain-up (fortunately I'm wearing Edgar's costume!).

1 p.m. We inch into a station – backwards. I change trains and direction.

1.03 p.m. We break down again: more graffiti, same names. Subways are supposed to be dangerous – I'm certainly feeling murderous. O, for the District Line. Fellow passenger, drama student, tells me his plans to study with Grotowski – I feel we're both currently performing in Kafka.

1.24 p.m. We clatter to my station in time to apologize to my understudy and face the critics, who presumably take cabs to Brooklyn. Between shows, I discover a hot shower, 100 yards and two elevators away from dressing room. Snacks ordered from Steve's Café across the avenue. My palate has reverted to childhood and adores American food – sandwiches, malted milk, pecan pie, jello – all kid's stuff, all delicious. Why can't Britain make American ice-cream? Today's temperature is 12 below freezing.

4th: Stage staff hang the string – actors free. Television traps me – as childish as the food. Six hours of Lucille Ball on Mondays; chat shows, quiz shows, commercials. And soap operas – 20 minutes of dialogue rehearsed every weekday, read from prompt-boards, and pulled out by tortoise camera work and tautological grimaces to last an hour. If the action speeds up, a commercial has intervened. On quiz shows I admire the overreactions of contestants as they win, lose and win again holidays to Miami, automobiles, etc. A friend, from experience, explains that younger participants are often out-of-work actors fraudulently engaged as anonymous students, salesmen, teachers because they react reliably on camera, look presentable and need the prizes.

As usual we share out publicity assignments. I talk to BBC in an attic off 3rd Avenue – tape batteries are weak and my voice, deep as Robeson's, dispatched to Portland Place. Then an hour's interview for New York's only radio station without adverts (financed by listeners' contributions) – four of us record underground in converted chapel with cardboard walls and broken chairs. Not enough listeners perhaps.

Through snow, past suspicious doorman and up twenty storeys above Central Park, I'm to be interviewed for a glossy theatre magazine which, judging from its photographs, isn't found in many normal doctors' waiting rooms. My interviewer is a diligent hostess, inviting me to remove my boots, to have wine and Danish and to peer through the blizzard at the YMCA's sun-roof – 'That's why I took this apartment – fun!' She wants to photograph me but has no film. I admire her pictures in numerous dance journals. Our chat is taped (– for posterity? She has kept her Anthony Hopkins interview and replays it for comfort and amusement). I talk on about my work, background and the Actors' Company. Am given more wine and urged to be indiscreet about myself . . . about the company, then . . . about anything! ('Hopkins told me a lot about everyone!') Do I have any secret desires? No. She does – and tells me about them. Two hours later – I've read her poetry by this time – the tape is as exhausted as we are. 'Look, why are you so darn happy? Can't you give me just a bit of sensation? My readers don't want . . . you can't be that happy!' I apologize and suggest it might be a change for her readers. She will send a photographer round next week. I promise not to smile.

Edward Petherbridge, adaptor of *Knots*, and others in the cast do a couple of early morning TV excerpts (5 a.m. at the studio): hoping also to talk about the company. Interviewer interested only in Robert Morley and Olivier, also in the programme – on commercials! I don't think the media have quite caught onto the Actors' Company!

But theatregoers have – our notice-board is covered with congratulatory letters.

13th: First night of *Way of the World* sells out; unknown since Nureyev first danced at BAM. I play four-line footman tonight – just as Petherbridge walks on in *Wood Demon* – any of us does when required. BAM asked for half as many performances of Congreve as the others – underestimating the attraction for Americans of an English cast in an English classic, not seen here for 20 years. Shakespeare is the same – though there has been a black King Lear on TV during our stay.

24th: Last two performances. Lear dies (now in full costume), audience cheers (will they in Wimbledon?), curtain falls and from the wings emerge all the American stagehands to applaud the company. Genuinely fond farewells.

Postscript:

The season at Wimbledon, which followed our return from New York, is another diary. But we kept seat prices down and over 50000 people came to see us – so that twice we broke the theatre's attendance record. The national Press was unanimous. My favourite quote is from Frank Marcus (*Sunday Telegraph*): 'After their exciting season at Wimbledon, which established them beyond doubt as one of the best companies in the country, we must keep our fingers crossed. Let us hope that they will find a London base in the Old Vic, which is soon to be vacated. The spirit of Lilian Baylis would rejoice.'

Notes from the Underground

A report by the editor of Plays *and* Players *and author of* Disrupting the Spectacle *a newly published account of alternative theatre.*

An observant visitor to the King's Head one August evening in 1973, might have noticed an unusually assertive crowd gathering in the bar of this enterprising pub theatre situated in the London borough of Islington. The occasion was a special benefit performance of *Vampire*, an ingenious play written by Snoo Wilson for the much travelled Paradise Foundry group, which was thought to have been unjustly neglected by both critics and audiences. The evening was designed to show us minority theatre at its most vibrant and risk taking (*Time Out* had asked its devoted readership to turn out in support), yet paradoxically the event served merely to highlight the incestuous nature of many of the fringe's most publicized activities. Few outsiders, for instance, could have stomached for very long the self-congratulating sniggers which accompanied every other line of dialogue, or the familiar die-hard sense of complacency which heralded this night of supposedly radical and provocative theatre. It was the perfect alternative version of a chocolate-box première at the Haymarket – a theatrical opportunity for meeting your friends and having your prejudices confirmed on a stage.

   Vampire, in its King's Head transformation, took place at a peculiarly demoralizing time for the fringe. There was a general suspicion, voiced most strongly by Pip Simmons, that five years of energetic activity had led the majority of practitioners towards

something of a blind alley. The most prestigious groups created by
the post-1968 movement – Portable Theatre, Freehold, The
Traverse Workshop, and Pip Simmons himself – had chosen to
disband during the first six months of 1973. One was left, or so it
seemed, with the occasional dying flame from a once active constel-
lation – like the visit of Joseph Chaikin's Open Theatre to the
Round House – but on the whole it appeared that the fringe was
running dry of artistic adrenalin. Yet twelve months later it is
possible to view the progress of the fringe from an altogether more
hopeful angle. Not only have the lunchtime theatres become as vital
stops on the American tourists' itineraries as the RSC or National,
but critics have become as willing to devote their columns to an
interesting product of the basements as to a more conventional
revival at Stratford-upon-Avon. More decisively, it can be argued
that the year in question was marked by a growing cross-fertiliza-
tion between the fringe and our more traditional areas of theatre-
going.

It was, for instance, the year of the Theatre Upstairs. Since its
inaugural production in 1969 the upstairs auditorium of the Royal
Court has housed most of the more prominent fringe writers and
groups. The Theatre Upstairs's most notable original contribution
to the fringe, prior to last year, had been the première of Heathcote
Williams's astonishing *AC/DC*. Yet in his final twelve months as
artistic director of the Theatre Upstairs, Nicholas Wright was able
to present a series of plays which began to give the tiny makeshift
auditorium a distinctive artistic flavour of its own. 1973 saw
Wright's theatre playing host to – among others – Caryl Churchill's
Owners, Michael Abbensetts' *Sweet Talk*, Sam Shepard's *The Unseen
Hand* and Snoo Wilson's *The Pleasure Principle*. These last two
productions were able to utilize the entire Upstairs auditorium to
create a bizarre series of environmental effects. In the case of the
Shepard play we were transported back to the 1950's for a nostalgic
trip to the land of AZUSA, the author's fictional title for his
memories of America. For the Snoo Wilson play, the auditorium
was decorated with images of carnival – fireworks, masks, paper
chains – making the point perhaps that the play was a reflection of
the main characters' elusive search for different kinds of pleasure.

'The Pleasure Principle' was also a suitable subtitle for Richard
O'Brien's *Rocky Horror Show* which opened as an experimental

musical in July 1973 and quickly transferred to the King's Road – converting two Chelsea cinemas into theatres in the process. At the time of writing *Rocky Horror* is still enjoying a triumphant commercial run, proving that a minority fringe cult can be converted into a majority hit at the box office. The show was voted best musical of the year (both by the *Evening Standard* and *Plays and Players*), completely outpacing such lavish Broadway imports as *Gypsy, Two Gentlemen of Verona* and *No, No, Nanette*. As directed by Jim Sharman and designed by Brian Thomson (the *Unseen Hand* team), *Rocky Horror Show* was one of the few instances of the popular culture of the young actually finding some kind of expression on a stage outside of a pop concert. The show was basically a spoof on a 1950's monster movie, but it also drew strongly upon summoning up a kind of post-Warhol world of mutant sexuality and inter-galactic intrigue. It spoke directly to a generation spawned on androgynous pop singers (similarities between Tim Curry's transexual performance as Frank-n-furter and David Bowie did not go unnoticed), a culture of midnight movies and revived 45's. After *Rocky Horror* managements can begin to think of the fringe in terms of commercial as well as artistic gain.

The Theatre Upstairs also provided another, even more unexpected transfer to the West End. *Sizwe Bansi Is Dead*, devised by Athol Fugard, John Kani and Winston Ntshona, opened at the Theatre Upstairs to what were probably the most enthusiastic reviews of the year. After Christmas the production transferred to the downstairs theatre (itself a precedent) and was joined in repertoire by *The Island* and *Statements* – eventually being picked up by Ray Cooney (with *The Island*) for a season at the Ambassadors, as the first presentation following the departure of *The Mousetrap*! The arrival of the South African Serpent Players in London not only made us revalue the place of Athol Fugard as a playwright, but also provided a clear example of how a fringe performance need not be deprived of a wide popular audience. Both Kani and Ntshona came as a revelation to their audiences. They fitted perfectly into one of the basic fringe situations – namely, two isolated actors addressing an audience directly with little help from either props or scenery. The variation of their delivery, the movement outwards to the audience, followed by an immediate withdrawal into privacy, the humour and agonizing refusal to abandon their humanity – these performance values will not be quickly forgotten. In particular the figure of Ntshona, reeling in confusion over the cruel South African pass laws, tearing off his clothes in protest, in pain but refusing to relinquish his eloquence, provided an unforgettable experience. It was a fringe performance which will be remembered as long as any of Olivier's roles at the National.

Both *Rocky Horror* and *Sizwe Bansi* were fringe productions aimed at reaching wide audiences; the former through its grasp of the appeal contained within certain elements of pop culture; and the latter more incisively, perhaps, because it had something important to tell us about the South African situation. Another theatre which has managed to avoid the withdrawal symptoms common to much of the fringe is the Half Moon in London's East End. This theatre was created out of the remains of a synagogue in Alie Street and since its opening production (*Jungle of the Cities*, directed by Guy Sprung in 1972) has managed to sustain a remarkable record of performances under its main sponsors Maurice Colbourne and Michael Irving. For the year under consideration the Half Moon had the benefit of Steve Gooch's presence as resident writer. Gooch, an enthusiastic supporter of the theatre from the beginning (his play *Will Wat, if not, what will?* was one of the first shows), has helped to define the Half Moon's style of theatre in a positive manner. One of the features of Half Moon productions has been the size of its companies – though often unpaid, they are usually large enough to attempt epic, community centred productions which have become unique in the English fringe. This was certainly true for Gooch's translation of Brecht's *The Mother* which Jonathan Chadwick directed for the Half Moon with Mary Sheen playing the title role. The production was an object lesson in fringe performance values. Its sense of economy, the clarity of the playing, the coolness of its commitment, made *The Mother* one of the most successful Brecht productions to have been staged in London for several years. The play transferred to the Round House for a season and it was fascinating to discover that Brecht had finally found his audience in England. Here were young people, silent, serious, and completely absorbed in Brecht's debate on the nature of revolution. Equally, the young actors on stage (playing students rather than workers) played the polemical scenes with complete conviction – these were people, one felt, who might very

well print revolutionary pamphlets in oppressive times and who
had declared war on the more corrosive processes of capitalism. As
the mother, Mary Sheen made no attempt to directly impersonate
an ageing woman – rather she stood for *motherhood*, sketching out
the naturalistic details from a standpoint of inner control and
understanding. Equally compelling at the Half Moon was Gooch's
Female Transport which told the story of a group of women convicts being transported to Australia at the beginning of the last
century. The theatre was converted, in Ron Daniels' production,
into the vault and deck of a slave ship in which the women were
confined, beaten and chained. Again the emphasis was upon the
women's growing awareness of their situation – the need for some
kind of mutual, communal support in order to survive. Among
several other enterprising productions one has to single out *Fall In
And Follow Me*, a show on children's rights at the beginning of the
century written by Dave Marson and Billy Colvill. There was active
participation from local East End kids – both as performers and
audience. Unlike the Theatre Upstairs, the Half Moon has not
shown a direct interest in the commercial potential of their shows.
But it remains a committed, humane theatre – outward looking
and firmly geared to the interests of the community which it is
seeking to serve.

It's less easy to claim an equivalent sense of identity for much
of the other work taking place on the fringe. During the year in
which it has gained (and lost) its first permanent company, Charles
Marowitz's Open Space has proved something of a disappointment.
Its most spectacular effort was an underrated production by the
author of *And They Put Handcuffs on the Flowers*, Fernando
Arrabal's much abused account of his weeks spent in a Spanish jail.
Ian McDiarmid and Antony Milner both gave unforgettable performances as writhing, tortured convicts – giving full vent to their
fantasies and perversions in the true blue, sado-masochistic tradition of Goya, Dali and Genet. It's worth mentioning in this context
Lindsay Kemp's 'pantomime' for Jean Genet entitled *Flowers*
which was first seen in London last year. After a period of travelling
on the continent, then winning a sizable reputation in Edinburgh
and establishing himself as an avant-garde leader, Lindsay Kemp
brought his mime troupe to London's tiny Bush Theatre for a
highly successful season. Following the pattern of *Rocky Horror*,

Flowers transferred to the Regent (a new theatre conjured up from
the old Cameo-Poly cinema in London's Regent Street) where it
was condemned by the first string critics with almost as much zest
as it had been praised by the second string critics a few months
previously at the Bush (is there a growing conflict of taste on our
arts pages?). In combining the sacred and the profane, the erotic
swing from idealized beauty to grotesque degradation and humi-
liation, Kemp's company captured life (and death) in Genet's
homosexual underworld more completely than any previous performance which I have seen in England. It was certainly more
authentic than the trivialized version of *The Maids* presented at
Greenwich at the same time as *Flowers* even though the South
London company boasted the names of Glenda Jackson, Susannah
York and Vivian Merchant. It's true that the majority of reviewers
have little sympathy for a style of theatre which operates firmly
against the naturalistic grain. We tend to distrust powerful stage
imagery, fantasy or physical presence when it is divorced from a
clear-cut naturalistic context, a quasi-Ibsenite notion of coherent
debate and rational argument.

Charles Marowitz has always recognized this critical fact, seeking to combine the best of avant-garde techniques with those of the
more traditional theatre. He has committed the Open Space to a
form of gestural, non-verbal theatre, derived from the theories of
Artaud, which is also (hopefully) based on content as serious and
influential as a more conventional naturalistic play. This is the
guiding idea behind the collage versions of Shakespeare which crop
up annually in the Tottenham Court Road cellar. By using intelligent texts as the basis for his experiments, Marowitz hopes to
avoid the mindless extravagances of other Artaud-bound groups.
This year Marowitz focused attention upon a version of *The Taming
of the Shrew* in which Kate was kidnapped, tortured and raped into
submission by a chauvinist Petruchio and his leather clad henchmen. This cue might have come from the famous lines of Sylvia
Plath's powerful poem *Daddy* – 'Every woman adores a fascist /
The boot in the face, the brute/Brute heart . . .' Yet, in a largely
improvised sub-plot, we were also shown a highly liberated young
woman ruthlessly bent on castrating her shy young mate, verbally
rather than physically. Pertinent and entertaining as the idea may
seem, Marowitz's collages are starting to resemble a highly select

form of party game rather than a true source of innovating drama. Ironically, the Open Space's surest successes last year were both solidly grounded naturalistic works: Irving Wardle's *The Houseboy* and David Rudkin's *Ashes*. The latter was an eloquent account of a childless marriage in which a young couple, played by Peter McEnery and Lynn Farleigh, exhaust both themselves and their doctors in a desperate search for the secret of fertility. Pam Brighton's production walked an impressive tightrope of public and private agonies – a drama that could only have made its impact in a claustrophobic, intimate setting of the kind supplied by the Open Space.

Yet Marowitz is surely right when he insists that fringe theatre-going should differ in kind from an evening spent in Shaftesbury Avenue or at the National. Too often the lunchtime venues have little to offer except tired programmes of TV rejects or endless streams of adolescent melancholia in the form of overanxious first plays. The Soho Poly is certainly an exception to this rule, having provided, over the past few years, a consistently high standard of adventurous work. This year the theatre produced the first lunch-time permanent company, bringing a sense of continuity and cohesive planning to a season of new work. Yet it does seem to me that one of the most important achievements of the fringe is often neglected – namely, the development of the writers who have become identified with working in underground conditions. In particular the work of the playwrights associated with the Portable group – Howard Brenton, David Hare and Snoo Wilson – has matured greatly over the past year or so. They are now capable of producing work which combines an innovating technique with relevant content. Yet in some ways they have been handicapped in seeking new outlets for their work by being compartmentalized as 'fringe' writers.

Messrs Brenton, Hare and Wilson were pioneers, of course, in creating the kind of short, compact and controversial play that was perfectly suited to the small scale demands of a fringe auditorium. Works like Brenton's *Revenge* and *Christie In Love*, Hare's *Slag* or Wilson's *Vampire* were ingenious do-it-yourself kits of fringe production and playwrighting techniques. Interestingly, the plays tended to be thematic variations on the decaying qualities of English life. In particular Howard Brenton's early work was peopled with politicians, criminals and policemen who were seemingly bent upon some hideous, yet parochial course of self-destruction in an England that was facing the steepest of moral declines. But just as these writers were becoming identified as promising products of the fringe, they began to abandon writing for small theatres in favour of more ambitious outlets for their work.

In this sense the première of Howard Brenton's full length *Magnificence* at the Royal Court (the downstairs auditorium) proved to be a turning point in the development of the fringe. Although *Magnificence* falls, strictly speaking, outside the scope of this chapter it demands inclusion for, like *Rocky Horror Show*, it helps to define the interests and obsessions of the generation who helped to set out the tracks of our underground theatre some five or six years ago. For the magnificent point about *Magnificence* was that it created a real talking point among the professional sectors of its audiences. Writers, directors and actors who had previously been confined in tiny environments began to measure the possibilities of working in a larger kind of theatre – of reaching wider audiences. As the actors began to occupy the stage the effect was of a new generation taking command of a stage. The play contained an interesting message for its audience: it told the story of a group of young people who try to set up an alternative way of life, by way of a squatting expedition, in isolation from the rest of society. The squatting mission fails rather disastrously and one of the group, Jed's, reaction is to attempt the assassination (on Angry Brigade lines) of a post-1970 Tory Minister named Alice. Jed winds up in Alice's garden with a bag of gelignite which refuses to go off until the last moment of the play. During his powerful confrontation with Alice, Jed refers to the title of the play:

. . . Can't get rid. Can't shake it off. Magnificence, that it would be magnificent to have you bleeding on the lawn . . . I am deeply in contempt of your English mind . . . the sticky mess of your English humanity that gums up our ears to your lies, our eyes to your crimes . . . I dunno, I dunno, what can a . . . What can a . . . Do? To get it real. And get it real to you . . .

Brenton has stated that the play can be read as a metaphor of waste – the way in which revolt and anarchism, if not properly pondered, can lead to futile useless acts of violence. At the crucial moment of confrontation Jed is unable to evoke a 'real' act which will destroy his enemies. With hindsight it becomes tempting to read *Magnificence* as a kind of critique of the fringe movement – the inability 'to get it real'. The sense of alienation, the attempt to create a different style of life, the increasing reliance on images of violence and theatrical terrorism to make an impact, the final sense of political impotence, that mere anger and aggression are wasteful – these thematic strands in the play encapsulate a dilemma facing the entire fringe in this country. Although *Magnificence* received mixed notices, I believe it to be a key piece of fringe writing – refusing to limit its perspectives to conventional ideas about the appeal of underground art.

David Hare is another writer preoccupied with gaining wider audiences for fringe work – his own included, of course. His appointment as resident dramatist at Nottingham Playhouse last season led to the première of *Brassneck*, a play written by Hare in close collaboration with Howard Brenton. *Brassneck* was an ambitious, panoramic view of post-war corruption and political sellout in a fictional Midlands town called Stanton (not a million miles away, one felt, from Nottingham itself). Against all prediction, this complex fascinating play not only won near unanimous praise from the national critics, but the Playhouse was also packed throughout a fairly substantial run. The success of *Brassneck* ensured that Richard Eyre's temporary appointment as artistic director at Nottingham (it was Eyre who appointed Hare) was extended indefinitely at the end of the season. For the first time both critics and the public became aware of what talented fringe writers could achieve given the resources of a theatre like Nottingham Playhouse. For instance, an elegant series of back projections managed to suggest the flow and implied decline of post-war England – ranging from an ironic portrait of Churchill in 1945 to the face of Mick Jagger (accompanied by *You Can't Always Get What You Want*) for a bankruptcy scene. The Portable writers are as avowed enemies of naturalism as Charles Marowitz. *Brassneck* focused upon the career of the ruthless Bagley family and charted its rise, corrupt success and eventual decline – but never on a purely documentary basis. There were scattered references to the ruthlessness of the Borgias and, at one point, Alfred Bagley mounts his throne at the local Masonic Lodge in the guise of an actual Renaissance Pope –

opening the play out to more generalized impressions of public corruption, greed and wealth accumulated through family intrigue.

Certainly such surreal, comic moments have often puzzled the reviewers. In *Magnificence*, the squatting episode was conceived on pure Royal Court terms of stage naturalism. Yet the second half of the play opened out to much more surreal effects – at one point Lenin arrived on the stage amidst a blazing fanfare! In Snoo Wilson's *Vampire*, Freud and Jung mysteriously turn up during a scene – the vampires of the title being both real and figments of the mind (they include a nineteenth century Heathcliffe figure, a World War One soldier, a Bowie-like pop singer, and Enoch Powell emerging in triumph from a coffin). Such shifts of perspective, varieties of tone and style, in the course of a play are a distinctive feature of the best of the new writing. Howard Brenton insists that these kinds of technique were common practice for Shakespeare and the Jacobeans – they would certainly seem out of place in a Pinter or Osborne play. David Hare's *Knuckle* (which Michael Codron bravely mounted in the West End during the spring of 1974) certainly confused several of the reviewers with its subtle parody of a Raymond Chandler-cum-Ross Macdonald thriller contained within an exposure of corruption in the Home Counties.

There is some evidence that we have neglected the real point about the fringe. Consider, for instance, the recent creation of studio theatres in reps across the country. These are tiny auditoria tucked away inside the vast structures of new civic edifices like the Sheffield Crucible and the Birmingham Rep. The theory is that new writing must be of minority fringe interest – that main stages must be safeguarded for safe revivals of classics or West End spin-offs. The success of a play like *Brassneck* at Nottingham makes nonsense of this peculiar notion. It's not only the writers who are condemned to this kind of solitary confinement but also our younger directors. On the whole the new generation of directors, at least the most adventurous, have tended to cut their teeth on the fringe writers. Hence directors like Chris Parr, Pam Brighton, Max Stafford-Clark, Walter Donohue, Pip Simmons and Ron Daniels have been denied opportunities to work in mainstream theatres and auditoria. Just where are the new Bill Gaskills, Peter Halls or Lindsay Andersons going to come from – if we don't allow young directors the right to experiment in properly equipped theatres? It is time that some serious thought was given to plugging the generation gap in our theatres. *Rocky Horror Show, Sizwe Bansi Is Dead, Flowers, The Mother, Brassneck, Ashes* and *Magnificence* – I hope I've been able to suggest that the term 'fringe' need not imply the kind of incestuous event described in my opening paragraph. It would be a disaster if we were to confine our most talented new writers and directors to organizing benefit nights for themselves at the King's Head.

Digging up Legends

A cautionary confession about the writing of theatrical biography.

When I agreed to attempt the biography of Lilian Baylis nearly twenty years ago, at the instigation of Patricia Strauss, one of the Old Vic governors, I was – like most beginners in life-writing – blithely blind to the Andes in my path. After my last mazy expedition into theatrical history no terrain, it seemed to me, could be as difficult to explore as the lost world of Regency pantomime: I had recently written the first biography of Grimaldi since 1838. To do this I had spent most of my spare time for two years sifting through hundreds of newspapers, periodicals, books and prints for tiny shreds of fact, anecdote and opinion, sticking them more or less together into a jigsaw with a lot of guesswork, background colouring – and empty spaces. Until I started to burrow in the British Museum, the Enthoven Collection and elsewhere I had not realized how high were the class barriers between straight actors and pantomimists. Small part comedians of merited obscurity were – so long as they were 'legitimate' – often documented in detail by the contemporary authors of reviews, gossip paragraphs, and theatrical biographies; while clowns, harlequins and pantaloons of apparent brilliance and incontestable popularity were dismissed as beyond the pale of educated attention, at least in the printed word. It is rather as if the entire Press today reverently chronicled the careers of the smaller fry with the National and the RSC, while ignoring Danny La Rue, Frankie Howerd and Morecambe and Wise, apart

from recording that their simple buffoonery had, as usual, tickled
the fancies of the mob. Whatever doubts may be harboured about
current priorities in criticism and reporting, those obtaining in the
period between 1800 and 1815 (Grimaldi's heyday) were unhelpful
to naifs like me who thought that digging up the history of the most
persistently popular and profitable of all theatrical diversions
required no more than appetite and stamina.

In the last five years of Grimaldi's working life (he was burned
out at forty-four, in 1822) his genius, and the vitality of the pop
culture in which he exercised it, was discovered by enough intelligent observers, writing in sufficiently vivid detail, to convince the
twentieth century reader that he was as good, even as great, as the
people of Regency London believed him to be. But if such a reader
wanted more than the fragments in Maurice Willson Disher's
splendid book *Clowns and Pantomimes* (which had spurred me into
my own quest) he would have to conduct his own excavations.
There was little evidence of Grimaldi's greatness in his so-called
Memoirs, transposed by clumsy hackwork from the first to the
third person singular, and edited (at second hand) by Dickens –
who was twelve when the King of Clowns retired – into one of the
most disappointing and tantalizing books of its kind. Outside it, his
private identity was virtually invisible.

I had started on the search for Grimaldi for the simple and (so
it seemed) sufficient reason that I wanted to know more about
what he actually did, that made so many people think he was a
Kean of pantomime, and what he was really like behind the grin-
ning mask of Joey. A similar impulse prompted me to accept Mrs
Strauss's invitation to write about Lilian Baylis. Although I had
never met her, I had seen her in her box, during my schooldays, from
the Old Vic gallery; and since then I had come, as a critic and
amateur historian of the theatre, to marvel at her achievements, of
which the books I had read and the anecdotes I had heard seemed
to provide no satisfying and reasonable explanation. The Baylis
myth, like the Grimaldi legend, led me on; and there was one seduc-
tive (though, as it turned out, misleading) difference. She had died
precisely a century after Grimaldi (with whom she shared a devotion to Sadler's Wells) and many of the people who worked for her
were still irrefutably alive. The evidence must be there, I assumed,
for the taking, from diaries, letters, cuttings and memories, apart

from the hardcover hagiography. Nothing could be more respectably legitimate, moreover, than 'the home of Shakespeare and opera in English' that she had miraculously created in a dingy, understaffed, overcrowded, Victorian temperance music-hall in a Lambeth slum, with virtually no money, equipment, resources or experience. So, armed with a tape recorder lent by the generous Pat Strauss and with an unteachable faith in the accessibility of the past, I began to read, to interview and to put out feelers, gropingly and very tentatively, towards that buried life into which – I had the temerity and the hubris to believe – I could intrude, and plumb its mysteries.

Two things rapidly became clear to me. To write the life of Lilian Baylis I should not only have to listen to a great many people, but also to follow the history of the Old Vic since 1880, when her aunt Emma Cons took it over as a teetotal centre of purified entertainment (including ballad concerts, temperance propaganda, lantern-slide lectures and music-hall turns purged of all unseemliness in word and gesture). For a spare time book writer with a full time job, this was likely to take at least as many months of self-immolation as *Grimaldi*. But I also discovered that my fascination with Lilian Baylis was not quite matched by publishers, whose polite interest went no further, contractually, than a readiness to advance the equivalent of two weeks' salary. As the fledgling father of four children (three had arrived at once, in my sole theatrical *coup* to date) I very regretfully decided, as the magnitude of the job and the meagreness of all but the spiritual rewards became evident, that to write a biography of Miss Baylis was a luxury that I (and my family) could not afford.

This was a decision about which I felt both sad and guilty, off and on. Nobody else took up the job, and during the following years the obituary columns frequently served to remind me of what was being lost to theatrical research, with the death of witness after witness who might have held part of a clue to Miss Baylis's complex character. Then, two years ago, I returned to the excavations, prompted by the imminence of the Baylis centenary. Now that my family had grown up, it was something that I could more easily afford to do. In any case, I had to do it. So I started again to interview the dwindling band of survivors from the early days of Miss Baylis's regime, and to search the official records. But I was obliged, shortly, to stop again – because of sudden pressures on spare time from my newspaper job, and the less predictable theft of my car, with a briefcase containing files of notes and recorded transcripts. I got the car back, smashed, but not the briefcase; and although I traced the thief to Wormwood Scrubs and enlisted the governor's help in trying to jog his memory, he was unable to assist our inquiries. These are scarcely common factors in the making or unmaking of theatrical biographies, but they illustrate two essential maxims for authors: never be optimistic about deadlines, and never leave anything in a car.

When I started yet again in the summer of 1973, and the book began to take shape, several problems emerged that postponed the crystallization of the woman behind 'the Lady'. That term, which Mrs Strauss had originally suggested as a title for the book-to-be, may serve as a tiny example of the snares on the trail. 'The Lady' was, I had been assured, the name by which Miss Baylis was generally known at the Vic, and I found that it was still used with reverent affection by some of her closest colleagues and warmest admirers, among whom it was ascribed to the spiritual authority and self-sacrificing devotion that she displayed in the Waterloo Road (not a few, at her death, invoked St Joan and St Teresa). But the name, it seems, was introduced in the 1920's by Miss Baylis's secretary, Evelyn Williams, partly to discourage the tendency among the backstage staff to call the manager 'Mother' (or, rather, 'Muvver'), which didn't seem quite the right way to address an honorary M.A. (Oxon) who wore her cap and gown on every possible occasion. According to some witnesses, Williams – as she was always known – was prompted to this accolade not so much by devotional loyalty (though she deeply admired Miss Baylis) but rather by ironic Irish humour; for 'the Lady' was (luckily for the Vic and the theatre in general) very far from being lady-like in her background, manners and life-style. She made no attempt at camouflaging her lack of conventional culture and the social graces of gentility. During moments of crisis during the early pioneering days at the Vic Miss Baylis was, indeed, inclined to explain vehemently that she was badly educated, knew nothing about Shakespeare, and wasn't a real lady.

In the larger sense that Williams also, no doubt, had in mind, Miss Baylis was certainly 'the Lady' of the Old Vic; and, whatever its origins, the term caught on among the staff, although they often talked about her (and still do) simply as 'Baylis' (common usage at the Vic, this, with no particular feminist connotations: 'We're democratic down here,' the Lady is said to have said. 'No Mr and Mrs at the Vic.'). But would 'The Lady' be a proper title for my book, when so few of the actors, singers and dancers who worked for her appear to have used the name, and most knew her only and always as Miss Baylis? Such intimates as Dame Sybil and Ernest Milton called her Lilian or Lil; but, as I was to discover, she made only a handful of fairly close friends among her companies during her 39 years in management. Outside the theatre Miss Baylis's intimates were mostly 'holy ladies' (as one of her staff sardonically described them). She had a wide range of acquaintances among Mothers Superior; she went into retreat frequently and fervently; and if she hadn't been called by God to the Vic, she would (Ninette de Valois believes) have found her vocation in a convent.

That in itself suggests one of the hazards of conceiving any study of Miss Baylis simply as a 'theatrical biography'. She was a deeply, intensely, naturally religious woman, and the most important and intimate relationship in her life – with God – was beyond my reach. But I found some clues in the life of Father Andrew, her spiritual confessor and main intermediary with the Almighty for over twenty years. This tall priest in a Franciscan habit was a familiar figure backstage at the Vic: some people recall him as being sinister and Mephistophelean, while for others he was a jovial Friar Tuck. Miss Baylis's custom of shutting herself up with him in the office for emergency sessions of prayer and meditation was the source of ribald gossip which has become embedded in the underside of the legend. Yet although he was often resented and ridiculed (out of Miss Baylis's hearing), Father Andrew seems to have been almost as remarkable in his priesthood as his 'dear child', Lilian, was in her management. He founded a new religious order, the Society of the Divine Compassion, and the only lepers' colony in England (Miss Baylis's favourite cause, after the Vic and Sadler's Wells); he was an enthusiastic author, director and designer of religious drama; he was an accomplished artist, a less accomplished poet, and wrote many popular and influential devotional books; and he knew more about Lilian Baylis than anybody else. How I wish that

I could have met him, but he died before I had first thought of writing the biography.

Apart from the absence of crucial witnesses, I was handicapped by the absence of autobiographical material. The only diaries extant record nothing more than appointments and telephone numbers, and I doubt if Miss Baylis ever kept any other kind (apart from some matter-of-fact notes on her rare holidays abroad). Most of her letters were brisk, business-like and impersonal. The personal ones that I have seen are seldom self-revealing, although they show her to be a far warmer, kindlier, nicer woman than was often supposed by those who suffered from the blaze of her temper, the lash of her tongue and the implacable squeeze of her economy. Towards the end of her life she began to dictate some autobiographical notes to her companion-secretary, Annette Prevost, but she did not get very far or go very deep. Miss Prevost, who gave me the most generous, valuable and illuminating help that any biographer could wish for, was going to write the book herself, but had to give this up when her husband fell ill.

Moreover, Miss Baylis's memory was – like so many other things about her – eccentric. She misremembered names and dates throughout her career, and also generated stories about her life which, one suspects, owed more to romantic fantasy than to autobiographical fact, though this was beyond verification. Consider, for instance, the cause of her slightly twisted mouth, which every actor or actress still mimics in telling a Baylis story, and which may be the clue to some of the complex defences behind which this intensely lonely woman survived. The most common explanation of that minor deformity, recorded in an anthology of posthumous recollections, is that while swimming in South Africa – where she lived from the age of seventeen for six years – she was swept out of her depth, and suffered a slight stroke from shock and fright. She told some people, however, that the stroke was due to a horrifying experience in Johannesburg, when a naked African – whom she said was a notorious murderer – broke into the family bungalow in the middle of the night. He took flight when Lilian grappled with him – according to one anecdote, God told her, 'Throw the pot at him, Lilian', and she did – but her face was never the same again. Among the other explanations she is said to have given is that the stroke was due to a broken romance in South Africa. Yet in the material passed on to me by Annette Prevost was a photograph of Miss Baylis taken in London before she went to South Africa that seems already to show that twisted mouth. Moreover, none of her diagnoses seems medically credible. She had probably suffered from an attack of Bell's palsy.

In trying to fill out the portrait of Miss Baylis I listened, with great pleasure, to the recollections of many graduates of the Old Vic, some long forgotten (except by their old comrades), others still at the head of the profession. The people I met were, without exception, remarkable personalities with remarkable things to say – but not, on the whole, about Miss Baylis. It was borne in upon me, after some fruitless expeditions (however enjoyable) around the Home Counties, that I had underestimated the difficulties of writing about a manager – a manager who did not direct, or design, or buy new plays or mix much with other managers, whose authors were (with a few exceptions) safely dead, and who left the production (cash apart) to her producers. Lilian Baylis attended auditions and interviewed new members of the company. She sat up into the small hours to watch dress rehearsals. She would make cutting (often) and encouraging (rarely) remarks. But for most of the companies most of the time she was a background figure in the box and the office, already a legend: 'a power and a joke', as Peggy Ashcroft says.

They had little to do with her, and knew next to nothing about her, apart from the snowballing legends.

The fact that Miss Baylis was a century closer to me than Grimaldi did not, after all, make nearly as much difference as I had supposed. I had overlooked one occupational hazard of all biographers, and perhaps particularly troublesome to those working in the theatre: memories often die long before the objects of those memories, and what many people remember is not first-hand experience but what they have read and heard. The legend tends to cover up the facts, deeper and deeper, every year. Just as in Grimaldi's case, many essential documents had disappeared from view – like the records of governors' meetings at the Old Vic in Miss Baylis's first decade. Sir Tyrone Guthrie appears to have read them, if his autobiography is to be believed (although in matters of fact he was not always more reliable than Miss Baylis); but they must be written off as a casualty of the war – not only at the Vic, but, more surprisingly, at the offices of those other bodies which received copies of them. In some ways, indeed, the reality behind the legend seemed to have gone as irrecoverably beyond recall for Lilian Baylis as for Joe Grimaldi.

I have emphasized the difficulties of writing about 'the Lady', but in spite of them – partly, perhaps, because of them – I was happy in my work while it lasted. Now that it is over, I try to block out the certainty at the back of my mind that, in a year or two, somebody will discover the missing records; a suitcase of correspondence will be found among an actress's effects; Lilian Baylis will turn out to be a Marie Bashkirtseff, when her secret diaries are unearthed in a Welsh convent. (At the very end of my own researches, Miss Prevost found in her cellar the diaries kept by Miss Baylis's father during his years in South Africa.) I still feel restlessly concerned that I could dig up so little about Emma Cons and her family, in whose pursuit I spent an absurdly disproportionate amount of research time and emotional energy. But I look back with relish on my bewildered and obsessional excavations; and I am obliged to confess that I would do it all over again. The prime moral of this cautionary tale, indeed, is that you take up with theatrical legends at your peril. They will never let you go.

Lilian Baylis to be published next year by Allen Lane

Bricks on our Shoulders

The theatre in Scotland, and the need for a Scottish theatre, as seen by the associate director of Edinburgh's Royal Lyceum.

When the train from King's Cross climbed slowly over Beattock Summit a great roar erupted from the bar, 'Scot-laaand, Scot-laaand'. It reminded me of my childhood, coming back from Wembley, celebrating one of my country's rare victories over England. The year of Jim Baxter's goal. We had been defeated many times since then but I didn't think of that, neither did the men in the bar. There were no border guards in kilts to check our passports but, there was no doubt about it, we were entering a whole different country. I knew. I was going home.

I had been assistant director to William Gaskill at the Royal Court Theatre. There I had learned an attitude to my work. I was and still am a believer in the writer's theatre – the theatre of new plays, of living authors. I wanted to take as much as I could of the personality of that building and the workers in it back home with me. I had never worked in Scotland before. It seemed ridiculous. Now I had been given the chance. Clive Perry and Richard Eyre had invited me to be associate director at the Royal Lyceum Theatre in Edinburgh. The theatre had a good reputation, both for the high standard of work and for the beauty, splendour and comfort of its Victorian interior. Now that I have been there for nearly three years I can only applaud the famous Sunday critic who described the Lyceum as just about the most delightful place in the country to watch a play in. It was my job to change the Lyceum in some way. Every director tries to bring his own personality to bear on his theatre. He brings to it what he is and what he stands for. I was Scots and I was from the Royal Court. I believed in new plays, new writers. Very early on I had a chance to commit myself. I had a new play by a living writer that I believed in. It was a Scottish play and could only be done properly by a talented company of native actors, *The Burning*.

This was a play dealing with King James VI, and witchcraft. It was written by the young Glasgow poet, Stewart Conn, who has since become literary manager of the theatre. I wanted to start rehearsals immediately. But where were the actors?

My memory of the Scottish theatre was hopelessly dim. I had seen some performances years ago at the Glasgow Citizens but one triumphant event stood out in my memory. This was Tyrone Guthrie's production of Sir David Lindsay's morality *Ane Satire of the Thrie Estaitis* which I had seen at the 1959 Edinburgh Festival. It was performed on an open stage in the Church of Scotland assembly hall on The Mound. The ensemble work and the individual acting of people like Roddy McMillan, Tom Fleming, Lennox Milne and a truly great actor, the late Duncan Macrae, completely staggered me. For three weeks the Scottish theatre was lauded, then it seemed to vanish into thin air. This collective of talent disbanded and went their separate ways, mostly to London and to television and films. But it had happened and I had seen it. Therefore it could happen again. These same actors and younger players coming out of drama school in Scotland could and must be brought together again so that a truly Scottish theatre could exist, expressing Scotland for the people of Scotland. This had happened in Ireland years before with the great Abbey Theatre Company in the days of Sean O'Casey, Sara Allgood, F. J. McCormack and Barry Fitzgerald which astonished Dublin, and then the world. The challenge was irresistible.

The actors were there. Many were living and working in Scotland. Some in radio and television, some were already members of the Royal Lyceum Company. Others caught a plane from Heathrow to Turnhouse. The first performance of *The Burning* was concrete proof that a talented ensemble of Scottish actors in a Scottish play was a unique experience. Watching this performance was not like watching English actors or German or French. It was neither better

nor worse. It was different. The success of the playing was capped
by the fact that the people of Edinburgh came to see it. We played
to full houses. Without, in any way, having to popularize we were
popular. We only played the play for about fifteen performances –
a crime in the circumstances. It has taken a long time but, even on
that first night, I feel that Clive Perry and I knew that the company must eventually play in repertoire. It is perhaps unfair to
single out individuals in an organization that is passionately a
company but the performance of John Grieve as the jester singing
Stewart Conn's melancholy lyric 'I'll bind marigolds in your hair'
is forever with me and I am sure with the men, women and children
who saw it. Next year we can perhaps go into repertoire. Again, we
can do *The Burning*.

Before leaving the Court I had written my first play, *Willie
Rough*. When I showed it to William Gaskill at the Royal Court it
had no claims to be the best script he had read as director of the
theatre but it was certainly the longest. After much good advice
from both him and Roddy McMillan, it was pruned and made much
stronger. The play is centred around the February strike of 1916
which paralysed production in every shipyard and factory on the
Clyde. It took place in Greenock, my home town, and the leading
character was based on the memory of my grandfather. I knew
exactly what actors I wanted to play every single part in the script
and a rare thing in the theatre happened. If we could wait they
could all be free. We waited and rehearsals began just after the New
Year of 1972. Bringing *Willie Rough* to performance is by far the
most exciting thing that has happened to me as a director. The
company were an ensemble from the first day. They had all worked
together before and their mutual respect was most apparent.
Fulton Mackay, Roddy McMillan, Joseph Brady, James Grant,
John Cairney, Eileen McCallum, Paul Young, Clare Richards,
Callum Mill and young Andrew Byatt brought the play to life.
Only very occasionally does a situation arise when every single
actor understands the man or woman he is playing down to the last
nuance. The other night Roddy McMillan asked me: 'Will we ever
do it again?' I think we will. We were on our own ground. There
was no company in the world could do this particular play better
than we could and we were being supported by the people. At the
Lyceum and thereafter on tour in Glasgow, Stirling and almost a

year later at the Shaw Theatre in London we packed people in to see us. In quite a short time we had become a Scottish company based in the capital, serving the nation.

I should say here that the Royal Lyceum Theatre Company of Edinburgh is not a permanent company on the European model. Even the large scale subsidized companies like the National realize that actors must be allowed out of the theatre to do television and films. They must make money. The public are too little aware of the fact that some of the very best theatre is subsidized by the artists who provide it. This free association for Scotland's actors must continue, yet a Scottish national theatre should be established. It is possible.

Roddy McMillan had written his first play in fifteen years, *The Bevellers*. It was set in the basement bevelling shop of a glass firm in Glasgow. Geoffrey Scott created an astonishing realistic set and Deidre Clancy dressed the actors in just the right clothes. It would be somehow insulting to call them costumes. Without these two artists it would have been impossible to bring the plays I am describing to life; and the director Clive Perry, and administrator, Charles Tripp, have created an economic situation in which progress can be made and in which the risks of doing new writing can be taken.

In *The Bevellers* an apprentice spends his first day at the trade. He is exposed both to the dignity of the craft and the violence of the workers. This uncompromising, primitive portrait of men at work was another success for the company. I felt that now we had to pass the big test. We had to go back to go forward. We had to perform the first Scottish play again. The Edinburgh Festival invited the company to perform *The Thrie Estaitis* in the assembly hall where the Scottish theatre under Tyrone Guthrie had had its great triumph. My production in a new version by Tom Wright wasn't a triumph. How could it be? The element of surprise had gone. You can't compete with legend. Many critics claimed that we had summoned the ghost of Guthrie rather than laid it but they had missed the point. This company was going to last longer than three weeks. It was a working organization. When *The Estaitis* closed we were busy in rehearsal. We were touring Scotland with a new version of *L'Avare* by Keith Dewhurst (from Molière), in which Rikki Fulton was an extraordinary Harpagon, and we were

taking *The Bevellers* to London. Rikki is one of Scotland's leading
music-hall comedians but now he is also an integral part of the
company. No one envied him the task of playing Flatterie in *The
Estaitis.* This was the role which had immortalized Macrae for the
Scots but I for one will never forget his exuberance, nor the gravity
of Tom Fleming as Divine Correction, the simplicity of Fulton
Mackay as John the Commonweal and the humanity of Joseph
Brady as the Poor Man. We did the play. The hall was filled by the
people of Scotland and abroad. There was no longer any need to
think in the past. New plays, that's what were needed! I had now
written my second play, *Benny Lynch,* about the greatest Scottish
boxer. There was a new play by Stewart Conn, *The Aquarium,* and
as I write this there's an interesting new work on the desk, *God Is
Good And The Republicans Won't Always Be Down* by a member of
the company, Sean McCarthy. There is talk about bringing *Benny*
to London after its tour of Scotland. I hope we can, but it is the
service to Edinburgh and Scotland that is important to the
Lyceum.

We need to expand. We need to commission and develop the
writers who are working in Scotland. We need to present the
company in international drama. These actors are custom built for
the plays of Gorki, O'Neill, O'Casey and Brecht. 'I carry a brick on
my shoulder in order that people may know what my house was
like.' Brecht said that. That is what the Royal Lyceum Company
is for – to show Scotland to Scotland – her past and her present –
to prepare for her future, which seems blessed by economic development if the oil under her waters is really there. To do this we
need to expand. This means repertoire, more touring, a second
auditorium, and more money. It can be argued that our theatre is
well subsidized by the Scottish Arts Council and especially by the
generosity of the corporation of the City of Edinburgh, but it is
never enough. It will never be enough until we think of the theatre
in the same way as public libraries and swimming pools. A vital
theatre is as important as a well stocked library or a championship
pool. A Scottish national theatre is the right of the people of
Scotland. If the subsidy for this is not forthcoming the Scottish
theatre will not die but it will have lost the moment. Today is the
time for growth and if we miss this great opportunity the next ten
years of Scottish theatre may be only an occasional outburst,

perhaps at the Edinburgh Festival again, punctuating deadly silence. Of course, here I am discussing the Scottish theatre not theatre in Scotland. No one serious about the theatre in Britain can deny the achievements of the Traverse Theatre Club under Michael Rudman and now his successor Mike Ockrent, or The Citizens in Glasgow. Here I am concerned with the Lyceum and its potential as Scotland's national company. The chance missed; the company breaks up. It will be like winning the cup, then putting the whole team on the transfer list. Of course, these players have worked in London before and they can do so again, but I for one would be much much happier if it was together and only for a spell showing our wares. We are first and foremost a theatre for Scotland. Our job is to make a Scottish theatre that stands up to be counted among the best companies in Europe. We are only beginning, but many movements of great potential in Scotland have died right there. The Scots truly 'don't know what they've got till it's gone'. Perhaps the Lyceum company will be an exception. The company is there to show the people of Scotland and elsewhere what it is like to be Scots and to live there – to demonstrate what makes it special. It is a whole other country. I was away for too long. Now I remember why they shout from the bar when the train crosses the border, 'Scot-laaand, Scot-laand'.

Repertory Round-up

The deputy drama critic of The Daily Telegraph *reports from the regions.*

If the theatre outside London was going anywhere in particular in 1974, it was going peripatetic: up and down the country, patiently, persistently, like Aristotle pacing up and down the classroom, spreading the word and waiting for the penny to drop. Of course it wasn't all carrying on like that. Most of it stayed firmly put. It had to. Your Nottinghams and Bristols and Birminghams and Stokes had a name for being where they were and (mostly) stayed there. So it was also with the lesser reps – the Salisburys and the Hulls, the Leatherheads and the Derbys: they knew their places, their audiences, their scope and stuck to them.

But it was coming to be accepted with less and less alarm that a repertory company under imaginative direction might – at the risk of a swollen head – pack its bags and start to move perpetually about in quest of audiences anywhere. It might, in fact, simply tour – not with a view to London but with a view to touring – as if touring might be an end in itself rather than a polite West End way of trying something out on the dog.

As a result the dog has been getting a better deal, and there is now more than one respectable theatrical company to be found on tour. It used to be just Prospect: a noble venture pitting its head (we used to think) against the celebrated brick wall of provincial indifference. Year in, year out it would tramp round the regions, taking one classic or another, and sometimes two or three, into various holes and corners. With subsidies, of course: no getting away from them. And no one except Toby Robertson and his henchmen and a few of the Arts Council visionaries ever supposed that anything much could come of it – not without stars, and it was well known that the stars (except for dearest Dulcie and Michael and Cicely and Jack) had stopped touring when the Thorndikes stopped – such a thankless task anyhow, trying to bring back to life to those faded marble halls long since past their heyday and too big for anything but opera.

Well, we were wrong. Something somehow eventually did come of it. The word began to get around, the penny to drop: the pacing up and down the country seemed to have paid off. And so it came to pass that the Prospect company became a respected name in the land. Some critics even left London to inspect it. More remarkable still the Prospect company grew and (in effect) multiplied, so that today we have in addition to it the Cambridge Theatre Company and the Actors' Company as direct descendants. All have a bias in favour of the provinces, each has a character it can call its own and between them they can muster a repertoire worthy of any national theatre, in title if not always in deed.

In other words we have here a trend, partly inspired by the Arts Council's desire to keep the No. 1 houses open, and partly meeting a public need for variety of tone and talent: something apart from the local rep, something extra. Not, admittedly, an all-star affair. Starriness is something which all three companies seem to be against as a policy. Anyway, they cannot afford it. They can however afford players of quality, people who enjoy the idea of loyalty to a company, of taking drama where it is needed and wanted.

But perhaps the most exciting fact in the existence of Prospect, the Cambridge and the Actors' is that just when we had mostly abandoned hope for anything in the provinces but civic based reps such as the last two decades had yielded with assurance, these troupes should have proved the need for strolling players. The Actors' Company at Wimbledon became quite the thing in the spring of 1974 with its nicely balanced repertoire of Chekhov (*The Wood Demon*), Shakespeare (*King Lear*), Congreve (*The Way of the World*), Ford (*'Tis Pity She's a Whore*), and Feydeau (*Ruling the Roost*). The Wimbledon Theatre is a big old house, off the beaten track: many a West End try-out dies there. Ask Eileen Atkins. But this company and this repertoire – especially Robert Eddison's Lear – renewed the management's faith in good theatre. For example, before this company turned up, how many playgoers could claim an acquaintance with Chekhov's *The Wood Demon*? Yet there they were at Wimbledon in sizable numbers one sunny Saturday afternoon in March, working out the difference between it and *Uncle Vanya*.

It must however be admitted that the Actors' Company has had something going for it for some time. I mean reputation. Ian McKellen's *Richard II* had set us all by the ears when first presented at Cambridge (I was charmed into forgetting my deadline); and when later he helped to establish a company of players, self-managing on a share-and-share-alike basis, his reputation rose politically as well. Whether his art went forward at a similar rate is a matter for critical disputation. The fact remains that he provided the leadership, and that – like Richard Cottrell with the Cambridge Theatre Company and Toby Robertson with Prospect – is what matters most with missions. Somebody up front in whom the rest have faith and (with luck) some say.

A say, that is, in the company's policy, or if not much say an instinctive sharing of basic belief. This is what Mr Cottrell – like Mr Robertson and Mr McKellen – uses as bait to keep a company together; and these days with the financial temptations of films and television it isn't easy to keep actors together for more than one show at a time, still less as tourists.

But there are snags. The theatres are not always right. A tour that takes in, for example, the Yvonne Arnaud, Guildford, the Crucible, Sheffield, the University Theatre, Southampton, and the Belgrade, Coventry, needs flexible designs and a versatile technique to fit itself to all the different shapes of stage. Then there are the audiences which tend not to turn up in heartening numbers until the visit is nearly over (an argument for early comebacks once the word has spread).

By and large, though, the system makes for more rehearsal time since a repertoire is sustained over months. Clumping together the titles offered by these same three companies in the spring of 1974 gives an idea of their broad mindedness: *The Royal Hunt of the Sun, Pericles, Twelfth Night* (two versions), *She Stoops to Con-*

quer, *French Without Tears, Fears and Miseries of the Third Reich,* and the aforementioned Wimbledon season of Chekhov, Feydeau, Congreve, Ford and *King Lear*.

To some extent therefore it may be argued that these companies are more national than our National Theatre if only because they get about more. The National, though, in its own small way contributes to the revival of provincial touring whenever it gets the chance. And never more notably, to my mind, than with Jonathan Miller's idea of *Measure for Measure* when it visited the Royal, Bury St Edmunds: a wonderfully cool updated appraisal of the comedy with all Freudian flags flying. Strange how this director in a subsequent season at Greenwich failed to enjoy the same artistic success with a group of what he was pleased to call family romances – *Ghosts, The Seagull* and *Hamlet*; and fascinating that Greenwich and Wimbledon should find themselves vying for the fashionable playgoer's attention.

Some of the year's best work however happened miles from London and – again – not always at the regular reps. The Sixty Nine Company of Manchester for instance in its temporary, tented theatre which arose amid the marble of the Royal Exchange gave us remarkable revivals of Eliot's *Family Reunion* and of Priestley's *Time and the Conways*, while at the Bristol Old Vic there was hardly a seat to be had for *Uncle Vanya, The Apple Cart* and Ben Travers's *Plunder*, or later for *Othello*. The reason is simple, Bristol has a way of inspiring a peculiar and nostalgic loyalty in its young players so that when they have grown up and grown famous they seldom hesitate to return for a season if asked. Which is how that season came to be a sellout. Peter O'Toole played Vanya, Magnus and D'Arcy Tuck, and Paul Rogers Othello.

The star system? Well, if the star is not a nuisance, why not? He may attract good players as well as audiences. Not that O'Toole took any conspicuous minor roles in the manner of Olivier or McKellen (which smacks of false modesty); but he managed to make the company still look like a team, and Edward Hardwicke, Nigel Stock, Sara Kestelman, Marie Kean and Penelope Wilton stood their ground with distinction. Mr Hardwicke proved especially memorable in the Travers farce, whereas O'Toole was not. He seemed too often to be sharing the joke with the audience, while Mr Hardwicke knew what farce was all about (which is solemnity).

But this Vanya – shuffling, weary, pale, unprofiteering – must be ranked among the best things O'Toole ever did. His sardonic indignation was superb, and his Magnus – indolent, elegant, condescending – played the correct kind of parliamentary havoc with Coward's inquisition on a king.

As for Mr Rogers, returning to the company after 24 years, one might say that he made a bold stab at Othello without drawing very much blood: good clear diction, a fair command of the verse, a dignified appearance (until the final scene when he was got up like a barber's pole in white and orange), and rather too abruptly jealous under Val May's swift direction. All of which remarks sound like an adjudication, whereas Othello is nothing if he cannot sweep such nice conclusions out of our minds in favour of a blazing passion. Mr Rogers blazed, in bearded indignation, but it was fretfulness rather than passion. In a word, he lacked the guns for this most challenging of roles which has defeated so many, even more accomplished actors. Gerald Harper's Iago consequently thrived theatrically in line with most Iagos. Neither player could however compete effectively with Graham Barlow's imposing setting of cycloramic, panelled doors which seemed to mystify us as much as the actors. Thus can a design occlude a tragedy.

Much harder, one would have thought to occlude the Meadows Players of Oxford, Frank Hauser's company which had for seventeen years supplied London as well as Oxford with a solid yet sensitive, middle-of-the-road and mildly offbeat attitude to the drama. Yet the Arts Council – which holds such sway over most of the repertory movement, large and small, static or peripatetic, fringe or famous, feeble or trendy – snuffed out the Meadows Players in a jiffy by simply cutting down its grant or failing to increase it, at a time of inflation, to a figure which to Hauser still seemed workable. Whether Hauser or his national patron was sulking, the pity of it was that a company's reputation – a company moreover which was inclined to tour in the tradition of Prospect Productions – should not be strong enough to save it. It takes after all a long time to build a name, to win a regular following for a theatre; and that is what Hauser had achieved at Oxford. He may have cast productions with an eye on the West End; but his heart appeared to be tuned to the regions. He was not against touring; he was not against reviving plays which people have not heard of. If *Dear Brutus* and

Dr Knock and *The Merchant of Venice* did not exactly set the Isis
on fire, it seemed ironical that his discovery of Ferenc Molnar's *The
Wolf* should have done almost that to the Thames: a fittingly fantastic swan song to an imaginative director's reign; a pioneering
director, some would say, since Hauser was on the scene at Oxford
long before most of his contemporaries.

Still, there have to be changes; and one of the great changes
that seemed to be coming over the regions in 1974 in addition to
the tendency to tour was the growth in popularity and achievement
and sometimes imagination of the studio theatres, one of which
was usually appended to each rep. A lot of their work was rather
wild and way-out-ish. Youth was all too evidently having its
fling. Efforts to shock seemed sometimes a bit naive and depressing.
But the quality of stuff which I came across at Birmingham,
Leatherhead, Derby and Sheffield was almost as high as in the
main auditorium. Some of it was also stuff on the move. *The
Speakers*, for example, taken from a tape-recorded sort of book by
Heathcote Williams, made an unusual evening at the Sheffield
Crucible studio with the audience and actors mingling and moving
round a shadowed hall in imitation of Hyde Park orators; and the
discipline of the players jointly directed for the Joint Stock Theatre
Company by William Gaskill and Max Stafford-Clark cast a properly hypnotic spell. This strange, taut, experimental entertainment visited several towns in its attempt to see behind the men on
soap-boxes. Whenever I looked behind one I saw Mr Gaskill or
Mr Stafford-Clark trying to behave like spectators.

Odder still in some ways was *The Supermale* at Derby Playhouse studio: another derivation from a novel, this time by
Kenneth Frost who had sliced up Alfred Jarry's dinner party
debate on the obsessive issue of perpetual masculine potency. Since
Jarry unwittingly and with characteristic rudeness founded the
Theatre of the Absurd, or so we are taught by Mr Esslin to believe, the devotion of an evening to an almost scientific search for
the unfailing erection raised at least a few eyebrows not at the
subject matter but at the elegance and lightly fantastic style of
Jarry's surrealistic writing – admiration too for the way in which
the company and the transformation of its sexes conveyed both the
discussion and the voyeuristic experiments with such a discreet
verve.

Discretion, of course, is essential at Leatherhead where Hazel Vincent Wallace who never actually directs has always seemed to know what the people want before they have known it themselves; and so while *Long Day's Journey Into Night*, much cut, was trundling along in the main auditorium – much cut but still too long for certain Surrey tastes – the art of René de Obaldia, rather a fringe taste in Britain, was making itself known in the studio at the back. *The Baby-Sitter* and *Two Women for a Ghost* had enjoyed some seasons earlier a decent run in Paris; and we were all visibly straining to make the same double bill go at Leatherhead. But it proved persistently slight and whimsical, just a couple of prolonged drawing room sketches – acted though with excellence by Pamela Strong, Lucinda Curtis and Peter Cartwright.

A similar sense of disappointment was unavoidable at the Birmingham Rep studio, known as Brum Studio, a few nights later. David Rudkin, so well remembered for *Afore Night Come*, seemed to be making a comeback in 1974 with plays on television and the West End fringe. So we all sat up hopefully for *No Title* in which a conventional and innocent young man finds himself drawn into the tenancy of a flat of such dismaying discomfort and crazy fixtures, not to speak of the dottiness of his fellow tenants, that only a half-wit or an author's puppet would have put up with it for a moment. Kafka, Pinter and Lewis Carroll came to mind in watching the sinister-jocular fantasy.

Eventually a sort of theme oozed through the sententious and farcical action – something to do with the liberty of the small individual in a large authoritarian state. Still, Rudkin remains always a writer to respect whether he is stylistically out of his depth or not; and it is after all one of a studio theatre's functions that it permits a writer to go out on a limb. The very flexibility of the auditorium which makes possible any kind of staging adds a dimension of excitement and novelty unobtainable at ordinary theatres – even if some playgoers like myself are still stuck with the belief that when it comes to the dramatic nitty-gritty the writing is what basically matters – not just a feeling for words but the shaping of a tale in theatrical terms.

Which is why, with something of a sigh of relief, it is good to get back to the Palace Theatre, Watford, to the works of Somerset Maugham, John Osborne and Noël Coward which can be acted in any shape of theatre you like, because they have the courtesy not to leave us befogged. First rate revivals of Maugham's *The Letter* – with Jill Bennett and Edward Hardwicke – of Osborne's *A Patriot for Me* and of Coward's *Fallen Angels* (Fenella Fielding and Penelope Keith) kept this agreeably uncomfortable Victorian suburban theatre firmly on the map.

For sheer off-the-mapness the Northcott, Exeter, takes some beating. Its remoteness may be a reason why its policy ran up against the tastes of the town hall. For it is the only theatre within reach of anyone living within reach of it; and its policy – since its director was a Royal Court graduate – of emphasizing writers like Howard Brenton and Edward Bond stirred some local resentment. All the same, its staging of two Bond plays, *Pope's Wedding* and *Bingo*, proved well worthwhile – the second (and new) piece went on to attract John Gielgud to the role of William Shakespeare for a London production; and *Pope's Wedding*, which I happened to see at its first Royal Court production twelve years ago, must still be ranked among his best plays; yet this was its first revival since that single Sunday night.

Here, of course, is a great argument for the reps and for their having studio theatres attached to them. Good plays need not be neglected simply because their appeal is limited. At the same time, there has to be a balance. It is no good, so to speak, emptying theatres so that critics and directors can indulge their esoteric tastes. The average playgoer has neither the time nor the inclination to swot up a text before he pays to go and see it or to acquaint himself with an author's background or to grapple with mysteries which are no longer mysteries to the professionals.

If he lives in the Midlands (say, Ashby de la Zouche) where every week there is on average a choice of two or three new productions, the playgoer can go to Nottingham, Coventry, Birmingham, Leicester or Derby in half an hour by car. Coach parties are also the coming thing. Round Exeter, alas, there is nowhere else to go: which means either that you supported Jane Howell's courage in not pandering to conventional, middle-class tastes, or felt frustrated by her single-minded, Sloane Square, leftist notions of what constitutes 'relevant' drama.

This is a widespread problem. Do you as director do what you like (and what you can with budget and casting limits)? Or do you do what the people like? The two ideas seldom coalesce; and in the consequential compromise many likely directors are apt to come unstuck. Miss Howell is no longer at Exeter. Bill Hays is no longer at Leeds. Stuart Burge is no longer at Nottingham. John Neville is in Canada. So is Robin Phillips. Peter Dews left Birmingham almost as soon as it opened. Colin George has gone from Sheffield. And so – defectingly – on. It isn't that they all got the boot or chucked it in. There are, after all, temptations beyond the reach of reps and no one should blame a director for going after them. But there is something wrong with a system which cannot retain for more than a few years at a time the men who run its main theatres.

We know it cannot keep its actors. We see that every season at Stratford-on-Avon, at the National, the Aldwych, the Royal Court. The defections are more marked at the reps, though it has yet to be proved that a permanent company can function for long without the civil service spirit of security and envy turning it into a mildewed institution. With directors it is different. They create policies. Their leadership is crucial. They give confidence, continuity.

So, one keeps one's fingers crossed for Stoke-on-Trent and Bristol, for Leicester, Liverpool and Guildford, where the directors have been in office for ten years or more. At Leicester Robin Midgley has two theatres in his care: the cosy Phoenix, best of all open-stage theatres; and the newly opened and splendiferous Haymarket, nearly three times the size and nicely appointed by an architect who must have meant it for spectaculars rather than the bulk of modern drama. It's yet another wide stage with amphitheatrical seating: a whole firmament above the players. As if to emphasize the point the theatre opened with *The Recruiting Officer* plus military band; and came on a week later with John Hopkins's closet drama *Economic Necessity* which fastened our attention on a middle-aged, middle-class, absent-minded man who suddenly drops out from the rat race. Forgive the clichés but they are the terms in which the piece was conceived, though it presented that good actor Anthony Bate with a fine, intense part as the broodingly confused paterfamilias who goes into such a brown study. Here, if ever, was a studio-type play – the television studio, really. Subsequent revivals of *Cabaret* and *The Caucasian Chalk Circle* looked likelier on this gaping stage.

The Mercury at Colchester also suffers somewhat from the

curtainless trend, making scenery difficult and exits and entrances lengthy. But somehow the Mercury is undeterred from disinterring a rare Victorian comedy every year. In 1973 it had been Henry Arthur Jones's *Liars*. In 1974 it was Tom Robertson's *Ours*, which proved so witty, stylish and gently satirical that it must surely turn up in London soon, if not in the Mercury's admirable production, why not at, say, the Mermaid?

As for new plays which were not specific try-outs, the reps had a thinner time than usual. The most exciting new piece I came across was *Brassneck* by David Hare and Howard Brenton at Nottingham Playhouse. This described the rise and fall of two provincial families – one posh, one poor – in terms which made the usual fun of capitalism and its corrosive tendencies, character corrosion, that is; but the vitality of the writing and scope of the theme made a fascinating evening of class-consciously political satire, English to the rotten core. Peter Cheeseman's company at Stoke-on-Trent characteristically inquired into the molten history of a local steel works threatened by closure. *Shelton Bar* recreated in summary and mime the events which were still causing much worry, and the actors had gone round and about with tape recorders to try to get the facts and feelings right. If it remained a sad story sadly underdramatized – community-based, agit-prop theatre, better suited to journalism than the stage – it was crammed with concern for the people of Staffordshire whose jobs had thus been jeopardized, and the sincerity of the enterprise and the humanity of its cause made aesthetic objections seem churlish. All the same they existed as they did not exist for Joyce Cheeseman's latest tribute to Arnold Bennett, *The Card*, which she adapted from his novel. Not to be confused with the musical comedy running in Shaftesbury Avenue at about the same time: indeed it would be hard to illustrate better the differences between regional and West End theatre (or should I say show business?).

The musical had been imported from the Bristol Old Vic company under a West End manager's watchful eye. You seldom see a West End manager's watchful eye at Stoke-on-Trent. They would wonder what he was doing there and so would he. But suppose, just for a lark, that both those *Cards* could have been staged in adjacent West End houses. I offer it as the year's mind-boggling notion in the theatre. On the one hand, the company which does its own thing, its own authors, its own history in its own style; and on the other, the company which does the Shaftesbury Avenue thing. The difference is – well, card-ish.

Myself I like both. There is room for both. But not, I fancy, in London, instructive though they would be side by side. Indeed, the idea is often mooted that the capital ought to have a regular opportunity to inspect what it is helping to subsidize in the desert beyond Hyde Park – that the reps should be brought to it from time to time. Well, let them try. It has been tried before – but remember, the more regional a rep becomes the more it is likely to create an impression of a fish out of water in London. Better to let the Fopling Flutters go to the provinces and see for themselves, if they care so much.

The Last of the Actor-Managers

A wryly affectionate tribute to Robert Atkins by the actor and author who was a member of his Open Air Theatre.

The sad thing about Robert's death in 1971 is not that it happened but that it caused so little comment in the world. *The Times* dutifully published the routine obituary which had been lying for years in their literary morgue in readiness for the occasion. It was written in a fact-filled, impersonal sytle and conveyed, alas, little of his character and personality. *The Stage* followed with a discreet paragraph: for the next month I kept a watchful eye on the press but nothing else appeared – no other obituaries, no comment, no nostalgic memories from old actors, no retrospective programmes on TV or radio. Poor Robert! Like Enoch Soames he has disappeared from history virtually without a trace. I think he deserved better than that.

And yet what a sombre, dominating, colourful figure he was in the lives of so many actors. How we shuddered and trembled under his rages. How eagerly we exchanged jokes and stories about him, for whenever actors get together to gossip and reminisce, the Robert Atkins stories will be told and retold and will gain in the telling – his tempers and his tantrums, his passionate singleminded love of Shakespeare and his disdain for any play written after 1800, his appalling language, his contempt for all his rivals, his alarming behaviour during rehearsals and his extraordinary sweetness after them, his loathing of all modern ideas, his cruelty, his kindness, his intolerance and his patience.

Now that he is no longer with us, who, exactly, do we mourn? Is it the loss of a robustly traditional actor, or a tenacious impresario, or a respectfully conventional director? It is a little difficult to assess his position for even more than Donald Wolfit, the *noire*-est of all his *bêtes*, Robert remained relentlessly unfashionable. It could be argued that he started the Open Air Theatre in Regent's Park, and kept it going season after season without missing a year even during the war. You could say that he was the Director of the Old Vic and Stratford during the traumatic twenties and the frumpish forties. But these institutions have had many directors and his achievement in the Open Air, though to his eternal credit, was not unique.

As for his acting, very little was ever said about this in his lifetime and the matter was one which was never discussed. Was he a great actor? There were times when one wondered if he was even a good one. And yet there were other times when one felt that greatness was hovering dimly in the air and that something titanic and earth-shattering was struggling to get out. One always felt that he should have been great but mysteriously and inexplicably was not. A blanket of dullness would descend; the outward mechanics of acting would continue to perform while the inner feeling was absent. He did not stoop to impersonation, for versatility was not a virtue he admired or practised – how could he, since Nature had equipped him with a voice and appearance which no make-up or actor's trickery could change. His Bottom had more than a passing resemblance to his Toby Belch which in its turn had a distinct likeness to his Falstaff which was very like his Shylock. Whatever the part, the voice would drone and boom, the eyes would flash, the eyebrows would semaphore and the face would grimace and glower. This is not to sneer, for some of the most popular actors have given the same performance all their lives to everybody's satisfaction. Robert had no interest in the art of acting as such. As he saw it, acting was simply saying the lines loudly and clearly and letting them work their own magic, a heresy which he appeared to have learned from William Poel. This, plus the bits of traditional business picked up from the early actor-managers of the century, constituted a performance. This is what he gave and what he expected his actors to give.

As a director he was equally hidebound. The costumes were

always Elizabethan, always simple and always the cheapest, and while not actually tatty, they were dull and drab. But not Robert's: whatever the company wore, his own costumes were always splendid. He wasn't interested in production as we nowadays know it. The lights, when it became dark, were always full up and fixed. 'Lighting effects, lot of bloody nonsense. Shakespeare never bothered about fancy lighting!' If he did a production indoors, the lights would be turned full on and left untouched. 'Did Shakespeare ever bother about lighting cues?' he would say aggressively. He had no visual sense, no pictorial imagination. The trees and bushes of the park offered splendid opportunities for striking and beautiful effects, as was later made clear by future managements, but Robert would have none of them, and they remained unchanged year after year.

During those summer seasons, Robert gave endless employment to actors. In the years in which I knew him, from 1953 to his death, his standards were not high, the money was low, and, as a result, it became increasingly difficult to get actors of status and quality. The company then consisted largely of old tats and young hopefuls. The old tats were very tatty and the young hopefuls exceedingly hopeful. The old tats were a nucleus of old actor laddies whom Robert had known for years, survivors of the William Poel and Charles Doran days. They were all as old as he was and touchingly loyal. Every year they joined the company in April and creaked and boomed their way through parts of the Antonio, Leonato, Theseus and second grave-digger category. The season would end in September and then most of them went into *Peter Pan* as pirates or crocodiles. This, with the tour, took them up to April, time for a short rest before joining the company at the park. *Peter Pan* all winter and the park all summer. 'Park-Panning, that's what I call it, laddie,' said Clement Hamelin to me – he was the oldest of the group (yes, there was a time when old actors would address younger ones as laddie and I just caught the tail end of that era). Robert was unfailingly loyal to them as had been all the old actor-managers. Old and tatty they may have been but they were reliable. They spoke the same language and they could have long cosy chats about Ben Greet and Lilian Baylis between the shows in the Volunteer Arms in Baker Street.

Happily, there was always a small nucleus of good, experienced actors to carry the play, and the company was then filled up with young hopefuls usually fresh from drama school who could safely be paid the minimum. 'RB' as the actor laddies would call it, standing for rock bottom. Robert didn't like employing them more than once and after one season the young hopefuls weren't too keen either, which meant that with such a turnover about a dozen of them could be employed each season.

Getting a job with Robert wasn't at all easy. Competition was fierce. What it required was not so much talent as tenacity, which is a much rarer commodity. You had to start your siege in January for the season which began rehearsals in April. Most of the young hopefuls began by writing a letter. 'Dear Mr Atkins, I have just finished at RADA having won the Edith Evans Award for Good Diction. . . . I have just played Othello with the Harry Hanson Players in Bootle. . . . I haven't worked for two years since I left the Rose Bruford and I need a start. . . .' The letters varied from the business-like to the pathetic: all wasted, for Robert never answered letters and it was a matter of some doubt if he even read them. Old hands at the Atkins game would advise young hopefuls, sipping their cup of coffee in the basement of the Arts Theatre Club (for years the unofficial meeting place of the unemployed of the profession), to telephone Robert. It had to be nine o'clock in the morning, sharp.

I made my first telephone call to Robert's flat in Ivor Place at the appointed hour. 'Yes?' snapped the voice. 'M-M-M-M-M-Mr Atkins?' I quavered. 'What is it?' 'My name is Richard Huggett. I wrote to you and sent you a photo . . .' 'Give me a ring next Tuesday,' snarled the voice and that was that. Next week at precisely the same time I made my second call. 'Yes?' roared the voice. 'Mr Atkins, this is Richard Huggett, you told me to phone you . . .' 'Ring me next week. . . .' At the end of March, after ten more phone calls, there was a new development. Most young hopefuls retired discouraged from the scene after this treatment but I did not and I received my reward. 'Come and see me tomorrow midday,' he said. 'In your flat?' I asked naively. There was a rumble of cynical laughter. 'Certainly not! I don't want my flat crawling with actors,' he said in a voice of disgust as if we were all infected with an unmentionable disease. 'Come to Dinely,' and he rang off.

The Dinely Studios, as I learned from the old hands, were two huge crumbling Victorian terrace houses fronting onto the Marylebone High Street. They contained about thirty rooms each fitted with a wall-mirror, an upright piano and a lot of floor space. It was very popular for auditions. At any hour you could hear somebody rehearse *Carmen*, the girls from a provincial panto doing their tap routine, and the young hopefuls hopefully declaiming their bits of Shakespeare. It was an intensely depressing place but few actors could avoid it.

Robert was waiting for me in a room on the second floor overlooking a dank, dark garden. He wore a three piece suit of indefinite material and uncertain age. It had wide lapels and big turn-ups and was of a strange mixture of grey and brown. This was his standard uniform and I never saw him wear anything else. With a brown derby hat perched on the back of his head he could have stepped straight out of any backstage musical of the thirties.

The minute I saw his face in close-up, I realized that it was not merely more noble, more distinguished, more impressive, more actorish than any other I had ever seen, it was a completely different type of face, belonging clearly to a category which stemmed from an earlier age of theatre. The bald dome, the shaggy eyebrows, the fierce blue eyes, the craggily high cheekbones, all added up to a face which was unlike any other I had ever seen. They don't make faces like that any more. Even in 1953, the breed was virtually extinct.

Happily, he was in a good mood. He greeted me cordially and waved me to an open space by the window. 'Show me a taste of yer quality,' he said, and I embarked nervously on my stock piece of Shylock: 'Signor Antonio, full many a time and oft . . .' Halfway through my voice trembled to a halt and my memory failed me. Robert picked up the speech for me and finished it in a voice which rumbled and boomed round the room making the chandelier tremble. I apologized abjectly and fully expected to be sent away, but instead he nodded and said in the friendliest possible manner, 'Not bad, not bad at all, come and see me next week in the park.'

Next week, in early April, I was invited to repeat my performance in the park. 'Just to let me hear how yer voice carries,' he explained. The microphones were not switched on; there was a strong wind and if my audition was bad at Dinely Studios it was a hundred times worse in Regent's Park, in that dank dampness, dripping with early morning dew, the green-painted metal seats stacked up at the side and the animals in the Zoo howling all too audibly in the distance. To my astonishment Robert seemed satisfied and invited me to join the company. 'I can't afford to pay yer much,' he said. 'In fact I can't afford ter pay yer more than £8 a week.' I later discovered that this was the Equity minimum and that most of the company were getting it, but it was considerably more than I had ever earned and I was delighted.

The season was to last from May till September and the plays to be presented were *Twelfth Night, Love's Labour's Lost* and *A Midsummer Night's Dream*. We rehearsed the first for four weeks in a punishing heat-wave and I was able to see Robert work and to observe the excesses and contradictions of this now legendary figure.

Like all autocrats, he had his favourites and his whipping boys. These likes and dislikes were completely irrational and very bewildering to the rest of the company. In this production of *Twelfth Night*, the whipping boy was a likeable young actor called Charles Hodgson whom Robert had seen in a play at Guildford and had invited, without audition, to join the company. Having done that he proceeded, for some strange reason which nobody could understand, to persecute him systematically and savagely. He would shout and hurl abuse, push him around physically and do everything he could think of to humiliate him. It was wickedly unjust for Charles was a good actor who succeeded in doing something which very few actors have been able to do – to give some glimmer of theatrical interest to Fabian, which is surely the dullest small part which Shakespeare ever offered to the theatre. But Charles could do no right: every time he opened his mouth to say a line, a volcanic roar would echo through the park. 'Chrrrrrist almighty, what the bloody hell do you think you're doing? Can't you do anything right? . . . you're just a bloody amateur . . . you can't walk, you can't stand, you can't speak, this is Shakespeare, not bloody Agatha Christie . . .' To his infinite credit, Charles bore it all politely and uncomplainingly. Tactfully, he never attempted to argue or answer back: he just stood there patiently until Robert had run out of breath and then continued to rehearse with an unflappable calm which Mr Macmillan would envy. In the lunch hour we would go with him to the Volunteer Arms in Baker Street and offer him beer and sympathy, but he would not be coaxed into complaining, and in all the time we worked together, I never heard him utter one word against Robert, neither then nor since.

Robert's favourite in the company seems to have been myself, a choice which bewildered me even more than the others. At twenty-three, I was totally undistinguished. I had been in the profession for barely two years and such talent as I possessed was then very much in embryo. Neither could my bespectacled, greying, junior don, appearance be described as interesting. Yet Robert went out of his way to be kind and friendly to me and never spoke a harsh word even when, as on a couple of memorable occasions, I richly deserved it. There was one hot sunny afternoon when I had been standing for three hours without respite while the final scene was being rehearsed. I began to yawn and my attention wandered. For anybody else this could have had serious consequences but Robert merely laid his heavy hand on my shoulder:

Mister Huggett, we have come to that superbly theatrical moment when Viola and Sebastian meet on the stage for the first time and everybody in the play as well as everybody in the audience can see that they are identical twins. Even you, Mister Huggett, are mildly surprised by this and I would be exceedingly grateful if you could contrive, by some masterly stroke of acting of which I feel sure you are capable, of indicating this.

This was the nearest he ever got to sarcasm with me: it was said kindly and gently and everybody laughed, including myself. A greater mark of favour came in the final week of rehearsal when he took me aside and said: 'I want you to understudy me' (he was playing Sir Toby Belch). 'Thank you very much, Mr Atkins,' I stammered, excited yet alarmed by the prospect. 'The part's a real bugger,' he rumbled reassuringly. 'First half's not too bad but in the second you work yer balls off,' and away he lumbered. I conveyed this new development to Jill Macdonald, our hard working and much put-upon stage manager. She opened her eyes wide. 'Crikey,' she said in amazement, 'you certainly are favoured.'

Robert's attitude towards understudies was characteristic. He normally never appointed them, disapproving of the whole system, which he regarded as a pitiful example of the spoon-fed self-

indulgence which was softening and weakening the spirit of the
theatre. In the days of Ben Greet, actors were actors, Goddamit!
They were tough, resilient, formidably hard working, and were
expected to learn not only their own parts but everybody else's.
When he did, on rare occasions, appoint an understudy, it was a
reluctant concession to modern weakness. But no further conces-
sions were to be made; there were no understudy rehearsals.
Eager-beaver as I was and anxious to show him that I could do it,
I learned the part in two days and rehearsed it privately with Jill
whenever she had a moment. I suspect that one of the reasons why
he took a liking to me is that I wasn't afraid of him. The other young
hopefuls waited until he spoke to them, but although I had a very
healthy respect for him I had no such inhibitions. Talking to old
actors had always been one of my greatest joys. Discreetly and
whenever an opportunity presented itself I coaxed him into talking
of the good old days.

Robert always arrived early at the theatre and I remember a
sunny morning in May when I too arrived early and found him
sitting alone in a deck-chair looking happily at the empty stage,
filling it, no doubt, with productions and performances of indescrib-
able grandeur and classical simplicity. He was in a good mood
and he greeted me very pleasantly as I sat down in the next deck-
chair. A happy companionable silence lasted for a minute or so and
then he started to talk about Sir Herbert Beerbohm Tree and Mrs
Patrick Campbell, about Mussolini who had decorated him, and of
Ben Greet whose performance of Lear was unsung but unequalled.
'Mr Atkins, why don't you play Lear?' I said at this point. 'It
would go well in the open air and it's very much your sort of part.
I'm sure you'd be marvellous in it.' An innocent question, it might
be thought, but I had quite inadvertently touched a sore spot. He
turned slowly, looked hard at me and his face was like thunder. 'I
have played Lear, Mister Huggett,' he rumbled in a voice which
was like a Wagnerian bass tuba, 'back in the Vic in the 20's.' He
leaned forward and glared right into my eyes, jabbing me in the
chest with every word, 'and I was . . . considered . . . just . . . as
good . . . as . . . Mister Donald Fucking Wolfit!!'

Somewhere, some time, somebody had described Robert as a
poor man's Donald Wolfit. This had got back to him and it hurt
and angered him most dreadfully. The fact that it was true didn't

make it any less painful. Wolfit, many years his junior, had recently scored a huge and well deserved triumph as King Lear and everybody talked about it. Nobody talked about Robert's Lear and to this day I have searched in vain for anybody who had seen it or even knew that he had played it. Wolfit was highly favoured by the best critics and received columns of praise in the *New Statesman* and the *Spectator* and other trendily intellectual magazines. Robert was ignored by the press or written off as a rather boring annual tradition like the inevitable *Peter Pan* or Bertram Mills Circus. Wolfit became for a short time fashionable and popular, but fashionable people seldom came to Regent's Park, which remained obstinately the rain-swept mecca of school children, coach parties and old-age pensioners. Wolfit got a knighthood. Robert only got a CBE. To be jealous was only human. Whenever he spoke of him it was always 'Mister Donald Fucking Wolfit'.

The dream which all understudies alternately hope for and dread came true. A fortnight after we opened, the theatre celebrated its 21st anniversary. A distinguished audience had been invited to honour Robert and there was to be a party afterwards. I arrived at the theatre in a euphoric state which vanished quickly when I reached the dressing room. 'Robert's ill,' said Jill Macdonald quickly when she saw me. 'His old war wound's playing him up again.' 'Which war?' asked one of the young hopefuls acidly. 'Boer, Crimean or Napoleonic?' 'Take his dressing room,' she said, 'you're on in half an hour.' There was a little corner of the communal dressing room which had been curtained off and this is where I was pushed. I had just enough time to climb into Robert's superb velvet and lace costume, smear a generous amount of red and purple make-up on my face in the hope of suggesting Sir Toby's alcoholism, stick on the white Vandyke beard and moustache and cram two large lumps of cotton wool into my cheeks. I heard Jill make the announcement over the tannoy; I heard the groan of disappointment; I heard Brendan Barry majestically intoning 'If music be the food of love', and five minutes later I was walking across what seemed to be many miles of wet grass to the row of microphones. These were concealed by a low hedge and they separated the stage from the audience.

I was twenty-three when I should have been at least forty. I was thin where I should have been fat. I was inexperienced, unrehearsed and hopelessly miscast. My voice sounded impossibly thin and unboozy and to hear it coming back from two not very well synchronized amplifiers in the theatre was an eerie experience. The costume was far too big and since there was no padding for me to compensate for not having Robert's ample proportions, it sagged ludicrously at all the key points. Finally, I made rather rapidly the discovery which many actors make and which I suspect that Marlon Brando has made in his *Godfather* performance – that you can't act with a mouth full of cotton wool. Throughout the evening I steadily got rid of it in small pieces, getting visibly thinner in the face, and ending up without any at all, so the audience was treated to the spectacle of a Sir Toby who began the evening as if he had mumps and ended it as if he had lockjaw.

The company played up magnificently, waiting to help me if I needed it and supporting me in all sorts of small ways. Of course mine was a pitifully inadequate performance, but I can truthfully say that, apart from two brief moments of uncertainty, I did keep the play going. When I arrived at the final scene my relief that I had got through the whole of that traumatic evening without active disgrace was so intense that I found myself almost enjoying it. Afterwards, the company and well-wishers from the audience were very generous in their praise but all I could think of was – if only I had had some rehearsal, if only I'd been ten years more experienced, if only I hadn't been so horribly miscast, if only . . .

Robert was away for a fortnight. There was no question of my taking it over during his absence. Audiences at Regent's Park didn't get much for their money but there were limits. Next day Russell Thorndike arrived, smiling and dapper, and, with only one rehearsal, charged superbly through a part he had not played for over thirty years. Robert did finally reappear. He was still weak and there was no question of his resuming the part. Reports on my performance had evidently filtered through to the hospital. He looked at me sardonically, placed his arm round my shoulders and said gently: 'Well, Mister Huggett, I told you it was a bugger!'

It is the personality we mourn and miss – that robust, colourful, bawdy, disrespectful personality which has inspired so many legendary anecdotes. Actors will tell of the time an actor auditioned for the part of Charles the Wrestler in *As You Like It*. He stripped to the waist and revealed an astonishingly large development of his

7F–K RSC LONDON

7f (above) David Waller and Peggy Ashcroft in *Landscape*, Aldwych Theatre

7g (below) Nicol Williamson as *Coriolanus*, Aldwych Theatre

7h (above left) John Wood
and Philip Locke in *Sherlock
Holmes*, Aldwych Theatre

7i (left) Gareth Hunt and
Elizabeth Spriggs in *Duck
Song*, Aldwych Theatre

7j (above right) Colin
Blakely (centre) in *Cries
from Casement as His Bones
are Brought to Dublin*, The
Place

7k (right) Patrick Godfrey,
Judy Geeson and Harry
Towb in *Section Nine*, The
Place

9a (left) Ian McKellen in *The Wood Demon*, The Actors Company

9b (below) Robert Eddison, John Woodvine and Marian Diamond in *The Wood Demon*, The Actors Company

10a (right) Tim Curry in *The Rocky Horror Show*, King's Road Theatre

10b (left) John Kani and Winston Ntshona in *Sizwe Bansi is Dead*

10c (below) Paul Dawkins, Jonathan Price and Griffith Jones in *Brassneck*, Nottingham Playhouse

11a (right) Lilian Baylis, the Butler portrait (1926)

12a (above) Roddy McMillan, Joseph Brady, James Grant and Fulton Mackay in *Willie Rough*, Royal Lyceum Theatre, Edinburgh

12b (below) Claire Richards in *The Thrie Estaites*, Assembly Hall, Edinburgh

chest and pectoral muscles. Robert gazed at him in astonishment and then turned to his assistant. 'Do you think,' he rumbled quietly, 'that if that fellow were judiciously buggered he might give forth milk?'

And they will tell of the time when he was invited by the Flower family to direct at Stratford-on-Avon during the war. The Flowers, who virtually owned Stratford, were respectable churchgoing worthies and the owners of the famous brewery. It was inevitable that Robert should be at loggerheads with them and thus it turned out. Their chief objection to Robert was his language which was no less uninhibited in Stratford than it had been in London. Their disapproval found an unexpected outlet: they did not invite him to read the lesson during the memorial service held on Shakespeare's birthday which was the traditional privilege of the resident director. Robert was deeply upset by this and stormed angrily into the vestry after the service had finished. 'Can you give me,' he boomed at the rector, 'one single cogent reason why I shouldn't read the fucking lesson!'

After two years, the parting of the ways had come. The Flowers gave Robert his notice of dismissal. He sat in their boardroom while they explained at great length that there was nothing personal in the decision, it was a matter of policy to change the directorship every two years. Robert listened patiently, and then rose and surveyed his persecutors. 'There's only one thing to say, gentlemen,' he said, 'Flowers ale is all piss.'

His last years were very sad. The fate which all actors dread came to pass – he began to lose his memory which is always the first thing to go. Not only could he no longer learn new parts but he couldn't even remember the old ones. And then one terrible day, while playing in *King John* with the Old Vic at the Edinburgh Festival, his memory gave out completely. 'I was on the stage and I couldn't remember a bloody word,' he later told me bitterly, 'and it was a part I've known all me bloody life!' and that was the end.

In his last years it was total retirement. He would occasionally walk down the Charing Cross Road to the Arts Theatre Club where he would climb wearily to the upstairs lounge and sit in one of the big armchairs. I would sometimes see him there sitting bolt upright, gazing sternly out front like Tamberlaine surveying his lost empires, not speaking to people and, it seemed, not even seeing

them. The old fires had gone and he was now a sweet, smiling old
man anxious for company and touchingly grateful if anybody spoke
to him. I once told him of a season I had played at Butlins – 'Never
heard of it, me old son,' he rumbled – and how the plays had been
cut to an hour to fit them in with the tight schedule the camp
offered to its patrons. 'That's not cutting,' he said, 'that's castra-
tion.'

But old actors always make a comeback and so, in a sense, did
Robert. But not on the stage. Just before he died, the National
Film Theatre presented a single performance of a film we had all
heard about but had never seen, *Hamlet,* starring Sir Johnston
Forbes-Robertson, made in Walton Studios in 1913 in front of the
same medieval castle setting he had previously used at Drury Lane
Theatre and which had been transported, piece by piece, to the
studios. The audience which, chattering excitedly, filled every seat
and every inch of standing, contained all the Knights and Dames
and a complete roll-call of Equity. Vivien Leigh's green and silver
Rolls-Royce was parked outside and this gave an added touch of
glamour to the occasion.

The film lasted just over an hour and it was a very bizarre
experience. Sir Johnston, wearing the then accepted Hamlet
costume, contrived to look like a Roedean headmistress in a gym-
slip. He went through the motions of acting with an air of polite
bewilderment: he gazed and glowered, showed first one profile and
then the other (I remembered while watching that profiles were
fashionable in 1913). He clenched his fists, knitted his brows and
heaved his bosom. His lips moved silently and from time to time
a subtitle would generously inform us of the play's progress, 'To be
or not to be . . .'

About fifteen minutes after it had started a pair of curtains
visible at the back of the castle hall, set about twenty foot from the
camera, parted, and a familiar balding figure suddenly appeared
and started to act. There was a brief pause while the audience went
through the is-it-no-it-can't-be-yes-it-bloody-well-is routine, and I
wish I could convey through cold print the shriek of delight and
affection which echoed throughout the cinema when it became
evident that this was Robert as the Player King. In those primeval
days it was the camera which stayed still and actors who were
compelled to move in front of it. Robert advanced purposefully

towards the camera and continued to act in close-up. The eyes flashed, the brows knitted, the face twisted and contorted in passion and his right arm performed its familiar up and down shaking movement which was his one stock gesture. In fifty years he had changed very little for he looked and acted then very much as he did at the end of his life. It was very reassuring to discover that, in a half-century which had seen so many stars come and go, so many reputations crumble, so many styles of acting appear and vanish, one thing remained sternly unchanged. The audience roared with laughter and applauded like maniacs. After that the rest of the film was an anti-climax, and neither the sweetness of Sir Johnston's smile nor all his graceful gestures nor the studied expertise with which he negotiated those dreadful sets, could compensate for Robert's absence. And for the first time in the play's history, one wished that the Player King would return.

On and Off Broadway

The drama critic of America *looks back over a year in the New York theatre.*

New York critics are given to peregrinating, especially in summer, and especially to London. As well we might be – though New York remains a better place to live than to visit, rumours to the contrary. This year, however, the mountain (so to speak) came to Mohammed, though not to Manhattan, in the form of something called the 'British Theatre Season' at the Brooklyn Academy of Music, for some three and a half months, thereby providing both a few bright spots in an otherwise generally – by now, almost traditionally – dismal season and also a few mountain-malfunctions. All of which I'll get to (as Ian McKellen does elsewhere) a bit later on. First, however, some of the sorry (and a few cheering) Broadway and off Broadway details.

The major event of the year was the phenomenally successful Joseph Papp and his New York Shakespeare Festival taking over things theatrical at Lincoln Center after a decade of almost continual frustrations with the Repertory Theatre. All that goes up must come down and thus, to a certain extent, did the Papp balloon, both up and downtown (at the Public Theatre). Call it the Perils of being Papp, though Papp himself elected to call it the critics being out to get him. Although attention only began to focus on the Festival's relative fall from critical and box-office favour with the opening of its first Lincoln Center season, the law of averages had in fact begun to set in a good year earlier.

There's little point in raking up the past, however, and any listing of a string of unsuccessful productions would be little more than a waste of space. Suffice to say that the NYSF's last major success was with *That Championship Season*, which reopened on Broadway in the autumn of 1972, having previously premièred at the Public Theatre earlier that year. What followed over the next two years has been considerably less stimulating.

Two plays by David Rabe, author of *The Basic Training of Pavlo Hummel* and *Sticks and Bones* and clearly Papp's prize playwright, illustrate not only the problems the NYSF has been having but some of the reasons for them. *The Orphan* (at the Public Theatre) was the first. The third work in Rabe's *Vietnam Trilogy*, it was both more ambitious and vastly more flawed than the earlier two, dense in its imagery and symbolism, but without the intensity and cohesiveness of its predecessors. Rabe sought to interweave the Greek myth of *The Oresteia*, violence at home (in the form of the Charles Manson 'family') and at MyLai, hallucinogenic drugs and the scientific information explosion. Not surprisingly, it turned out something of a hodge-podge.

With some characters in modern dress and two actresses playing Clytemnestra, one tortured and essentially sympathetic, the other cruel and vengeful, the diffusion of image and impact seemed at times almost intentional, though surely misguided. Nor did the occasional rock numbers help. There was a murkiness and an intellectual clutter to *The Orphan* that should have consigned it either to the rewrite desk or, better yet, the playwright's closet.

Boom Boom Room, which launched the Papp regime at Lincoln Center, suffered from some of the same difficulties, and from another far more significant one, which I'll get to shortly. Rabe's play is about a Philadelphia go-go dancer who is trying 'to get some goddam order in my stupid life'. That Chrissy's *is* a stupid life is one of the play's major difficulties. If we're going to spend three hours with a character, she'd better be interesting and Chrissy, appealing and sympathetic in her way, isn't. Instead, she's yet another in a long line of Marilyn Monroe-like figures, wanting desperately to be taken seriously, unable to articulate her loneliness, unable to fulfil her needs. To compound matters, she's surrounded by a pretty shallow and unsavoury lot, from a father who spiked her milk with vodka and apparently sexually assaulted her when she was a child to a bisexual dance captain who would like to have an affair with her. As for her mother, she made her 'nearly an abortion'. *Boom Boom Room* is Rabe's fourth play, the first not about Vietnam, and it contains some fine and highly theatrical writing and some moments of power and humour. But they're hardly enough to lift it above tedium more than briefly in a work that is wordy, diffuse and ill-focused.

What was worse, if anything, was the production, a curious cross between realism and expressionism. After sacking the original director, Papp himself took over in the last days before the opening (which by that time was getting to be a habit). To go into the details of it wouldn't serve much purpose, but perhaps it will suggest something of the problem to note that even the theatre seemed wrong. I couldn't avoid the feeling that the play would have fared much better given the necessary concentration of resources and additional rehearsal and preview time possible in one of the festival's smaller Public Theatre houses. The honour of inaugurating the new play policy at the Vivian Beaumont may have been the worst thing that could have happened to this particular new play. (That I'm not alone in this belief is perhaps suggested by the fact that as I write Rabe's most recent play is having workshop performances at the Public Theatre.)

About other NYSF productions at Lincoln Center, perhaps the less said the better, though there have been a perfectly respectable *Dance of Death* (with Robert Shaw and Zoe Caldwell) and an erratically involving new black play, *What the Wine-Sellers Buy*, by Ron Milner. In the smaller Mitzi E. Newhouse Theatre, to which Shakespeare has been consigned, things have been disastrous, with a *Troilus and Cressida* that only a masochist would try to recall and a *Tempest* marked by appropriate sound and sand and little else. The most charitable thing to be said for the acting in both is that it occasionally rose to the mediocre.

Not surprisingly, the unfulfilled great expectations concerning Lincoln Center in combination with a generally poor season at the Public Theatre, have led to considerable speculation about whether Papp has finally overextended himself, on the one hand, and whether as a reviewer for the *Village Voice* suggests 'the Curse of the Beaumont, so terrible to Jules Irving and Herbert Blau, has [Papp], for the moment at least, firmly in its grip.'

All of which seems premature, though surely inevitable in view of the large stake everyone in the American theatre has in Papp's making a success of things at Lincoln Center. What is unfortunate is the prevailing 'Let Joe do it' attitude when it comes to so-called serious theatre. As the mutters of discontent increase – and even if they do not – the American theatre, not to mention the foundations and other sources of public and private funding, will have to take a far more serious look at whether it's advisable to place quite so many eggs in one basket.

One of the more encouraging things in the institutional theatre has been the emergence of the City Center Acting Company, which was formed in the autumn of 1971 with eighteen members of that year's graduating class of the drama division of the Juilliard School. The City Center Acting Company, under the artistic direction of John Houseman, who is also director of the Juilliard drama division, is principally a touring company and has played throughout the country, primarily in university, regional and community theatres. It has, however, now had two New York seasons, the first a six play repertory in a church near Lincoln Center, the second this year in Broadway's Billy Rose Theater with four plays in a four week stand.

If the first season could at best be termed promising, the most recent one showed at least some of that promise being fulfilled, though the company remains considerably short of international stature. *The Three Sisters* was deservedly the best received production during the company's second New York stay, largely because it was ideally suited to capitalize upon its most obvious asset: several extremely able young actresses, who, in Boris Tumarin's production, conveyed both the poignance of the play and a vitality seldom found in American approaches to Chekhov. Houseman's own production of *Measure for Measure* was marked by clarity and humour, though it did suffer from the fact that several of the actors were perhaps too young to achieve the full depths of their characters. Even so, it was intelligent, consistent and dramatically effective.

The Beggar's Opera and *Next Time I'll Sing to You* were less successful, but then they are also less successful as plays so, all in all, one had to be encouraged by the company's development in the short period of three years. They have, as Houseman admits, 'been successful beyond our wildest dreams. I never would have thought that we'd be playing in a Broadway theatre for a season in our second year. In part, it's sympathy for a young company. On the other hand, I'm prejudiced: I think they do the shows pretty damn well.' For the most part, one has to agree, and to hope that the lure of Broadway and film making won't exert so heavy a presence that the quality of talent will diminish.

In the commercial theatre – and what a misnomer that sometimes seems – there's been even less than usual to take comfort in, with only one new American play of any note and a comparable scarcity of quality (or even hit) musicals. Even the revivals – and there have been plenty of them – have been a pretty sorry lot.

Mark Medoff's *When You Comin' Back, Red Ryder?*, which started out at the off-off Broadway Circle Theater, then transferred to off Broadway, was easily the best new American play of the season. Set in a small roadside diner in southern New Mexico, it is in almost every sense conventional in structure, characterization and dialogue, yet sends off sparks in its confrontations, humour on its surface and a chilling realism from its core. It's six in the morning and young Steven Ryder – who desperately wants to be known as Red – is just getting ready to go off duty. As the girl who replaces him goes busily about, cleaning, getting ready for the appearance of the day's first customers, Red drinks yet another cup of coffee, killing time, complaining that Angel refuses to call him Red. So what if he doesn't have red hair?

A young couple come in and order breakfast, closely followed by the flamboyant and aggressive Teddy. At first he is only an irritant, then starts to become intimidating, begins to bend them to his will by the power of his presence, all the while remaining sardonically humorous, half serious, half putting them on. But there's more to Teddy than meets the eye. Initially simply a nuisance, he rapidly becomes a menace, creating an aura of fear that soon permeates the diner. Toward the end of the first act he pulls and fires a revolver.

On this level, *Red Ryder* is first rate melodrama, taut and suspenseful. It is also something else, just what becomes more clear in the second act. For Teddy in his way is a figure out of American mythology. Western bad man, hood, con man, the kind of guy who pulls his horse in for a shoot-out outside the Dodge City bank, he is violent, unstable, unpredictable. Vicious, even sadistic, he is not content to make off with their money, he must also make off with their dreams. For him, it is a game to make people crawl.

Red Ryder perfectly captures a mood and a milieu, adroitly communicating both the outbreaks of violence and the underlying currents and tensions. In another time, another place, Teddy might have been the bright, somewhat precocious, boy next door. But, living amid the violence, the disaffection and faltering sense of identity of modern America, he is what he is. It is a beautiful role, beautifully played by Kevin Conway.

After that, it's strictly downhill in terms of new American drama, with a disappointing new work by Mart Crowley called *A Breeze from the Gulf*, which passed about as quickly as a breeze; Arthur Laurents' slick and bitchy *The Enclave*, which departed the scene equally quickly; and the annual Neil Simon. This time it's called *The Good Doctor* and it represented something of a departure for the author of *The Sunshine Boys, The Odd Couple*, etc. But, alas, not enough of a departure. Simon has taken nine of Chekhov's early stories and sketches and, with Christopher Plummer as The Writer to link them, come up with something that's diluted Chekhov and second rate Simon. It had its enjoyable moments and some good performances, but it was hardly enough to make a satisfying evening for fans of either the good doctor, Chekhov, or 'Doc' Simon.

In fact, the '73–4 season was so lacking in plays of quality on Broadway that only four of a possible five best play nominations were made in the annual Tony awards, one of them to *Boom Boom Room*, which had been almost universally panned by the critics, the others to *The Au Pair Man*, by Hugh Leonard (which somehow turned up as part of Joe Papp's new American play programme at Lincoln Center), *The River Niger*, which transferred to Broadway after a successful Negro Ensemble Company run the previous season, and *Ulysses in Nighttown*, a vehicle for Zero Mostel, first ridden by Mr Mostel some 16 years ago off Broadway.

Fortunately, there were a few bright spots among the revivals and one of them wound up the hottest ticket in town, though originally only scheduled for a limited run. Jose Quintero's production of O'Neill's *A Moon for the Misbegotten* was quite simply the best production of a serious American play on Broadway within recent memory. It is, to begin with, good if not great O'Neill, done just about as well as I can conceive of it being done. Why it was so good is, of course, the most interesting aspect, since the play itself has had at best a star-crossed history.

O'Neill completed this, his last play, in 1943. It was, for practical purposes, a sequel to *Long Day's Journey Into Night*, following the life of Jamie Tyrone, the elder brother among 'the four haunted Tyrones'. It has, in fact, been called 'Jamie's epitaph'. *A Moon for the Misbegotten* has scenes of O'Neill at his best, but also others that remain determinedly earthbound, for O'Neill the poet almost always strove for something O'Neill the playwright, the craftsman, was incapable of. But there was torture and a scorching humanity beneath that struggle and, in the moments when it did succeed, there is an insight not only into what makes O'Neill's characters what they are but also into what we are. Yet, it is a play that requires great care in the production and especially in the casting if it is to succeed. Colleen Dewhurst has portrayed several O'Neill heroines and, here, she is almost perfectly cast. Miss Dewhurst is a large woman and a luminescent one. One can accept her as the great overgrown cow O'Neill constantly called for, yet be continually struck by her grace, her beauty and her sensitivity. She is both earthy and intelligent, never for a moment lapsing out of character, whether in her rage or in her dreaming.

Seventeen years have passed since Jason Robards Jr played Jamie in the superb 1956 Broadway production of *Long Day's Journey*, and Mr. Robards takes up very much where he left off: a portrait of self-loathing, of guilt, of drunken fear of yet another dawn in which the sun shines through yet another dusty windowpane to find him in the arms of yet another nameless prostitute. Although there are times when Robards seems only to touch the surface of this, at others he clearly has probed to its core.

Not a great play, then, but a great production, and it would be hard indeed not to take comfort from the fact that as such exploitative revivals as *The Women*, *The Desert Song* and *Gigi* foundered, *A Moon for the Misbegotten* became the biggest dramatic hit Broadway has had in several seasons.

Hits, as it happens, were in generally short supply on all fronts, if you exclude the Circle in the Square's all-star revival of *Uncle Vanya*, in which George C. Scott and Nicol Williamson appeared for a limited and decidedly overpraised run. Only toward the end of the season did a couple of musicals crop up to somewhat redeem things, and that after we'd languished through the likes of *Cyrano,* a musicalization of Rostand, starring Christopher Plummer; *Gigi,* the Broadway version of the London, Broadway, Hollywood, Colette show, which only went to prove the latest incarnation isn't necessarily the best; a rather tepid revival of *Pajama Game* and assorted others too enervating or shortlived to mention.

Over Here! isn't really very good – in fact, at times it's downright awful, if you're going to apply the usual critical standards. Its book hasn't enough substance to make a bookmark and its score (by Richard M. and Robert B. Sherman) is a pastiche of World War Two styles, songs that sound as if you've heard them before, though in reality you haven't. Even so, it had a lot going for it, starting with the Andrews Sisters, which proved a better place to start than one might imagine. Patty and Maxene (La Verne died several years ago) provided the show's preopening selling point and apparent reason for being, and the plot – which is being charitable – is set in a 1943 cross-country train taking troops to their embarkation point. It's also taking Pauline and Paulette, who are looking for another singer to complete their trio. They find her in Mitzi and Mitzi turns out to be a Nazi spy. That's the plot. To say there's no subplot borders on overstatement.

But plot isn't what *Over Here!* is all about. Rather, it is the innocence, the romanticism, the heroics of a period where there was a sense of living at a higher, fuller pitch. It is a musical not only for those who remember Glenn Miller and FDR, Betty Grable, Esther Williams and Sonja Henie, Joe Louis and the Stagedoor Canteen, but for those who, in an age of lost innocence, perhaps wish they did. 'My dream for tomorrow,' sings a soldier's girl, 'is to keep what I have today.' *Over Here!* has a sheer professionalism about it that puts many a new musical to shame. Tom Moore's direction, Patricia Birch's choreography, the sets, the costumes, the performances, are exactly right. And when the opening night audience cheered the Andrews Sisters as they came on at the end to sing some of their actual old hits, Broadway for one of the few times in a dismal season recaptured some of its long declining vitality and glitter.

Candide provided it with some more. Ever since its Broadway première in 1956, it had been a cult show. Or, more accurately, a cult record, since hardly anyone liked the original production. Harold Prince's 1974 version, originally presented at the Chelsea Theatre Center of Brooklyn (it wouldn't do to give Broadway too much credit), rescues it. With a new book by Hugh Wheeler, some additional lyrics by Stephen Sondheim and John Latouche and, most of all, a completely new production concept, to complement Leonard Bernstein's marvellous score and Richard Wilbur's original lyrics, *Candide* emerges as a considerable delight.

Instead of the proscenium stage that crippled Tyrone Guthrie's 1956 production, Prince employs wrap-around theatre, transforming the Broadway Theater into a world of ramps, drawbridges, catwalks and trapdoors, with one standard stage tossed in for good measure. It works beautifully, opening up the action for the many scene changes of the Voltaire-based plot and surrounding the audience with all the energy of Candide, his pilgrimage, adventures and love for the something less than virginal Cunegonde. We may not live in Dr Pangloss's 'best of all possible worlds', but with a few slight reservations in terms of questionable taste, this came close to being the best of all possible *Candides*.

Raisin, based on Lorraine Hansberry's *A Raisin in the Sun*, which won the New York Drama Critics Circle best play award back in the late fifties, was the only other musical of note. It has, for a musical, a strong and involving, though excessively melodramatic and diffuse, story line which by now seems a little dated, though it very likely is not. For Lena Younger, the $10000 cheque for insurance left by her late husband represents a way out of the family's Chicago ghetto, an opportunity for the next generation to live in circumstances far better than she has. But her son manages to lose much of the money when his would-be partner in a liquor store proves to be a con man. Walter eventually achieves some measure of maturity as white neighbours attempt to prevent the family from integrating their neighbourhood and there is, this being a musical, an upbeat ending.

What there isn't is much of a score, though some of the ballads, gospel numbers and African love songs are pleasant enough in a generally bland kind of way. What they lack is any trace of genuine excitement, any real power or originality. Although diverting enough from moment to moment, they are forgotten almost as soon as one leaves the theatre. For, despite an outpouring of rhapsodic reviews, *Raisin* lacks the final touch of creativity and verve that would have lifted it from the fleetingly engaging to the dynamic.

Lorelei, on the other hand, is the Broadway musical in yet another of its seemingly unending series of last gasps, though its sponsors make haste to assure you it does have Carol Channing. The latest musicalization of Anita Loos's 1926 best-seller *Gentlemen Prefer Blondes* is a close kin, very close, to the 1949 musical, also starring Miss Channing and, for those who might miss the relationship, even carries the subtitle 'Gentlemen Still Prefer Blondes'. It retains much of the original music – and that includes some good numbers, among them *Bye, Bye, Baby, Little Rock* and *Diamonds Are a Girl's Best Friend* – and adds a flashback framework which finds the recently widowed Lorelei Lee about to embark for Paris and recalling life with her late husband. Such success as *Lorelei* has had, however, is attributable almost solely to the vitality and enthusiasm of its star (which at times do get a little wearing). It hardly seems enough.

If it hardly seems enough for a season either, at least there have been some compensations, from the aforementioned British Theatre Season at the Brooklyn Academy of Music which, if it has received mixed critical notices, at least never was less than worth noticing, unlike most of what was going on on the other side of the Brooklyn Bridge. Things started off with the Royal Shakespeare Company in *Richard II* and *Sylvia Plath*, and *Richard*, at least, seemed to have lost something in the crossing, regardless of whether it happened to be Ian Richardson or Richard Pasco in the title role. Amid the elaborate hobbyhorses, the escalator-like stairways, the murky lighting and monochromatic black and brown costumes of John Barton's production, both Richard and Bolingbroke remained for the most part stubbornly symbolic figures, never for a moment really moving the audience, never suggesting the real agony, the real pride, the real challenge – or the real fall – of kings, of men or of angels. The production didn't deserve some of the slight booing it received on opening night; nor did it deserve some of the rapturous praise.

Without having seen the box office figures, I would guess that the Young Vic probably enjoyed the greatest response from the audience (though the RSC profited from a certain snob appeal). Of the three productions, Rattigan's *French Without Tears* came off least well, with *The Taming of the Shrew* and *Scapino* clear – and deserved – triumphs.

With the Actors' Company, there were two disappointments to go with two opening successes, Chekhov's *Wood Demon* and the adaptation of R. D. Laing's *Knots*, both of which had already been widely hailed in Britain. It was the season's lone première that fared least well, with Robert Eddison's *King Lear*, like David William's production itself, very straightforward, very clear-cut, but also regrettably lacking in inspiration. Although Eddison had some strikingly effective moments, he failed to rise to the role's grandeur, to the devastating impact of its emotions. It was Ian McKellen's Edgar who provided the evening with much of its intensity and dynamics, and I mean it as no criticism of him if I suggest that this at times did alter the shape and sense of the play. Of *The Way of the World* it is probably sufficient to say that up-dating of period is not per se virtuous and in setting Congreve in the Edwardian era, David William's production subtracted more than it added.

Again this year, then, the box score for both on and off Broad-way has wound up pretty anaemic. This is especially disheartening in terms of the latter, which only a few years ago was a continuing source of creativity, a place where both playwrights and directors, not to mention actors, of talent seemed regularly to be emerging. It is even more disturbing how little of genuine worth has been taking place off-off Broadway, where today one finds more classical revivals than new plays, and those new plays often self-indulgent and self-serving. And it hasn't even been a good year for movies.

Opera: London Lacks a Team

The Arts Editor of The Times *looks at opera in Vienna; at both ends of Floral Street; and elsewhere.*

Sometimes the seats in the Theater an der Wien can feel distinctly hard. Vienna's oldest theatre, now unfashionably tucked outside the Inner City and below the Ring, thrives on its past. It was here that *Fidelio, Die Zauberflöte* and a host of other operas first came to the stage. All too frequently when sitting in those stalls, which are scarcely upholstered for pampered late twentieth century behinds, I have found ghosts more potent than present players.

But not so at the end of May, 1973, on the first night of a new production of Donizetti's *L'elisir d'amore.* Even on paper before the first bars had been heard it looked to be a festival performance. Nicolai Gedda and Reri Grist, who took the leading roles of Nemorino and Adina, are two of the best actor-singers to be found today. Silvio Varviso was bidding to become the most improved opera conductor of the year: Covent Garden had heard him do a fine *Arabella* and his *Bohème* was to come, although that is strictly in the province of *Theatre 75*; Bayreuth was waiting for him to open their season with *Meistersinger.* The producer/designer team of Otto Schenk and Jurgen Rose is one of the most accomplished in Europe.

In the event that performance of *Elisir* surpassed its promise. It developed into one of those evenings the operagoer is always seeking and rarely finds, an occasion when eyes and ears are simultaneously dazzled, when theatre and music are harnessed together.

'Prima le parole, dopo la musica', or should it be music first and words second? The old argument of Strauss's *Capriccio* is only really solved when the two elements are run in tandem, as in that *Elisir*.

For all the credit that went to the musicians of the evening, and Vienna's audience is not one to sit on its hands when it is pleased, the greatest praise must be reserved for Schenk and Rose. Rose's Basque village preened itself in the autumn sunlight; flowers cascaded down from the balconies of the wooden houses; the cobbles outside Adina's farmhouse glittered in the heat. It was a pretty picture and more than that.

In the opening chorus Donizetti's villagers sing of the delight of getting out of the midday sun into the shade, although it is never actually suggested that they are working themselves to the bone in the fields. Rose's set placed the opera in context from the moment the curtain went up. Schenk, for his part, drew remarkable acting performances from his principals: Gedda's Nemorino, the country boy with tousled hair and brawny, clumsy arms; Grist's Adina, whose substantial farmhouse sets her aside in manner and manners from the rest of the village; Eberhard Waechter's travelling salesman, who will give anything a new name if it puts a few more cents in the pocket.

Otto Schenk and Jurgen Rose working together have a sense of style. So much will be known to the European operagoer, although alas not necessarily to the British one. Schenk proved his worth in 1972 with the *Freischütz* he did for the Vienna State Opera; he was even better when Rose joined him for Munich's *Rosenkavalier*, which survives even through cast changes. The style is both their own and that of the work. *Rosenkavalier* is Maria Theresa's Vienna, from the dark pastoral scenes on the walls of the Marschallin's apartments through to Faninal's glossy new glass palace, a miniature Amalienburg. The music, the time and the place are all woven together.

This feeling of unity is needed for all great opera performances. La Scala, which has had its poor years recently, is moving back towards it and in the process has become by far the most interesting house in Italy. Jean Pierre Ponnelle together with the house's musical director, Claudio Abbado, has been setting the style for the run of Rossini revivals, which began with *Il barbiere di Siviglia* and continued through *La cenerentola* to *L'italiana in Algeri,* seen just before Christmas. Here the emphasis is on speed and ensemble; the movement and the singing must be quicksilver and nothing is allowed to get in the way.

The qualities of *L'elisir, Rosenkavalier* and *L'italiana,* and they were the best productions I saw during 1973, come from teamwork, from having a group of people not only used to performing together but who positively bring the best out of one another. And teamwork is the very factor lacking in the London opera scene at the moment. This surely is the main reason why 1973 here was an off vintage year.

There was of course one major exception: the completion of the Sadler's Wells' *Ring* with *Siegfried* and the running of the complete cycle in August. London, and particularly the Coliseum audience, broiled while the four evenings ran their course twice round. But nobody minded the heat and there was not an empty seat in the house because the team had both played itself in and had proved its quality. Reginald Goodall was at the helm, and he quite rightly picked up the *Evening Standard*'s first award for the year's outstanding contribution to British opera; Rita Hunter and Alberto Remedios were singing their way towards the international league; Glen Byam Shaw, John Blatchley and Ralph Koltai quite rightly stuck right through to the final production by the concept of the *Ring* they had devised in the late sixties.

The *Ring* succeeded because there was no deviation from style, either musically or scenically. The tone was set and the tone was adhered to, whatever the critics or the public might say. And fortunately there were few dissenting voices.

Probably it was no coincidence that when John Blatchley left the team to do his own production of *Katya Kabanova* for the same house in the autumn the magic vanished. This *Katya*, despite some fine playing from the orchestra under Charles Mackerras, was far less successful than a much more modest staging of the same opera at Wexford the previous year. Blatchley seemed as impervious to the Russia of Ostrovsky and Janáček in *Katya* as he had been to the Italy of Mascagni and Leoncavallo when he produced *Cav* and *Pag*. Where was the Volga, where was the inbreeding of the village forced by its very isolation, where was the loneliness of Katya herself? The answer was nowhere. And too many people, perhaps still dazzled by the success of the *Ring* or bewitched by the sounds Mackerras drew from the pit, neglected to notice the fact. So *Katya* acquired a reputation out of all proportion to its actual merits.

At roughly the same time, down the far end of Floral Street, Covent Garden was in considerably deeper trouble with its opening production of the season, *Tannhäuser*. The Royal Opera House had recognized the team principles I have been suggesting, but unfortunately did not differentiate between good sides and mediocre ones. The trio engaged to stage Wagner's opera consisted of Václav Kašlík, Jan Skalický and Josef Svoboda. Together they had previously been responsible for *Nabucco* in the same house. Yet there was nothing in that *Nabucco* to indicate that they were capable of mounting a good *Tannhäuser*. The writing was on the wall. But, alas, it was not read.

Visually and dramatically *Tannhäuser* turned out to be a disaster. Nothing poorer has been *seen* since an attempt, a one-shot fortunately, to cobble together a production of *Manon Lescaut* from bits of scenery left over from other operas. The Czech trio did not linger in the theatre. Fortunately Colin Davis, Covent Garden's musical director, was on hand to rescue the ears and help close the eyes. He had two outstanding singers to help him, Jessye Norman (Elizabeth) and Karl Ridderbusch (Hermann). As the run continued the orchestra became better and better, raising plenty of optimism for Davis's forthcoming *Ring*.

But if nothing else the evening brought home the true significance of Peter Hall's departure from Covent Garden and the break-up of the Davis/Hall team. That word has to reoccur. The Royal Opera House was both without a regular producer and an artistic director; it was, in fact, without the sort of man whose responsibility it was to nip *Tannhäusers* in the bud before they started to grow on stage.

Some argued, with a good deal of right on their side, that there was not another Hall and that it was better to soldier on. John Copley had taken over two of the proposed Hall productions, *Figaro* with great success and *Don Giovanni*. Ironically, the latter opera with its glittering steel rods and speed of movement was much under the influence of Hall's *The Knot Garden* and the first night audience showed its displeasure. As all too often the reaction was wrong. On revival with a much stronger trio of ladies this *Don Giovanni* showed itself to be a workable and imaginative staging. And John Copley, with *La traviata* and *Mary Stuart* for the Coliseum under his belt, as well as a number of successes in Australia and America, went from strength to strength during the year.

Covent Garden's other new productions were a good deal more distinguished musically than they were dramatically. Solti made his annual reappearance at Covent Garden, this time for the new *Carmen*. Some of the critics spent a good time squabbling over the edition used and in the dispute overlooked the excitement Solti drew from the orchestra and neglected to register that Placido Domingo is the best José on stage at the moment. But they did register disappointment at Michael Geliot's dull production. Geliot, who has worked hard and well for the Welsh National Opera, was not given much time to prepare *Carmen*, but he scarcely seized the opportunities that were available. Colin Graham was given an equally difficult task in transferring Britten's television opera, *Owen Wingrave*, from the small screen to the wide stage. The mystery of the piece was lost on the way, and watching it from Covent Garden's Grand Tier was much like trying to pick out objects in the distance through a telescope.

Graham had considerably more success with Britten's other new opera *Death in Venice*, particularly at Aldeburgh. The austerity of the Maltings and its acoustics seemed to suit the piece well, and down on the Suffolk coast Peter Pears's Aschenbach was one of the performances of the year. In London, as in the case of *Wingrave*, *Venice* lost some of its effect, but possibly this was the price of having constantly changing casts for the three nights it was on.

The rewards of the year at Covent Garden, then, were principally musical. Davis, Solti, Domingo I have already mentioned. Then there were individual performances such as Sutherland's return in *Lucia*, Margaret Price's first London Donna Anna, Geraint Evans celebrating his 25 years in the house by playing the title role of *Don Pasquale* (Ponnelle did himself less than justice in this production) and Bergonzi appearing for a run of *Toscas* and *Aidas*. Yet always lurking in the background was the knowledge that there was no artistic director, no prospect of a resident team.

Down in Sussex, by contrast, the problem had been resolved. John Cox began his first season at Glyndebourne as director of

productions with Von Einem's *The Visit of the Old Lady*. The work
has taken some time to reach Britain and there is quite a lot to be
said for the view that the journey was never absolutely essential.
But there were no doubts about the quality of Cox's staging. Nor
indeed were there about the way he refurbished the *Capriccio* of the
mid sixties to make it a salon opera of great elegance. Elisabeth
Soderstrom's Countess, almost certainly inspired by Cox's guiding
hand, was even better than ten years previously and round her was
gathered a remarkably tightly knit ensemble. John Cox's Glyndebourne Strauss started with his *Ariadne* and goes on with *Inter-
mezzo* this season. Continuity is always likely to breed evenings
worth remembering.

While Cox was working on Strauss and Von Einem, Peter Hall
continued his Glyndebourne links, which had started so dazzlingly
with *La Calisto*, by staging *Le nozze di Figaro*. The opening performances were edgy: Elizabeth Harwood's Countess was considerably less assured than it had been at Salzburg with Von Karajan
and Benjamin Luxon's Count did not fit in with Hall's pattern of
things. And Peter Hall, with his regular designer John Bury,
always does have a pattern, a motif, an aim. This emerged later in
the season when the cast had changed and Hall's *Figaro* was revealed as an opera about opportunism, both sexual and social. The
second act finale, possibly Mozart's most complex and incisive piece
of ensemble writing for the stage, became the core of the evening
as the advantage passed at lightning speed from person to person.
Part of Glyndebourne always coincides with Wimbledon fortnight.
Now we knew why: this Figaro at its best was as rapid and as
exciting as a tie-breaker on Centre Court. The season ended with
Figaro and *Capriccio* alternating; both showing in their different
ways just what can be achieved by a company working together.

Out of London producers and designers have regular associations with opera companies: Cox, Hall and Bury at Glyndebourne,
Geliot with the Welsh National Opera, Anthony Besch with Scottish
Opera. Sometimes they have titles, sometimes they work on the
basis that they will always be remembered when future plans are
made. Yet the two main London houses refuse to make any
appointments.

Ironically, there has probably never been a time when British
opera producers have been in greater international demand. We

have a generation of men, whose age span runs roughly from thirty-five to forty-five, who have proved their worth on the lyric stage. Some, such as John Copley and John Cox, have spent most of their career in the opera house; others, such as Peter Hall and John Dexter (whose staging of *The Devils* at the Coliseum was a brilliant production of a meretricious work), take time off from the straight theatre. But are they sufficiently used and encouraged in this country? As I write, it has just been announced that John Dexter has been made an Artistic Director. Of where? The Met.

Ballet: Splendours and Miseries

The Financial Times *critic reviews a year of ballet – and its audiences.*

'The art of dancing', wrote William the Jew of Pesaro, a Renaissance dancing master, 'is for generous hearts that love it, and for gentle spirits that have a heaven-sent inclination for it.' 500 years later the words are still true – if not applicable to quite everything we saw during a very crowded year – but the visit to Britain of one of the gentlest spirits, most generous hearts, stressed a continuing problem with the audience for dancing.

The American dancer/choreographer Paul Taylor is one of the finest creators at work anywhere in the world today. His company is small, but it numbers some exceptional dancers in its ranks; his ballets are beautifully wrought, fresh, inventive, heart-stirring in their nobility and humour, and sometimes deeply disturbing by a kind of dark unease that can lie just below their engaging surface. A European tour had initially been made possible by an invitation from Granada Television (whom Heaven bless) to film a couple of dances for a *Parade* programme at the time of the Manchester Festival; thence Taylor was able to play Chester's Gateway Theatre for a single Sunday night performance, where he found an enthusiastic house (and several of the London critics prepared to brave all the delights of Sunday rail travel) before leaving for Paris and points east. The idea of a London season was mooted, yet previous visits had hardly smashed any box office records, despite a warmly receptive public and the admiring notices every company dreams of. The impresario Richard Graham went to enormous trouble to arrange a brief London season, but it was Rudolf Nureyev's generosity and willingness to join Taylor's company for five guest appearances that was ultimately to make a week's visit to Sadler's Wells possible. Taylor brought a splendid collection of ballets, including the serene *Aureole* and *Duet* (in which Carolyn Adams showed once again why she is one of the most exquisite dancers in the world), a revival of his bleak and disturbing *Scudorama*, and five new pieces that ranged from the zany fun of *Book of Beasts* to the lyric *Guests of May*, with Taylor himself tremendous in both. Thanks to Nureyev, who danced to excellent effect in both *Aureole* and *Book of Beasts*, the first five nights of the season were sold out. Came the Saturday matinée and evening performances, *sans* Nureyev, and – despite ecstatic notices and what must have been pretty good word of mouth – the theatre was less than a quarter full.

This dispiriting fact can, I suppose, be explained in several depressing ways; it certainly confirmed the view that there is now a marked and widening division in the dance audience, a polarization between the fans of old-style ballet, eager for swans and Tchaikovsky and fairies, obsessed with star names, and a younger modern dance public who mistrust these trappings of the 'opera house' idea of ballet. The new public throughout the country has developed a tremendous loyalty to Ballet Rambert and the London Contemporary Dance Theatre; in Europe these are the young who find Béjart in tents and circuses and stadia and know him as the Billy Graham of the dance. Quite irrespective of his entirely dubious choreographic merits, the award of the prestigious Erasmus Prize to Béjart was a recognition of his huge influence in 'giving new forms to modern ballet' and 'inspiring many young people to look for new means of expression in this sector'. The fact that Béjart shared the prize with Dame Ninette de Valois ('a driving force behind the renewal and resurgence of classic ballet throughout Europe') shows how widespread is this division.

In Britain this has also meant that the sharper the identity of a troupe – be it ancient or modern, home-grown or visiting – the surer the public's response. Louis Falco came from America to the Wells with a small way-out company, and found an audience appreciative of his very mixed offerings; Alvin Ailey has, over the years, taught his public to expect fizzing show-biz excitement from his dancers to counterbalance the very uneven quality of his dances, and certainly did not disappoint them during his three weeks at the Wells in June. A curiosity of this engagement was the appearance of Lynn Seymour as guest in a vehicle that Ailey had made for her in New York. *Flowers* told the brief, sad tale of a pop singer (to be identified as Janis Joplin) and allowed Miss Seymour to deploy some of her phenomenal artistry in an indifferent cause; but, as ballet audiences believe, it's not what the star does but the way that she does it which matters -- and Miss Seymour did it tremendously.

A guest star better served by her choreography was the angelic Natalia Makarova, who appeared with the Royal Ballet in the new production of *The Sleeping Beauty* and in *Romeo and Juliet*, in both of which she was partnered by Rudolf Nureyev. (This prior to the open air performances of *Swan Lake* in Paris in which the damp chill of the night air wrought its toll on Makarova's health and on her partnership with Nureyev.) Makarova's London appearances were superb. Nobility of schooling, lightness, ravishing placing of limbs, showed her as an Aurora in the grand manner; her Juliet was ideal, with MacMillan's creation perfectly understood in impetuosity, passion and finesse of playing. Later in the year Makarova returned for a brief visit, whipping through the nonsense of the *Don Quixote* pas de deux with adorable elegance, and illuminating the central duet of *Concerto* with lambent grace.

For the Royal Ballet's Opera House troupe this was a year of considerable activity which had begun with a major revision of *The Sleeping Beauty* by Kenneth MacMillan. The production was controversial, more especially because of the designs by Peter Farmer in which some of his decorative ideas went oddly amiss; in the main the choreographic text was given proper respect and the chief amendments were to be found in the last act, where the suppression of a little Petipa and a mass of later accretions should have been more welcomed than it was. Performances, led by Antoinette Sibley and Anthony Dowell, and then by Merle Park and Donald MacLeary, were in the best traditions of the company, and later Alfreda Thorogood and Jennifer Penney showed that the Royal Ballet continues to produce ballerinas able to sustain the most searching demands of the *danse d'école*.

One other performance must be noted for the record books:

Ann Jenner had embarked upon Aurora but was taken ill with appendicitis at the end of the first act. Brenda Last was in the audience, and on going backstage to see Desmond Kelly, who was making his first appearance as Florimund, she was able to offer to complete the performance. Herself barely recovered from a lengthy illness, Miss Last sailed through the rest of a ballet she had danced a couple of times, seven years before. The production was un-familiar, she had neither her own costume nor shoes, and only the briefest time for a warm-up, but sheer professionalism and a wonderful sense of duty to audience and company brought her faultlessly through the evening, to a standing ovation and – we hope – crates of champagne from the management.

Immediately after the *Beauty* staging the company left for a first ever tour of South America and a not surprising triumph, which included an audience of 19000 inside the Brasilia stadium and thousands more outside, baying to get in; the return to London marked another first – a month's season at the Coliseum in May. This proved a success, and raised once again the question of the company's need for a home entirely its own with the advantages of more performances and more chances for the dancers.

The very forward projection of the Coliseum stage suited most of the repertory well, and a series of revivals of Ashton ballets were given fine interpretations, while the return of MacMillan's *Anastasia* to the stage confirmed my long-time impression that this is one of the best of modern full length ballets, not least for Seymour's intense and moving incarnation of the central figure.

The company moved directly from St Martin's Lane back to Bow Street; a sad note – albeit a happy performance – was David Blair's farewell in *La Fille mal Gardée*. He danced Colas for the last time on 25 June, with all his old panache and charm; his decision to give up dancing saddened his admirers, but at least we never saw his powers in decline – his farewell was as bright and punchy and satisfying as his first performance.

The last novelty of the season was the first Opera House showing of MacMillan's *Seven Deadly Sins*. He had originally mounted the Brecht/Weill morality for an Edinburgh Festival programme by Western Theatre Ballet in 1961; this revised version seemed more diffuse in effect because larger in scale, but the staging (far more a production than a choreographic statement because of the fragmented nature of score and text) had a sharp, vicious energy, and plenty of feeling beneath its cynical surface, and it benefited enormously from brilliant designs by Ian Spurling. Spurling's 1961 decor had made prophetic use of the wilder aspects of Art Déco; fashion had seemingly now caught up with him, but his new designs were ever more in advance of taste – consummately witty capriccios on the styles of the early thirties. Jennifer Penney, and her successor Lesley Collier, were both delightful as the dancing Anna; Georgia Brown, and later Annie Ross, were admired as the singing alter ego; in a mass of tiny, outrageous characterizations the dancers had great fun as the denizens of various dubious locales, with Vergie Derman moping under a cascade of medals as a Tap Champ, and Lynn Seymour gleaming with vulgarity and sequins as a Cabaret Queen.

MacMillan garnered his by now utterly predictable batch of mixed notices, but he finished the year on a note of high personal success with his three act *Manon*, first given in March 1974. Bypassing the previous operatic and balletic versions, he returned to the Prévost original to show his hero and heroine as victims of the corrupt society of the *Régence*. The destruction of their innocence found its momentum in a series of flowing, impassioned duets, grandly stated by Antoinette Sibley and Anthony Dowell – whose CBEs in the New Year Honours List had been a fitting comment upon their artistry and their popularity. The other notable performance was given by David Wall as Lescaut, a role richly written and played with tremendous bravura; the duet for the drunken Lescaut and his mistress (the dazzling Monica Mason) was a hilarious present to all those who may have longed to see what would happen when a pas de deux found the male dancer as carefree as several newts. The ballet had some of the most fluent and diverse choreography MacMillan had made since *Anastasia*; he showed off his company with affection and pride, and audiences took it to their hearts. Nicholas Georgiadis' designing was characteristically opulent and responsive to the demands of the action, and the only drawback to the piece was the choice of Massenet music. Assembled from a whole catalogue of operas (not *Manon* though) and orchestral works, it failed variously to live up to the vitality of MacMillan's imagination and the power of the narrative, but it could not detract from the success of the ballet, which also benefited from a second cast (Jennifer Penney and Wayne Eagling) of touching innocence and grace. The only other Opera House novelty was the acquisition of Jerome Robbins' *In The Night,* an exploration of four Chopin nocturnes that was a happy pendant to *Dances at a Gathering.*

For the Royal Ballet's touring New Group the year brought journeyings that extended from the provinces to Israel, and a repertory of over thirty ballets to maintain. A final identity may still escape the section – the sort of positive personality that will attract consistently good houses in the regions – but the enthusiasm of its artists is beyond question. The development of the repertory was also somewhat checkered: David Drew's *Sword of Alsace* won little critical acclaim, although audiences have responded warmly to it, and I cannot as yet report on Ronald Hynd's *Charlotte Brontë,* first given in Bradford as a discreet homage to the proximity of Haworth parsonage. The revival of Andrée Howard's *La Fête Etrange* brought back a most sensitive work, far too long absent from the repertory, and the only other ballet new to the group was Hans van Manen's agreeable *Septet Extra,* which the company plainly enjoyed dancing, and we enjoyed watching.

The outstanding events for two other sections of the Royal Ballet were Ballet for All's *coup* in involving both Dame Ninette de Valois and Sir Frederick Ashton in the composition of a Harlequinade for a new programme, and the Royal Ballet School's annual Opera House matinée and subsequent appearances at Richmond and Holland Park. The school was in fine form, with promising young artists in the upper classes to shine in *Solitaire, The Dream* and *La Fête Etrange,* and a very sparky collection of junior boys who whipped through clog dancing and some beautiful folk items with enormous zest and a great deal of style.

Ballet Rambert continued to flourish throughout the year, making yet more adventurous departures in repertory and achievement, and winning awards, too. A season in April '73 at the Young Vic brought no less than eight works in progress designed for the thrust stage, in conjunction with already proven repertory pieces. The creative drive of the Rambert troupe is one of the continuing pleasures of the ballet scene and the very fact of undertaking this season was in itself commendable. Willingness to experiment has ever been a Rambert characteristic, and by the autumn the company braced itself for another challenge – the return to Sadler's

Wells after eight years, the first time such a visit had been made since the company was re-formed in 1966.

With seven of the best works in the repertory, plus three brand new acquisitions, the season was both an artistic and a box office success; the faithful audience who used to flock to the Jeannetta Cochrane Theatre came willingly to Rosebery Avenue (and until Rambert is given its much needed permanent home in London the Wells is entirely suitable) and the excellence of the company and of its ideals won new admirers and new laurels. Of the new ballets, Christopher Bruce's *Duets* had a quiet grace and an appealing lyricism; the American choreographer Louis Falco's first work for a British company – *tutti-frutti* – was a densely written exercise in group therapy that found its admirers and was very strongly danced; Norman Morrice's *Isolde* is best considered as a first draft of the more interesting work that will be shown after some re-shaping of its episodes – it had moments of rare insight, but seemed only half-realized at its première.

From the regular repertory Morrice's *That is the Show* and *Blind-Sight*, Tetley's *Pierrot Lunaire* and *Ziggurat* looked particularly impressive in their new home, and as a postscript to the season it is worth recording that Christopher Bruce's dancing throughout the year (outstandingly in *Pierrot*, in which he is a marvel of expressive power) and his choreography for *There was a Time*, given in January '73, and *Duets* rightly earned him the first Evening Standard Ballet Award by a unanimous decision of the adjudicating panel. And for Norman Morrice, Rambert's director, came the Royal Academy of Dancing's Queen Elizabeth II Coronation Award for his 'distinguished contribution to British Ballet'.

Festival Ballet, with its extensive touring commitments and its ever faithful audience both in London and the regions, made a serious effort to broaden its repertory during the year. It is a company that knows to a T what its large middle-brow public wants, and to survive it must continue to offer the standard classics, Diaghilev revivals, and its own particular brand of glamour. But the presence of a resident choreographer, the talented Barry Moreland, has already brought benefits: his *Dark Voyage* was shown briefly in Oxford, together with *Silver Apples of the Moon* by Timothy Spain, another member of the company; I was unable to see either since after a couple of performances they were tucked away until the April–May '74 Coliseum season, when Moreland's two act *Prodigal Son* was also scheduled. The need to give audiences yet more classical ballets brought the company's largest undertaking of the year, a version of Prokofiev's *Cinderella* by Ben Stevenson which, though a long way after Ashton in manner and, to my mind, stultifyingly dull, would present no problems at the box office. Much more attractive was Stevenson's brief lyric, *Three Preludes*, admirably danced by Gaye Fulton and Dudley von Loggenburg, and very touchingly choreographed. The major acquisition of the year was Antony Tudor's piercing version of the Lidice massacre, *Echoing of Trumpets*; first given by the Royal Swedish Ballet a decade ago, it showed how a master choreographer can shape an expressive dance language to explore the bleakest aspects of war.

There could be no greater contrast than another welcome arrival – Mona Vangsaa's production of Bournonville's *Le Conservatoire*, with its dulcet style really only fully understood by Peter Schaufuss, Mme Vangsaa's son and a product of the very Bournonville schooling that is the matter of the ballet itself. The staging of Massine's *Three Cornered Hat* was another happy stroke for the repertory, and Festival's artists were soon acclimatizing themselves to its vivid, sun-baked style. Rather less appealing was a companion piece by Massine that also stumbled into view: *Gaîeté Parisienne* is a tirelessly roguish item that keeps jigging about the stage in the fond hope that we shan't realize that it has been dead for years and just won't lie down (could it be reluctance to find eternal rest amid the mimsy Etienne de Beaumont designs?). It got the sort of dire performances such pieces receive nowadays – there are no replacements for Danilova and Massine who made the whole thing bearable by just appearing on stage.

At a gala in April 1973, three duets were also put on view: Balanchine's pretty *La Source* was done with utter musicality and wit by Violette Verdy and Helgi Tomasson from New York City Ballet; the balcony scene from Ashton's *Romeo and Juliet*, for Gaye Fulton and Peter Schaufuss, did not look its best out of context; Maurice Béjart's *Webern Opus 5* was created for Maina Gielgud and as danced by her and Peter Breuer from Düsseldorf was revealed as a sophisticated and highly nuanced work, excellently matched to Webern's mysterious sonorities.

Up in Glasgow Peter Darrell continued to build on sure foundations for his Scottish Theatre Ballet, both in large undertakings,
and in a concern for the small stages in Scotland with a concert
group and special works made for these special surroundings. The
completed *Nutcracker* had an extended season in Edinburgh at
Christmas (both the Royal Ballet and Festival were playing their
own versions elsewhere at the same time – a fact I record with
absolutely no comment); and a major nineteenth century classic
also entered the STB repertory. This was Bournonville's *La
Sylphide*, meticulously revived by Hans Brenaa, sensitively decorated by Peter Cazalet, and danced with loving enthusiasm for its
style and its dramatic power by the whole company. With only
thirty dancers STB yet contrived to provide three different casts
for principal roles, all pleasing, and in the case of Michael Beare's
James, outstandingly good in dramatics and buoyant clarity of
dancing. *La Sylphide* was shown in tandem with a modern Scottish
work: Walter's Gore's *Embers of Glencoe*. As always with Gore it
was excellently crafted, making brave use of a narrator and a strong
percussion score by Tom Wilson, and it charted the final avenging
of the Glencoe massacre with bold skill. The other important staging
by STB was Jack Carter's *Three Dances to Japanese Music*, which
received excellent notices at its Edinburgh Festival première, but
which I have not yet had an opportunity to see.

Our other regional company, Northern Dance Theatre, acquired
a decently spacious hall in its home town, Manchester – the new
Opera Theatre of the Northern College of Music. The company's
first season there, in May–June 1973, showed the stage well suited
for dancing, and the programme of novelties – revivals of *The
Green Table*, *Le Carnaval*, and a new ballet by Suzanne Hywel, *The
Teachings of Don Juan* – marked a continuing concern to extend the
company's range. I cannot pretend that the dancers were any
match for *Le Carnaval*, a masterpiece almost impossible to bring
off nowadays, or that I have any sympathy for Jooss's *Green Table*,
which I find wildly dated and unconvincing, though others of my
colleagues still find it pertinent, but Miss Hywel's piece was of more
than passing interest in its originality of inspiration and feeling for
dance-theatre. Very encouragingly NDT has already, in its brief
existence, managed to inspire choreographic experiment among its
dancers, and in addition to Laverne Meyer (NDT's director) and

Miss Hywel, Simon Mottram has demonstrated real choreographic understanding, and in Jonathan Thorpe a most intriguing creative intelligence has developed during the past three years. His *Part Exchange*, a duet played in silence, was allusive, thoughtful, and looked far superior to the thin jollity of Charles Czarny's *Brandenburg Three*, a novelty which had been originally staged in Holland some years previously.

South America may well have felt that it was undergoing an invasion by British dancers during the spring and summer of 1973, for, in addition to the Royal Ballet's visit, there was a tour by the London Contemporary Dance Theatre. Returned to its home at the Place in August, the company gave the first London showing of Robert Cohan's *Mass*, a collaboration between composer (Vladimir Rodzianko) and choreographer, in which the cast doubled as vocalists and dancers. Cohan's prime concern seemed an immediacy of expression, a comment in which his dancers are both witnesses and participants in the horrors of battle; the sharpness of the cry for liberation from suffering that rang through the work was its most interesting feature. A similar theatrical urgency has made Cohan's evening-long *Stages* a great success wherever it has played, and in a bold bid for greater recognition in London, LCDT came to Sadler's Wells for a week with *Stages*, and played to full and eager houses of young devotees.

When, for the Camden '74 festival in February, LCDT moved across the Euston Road from the Place to the Shaw Theatre, their audiences were again enthusiastic. New works for the season included experimental dances that had survived from the company's workshop programmes: Robert North's tribute to Raymond Chandler, *Dressed to Kill*, and Siobhan Davies's fresh, delightful *Pilot*. Richard Alston's *Blue Schubert Fragments* was a reworking of his *Lay-out*, seen during the previous summer, a luminously attractive study in which coolly eloquent choreography was beautifully organized, and beautifully danced; it showed up the anguished posturings of the other new work in the repertory – Anna Sokolow's *Steps of Silence* – as more than usually tedious. A collection of dances by Remy Charlip, given under the general title of *Mad River*, completed the season's offerings.

For the smallest but by no means least important troupe in the country, Richard Alston's Strider, making new dances was the thing. The manner is best described as post-Cunningham, and Alston and his six associates are tirelessly inventive, and vividly responsive to the possibilities of new dance activity. Alston is a choreographer of unquestioned gifts – his work has sure structure and a subtle feeling for line – and his colleagues, notably Christopher Banner, all show a readiness to explore new territory, and often come back from these artistic journeys with bright dance ideas. A five day engagement by Strider at the ICA Nash House theatre offered some of the most stimulating dances of the winter season.

If, in perspective, the year has looked busy – and rewarding – it must be recorded that visiting companies contributed not a little to the vitality of the ballet scene in London. A development of recent years has been the re-establishment of the Coliseum as a home for dance when the opera is away; in addition to the Royal and Festival seasons, the Australian Ballet roared in on the crest of a successful Eastern European tour in the autumn, and dazzled audiences with Rudolf Nureyev's staging of *Don Quixote*. The company was much admired in this farrago, and Lucette Aldous, Marylin Rowe and Kelvin Coe showed that Australia had stars of its own to rival the indefatigable Nureyev, who whipped through several performances and guaranteed full houses thereby. The houses stayed full for the later days when a triple bill brought a chance to admire Glen Tetley's *Gemini* which made a far more illuminating commentary upon the identity of the Australian dancers than Helpmann's *Sun Music* or *Ballet Imperial* which completed the programme.

The Royal Danish Ballet also came to the Coliseum (in April 1974) for a week's visit; much loved in London, the Danes offered *La Sylphide* and *Etudes* in one programme, and *The Whims of Cupid* – which dates from 1786 – in tandem with Flemming Flindt's mime drama *The Triumph of Death*. Flindt's adaptation of Ionesco's *Jeux de Massacre* was a big, super-efficient portrayal of the collapse of the world, complete with rock score, nudity and superb, fraught performances from artists who earlier could be seen tripping decorously through the eighteenth century humours of *The Whims of Cupid*.

Exotic triumph of the year was the Shanghai Acrobatic Theatre whose fortnight at the same theatre was a phenomenal success – but how could it be otherwise with a company made up of geniuses who can balance three eggs on top of one another on a bamboo wand on their noses (the eye constantly disbelieving throughout the evening) and cluster twelve on a bicycle, or ride a unicycle round a parasol? Peasant frolics were at a merciful minimum throughout 1973: the Georgian State Dance company also visited the Coliseum, with a great deal of practised charm and ferocious-looking chaps dashing about on tiptoe; and the Mexican Ballet Folklorico came to the Festival Hall, which presumably pleased people eager for Mexican folk-lore. The superlative Umewaka Noh troupe united the dance and drama audience during the World Theatre Season at the Aldwych; Maurice Béjart's school, *Mudra*, made a single Sunday night visit to the Coliseum, and the English Bach Festival must be held accountable for inviting the excruciating Folkwang Ballet from Essen, which glowered at us, choreographic-ally speaking, at the Round House. At The Place a small troupe, *Pilobolus*, offered an American combination of dance and gymnastics which had a certain muscular charm, but it was Sadler's Wells that was most importantly and significantly host to visiting troupes.

The scandal of the year was the fact that the theatre itself was in the grip of a financial crisis. An appeal fund to guarantee the building's future had been launched and had received most, though not all, of the support it needed; but a report by Douglas Craig, administrator of the Wells, to the governors of the foundation made quite clear that Sadler's was far from well. If the theatre was to continue its policy of providing a stage for distinguished visiting opera and ballet companies, a much larger subsidy to meet gallop-ing inflationary costs and to encompass serious planning for the future was needed. Without this, Craig could observe that 'unless a radical improvement is made in our subsidy from public funds we shall not survive beyond the next three years'. In an appendix to the report he published a letter from the director of the Nederlands Dans Theater which expressed regrets that unless a minimum guarantee were available for future seasons, no further visits could be envisaged: a season in April '73 had cost NDT £3500, despite excellent houses. The Wells, it was further noted, was the only theatre in the world in which NDT has not been offered a financial guarantee since 1968.

All this has to be considered in the light of the fact that during the year under consideration no less than thirteen dance companies

were seen at Sadler's Wells. In addition to appearances by the Royal
Ballet's New Group, Rambert, London Contemporary Dance, there
had been the impressive seasons by Nederlands Dans Theater and
the Dutch National Ballet, and by the Ballet-Théâtre Contemporain (with two fine Stravinsky/Stockhausen programmes). Among
smaller troupes the Joseph Russillo Ballet Theatre, the New London
Ballet, Alvin Ailey, Paul Taylor and Louis Falco from the USA,
and the Gulbenkian Ballet from Lisbon, had also found a London
showcase, as too the Bayanihan company from the Philippines.
Whatever the merits of some of these companies, and they ranged
from the superb to the insufferable, Sadler's Wells was making a
vital contribution to London's artistic life and to its theatrical
eminence, and Douglas Craig's request for an additional subsidy of
£1000 per week seemed positively too modest when compared with
the £225000 that is Paris's annual subvention to the Théâtre de la
Ville, the Wells' opposite number. The loss of the Wells is unthinkable to the dance and opera audience; the tragedy of our times is
that the unthinkable too often happens.

However, in far Pyongyang the Wells has its friends. In March
1973 the North Korean Mansudai Dance Company visited the
theatre, bringing a programme that contrasted a few merry acrobatic and juggling acts with an over-generous allocation of dance
scenes in which a cohort of inexorably smiling young ladies had
tripped about waving pink paper azaleas in a frenzy of patriotic
fervour, to give us a display of official folk art of the most simpering
and inscrutable quaintness. But at least *The Pyongyang Times*
realized how much we were affected by the season, even if we
didn't; in April its English edition reported that on the final night
the crowd round the box office were crying, 'Let's share the honour
to see the world summit of art which came to London for the first
time. We haven't seen it. The second time comers give way for us',
and other idiomatic choruses. One old docker was moved to testify
that '. . . the great rays of Comrade Kim Il Sung in the east shine
to ripen the red fruits in a corner of the Western hemisphere', and
a 'British official' observed that 'The Korean art is an art indispen-
sable even for the people of the thirtieth century'. With an audience
like that there's really nothing wrong with either the Wells or its
future that a few paper azaleas – and the journalists of *The Pyongyang Times* – can't cure.

Stephen Sondheim and the American Musical

A theatre historian and the former editor of Music and Musicians *look at the career of Broadway's most important contemporary lyricist/ composer.*

Musical comedy, it seems clear, is foreign to the British theatre. Over the centuries London has seen a variety of musical forms in the theatre: Purcell's semi-operas, *The Beggar's Opera*, the Savoy operas, the shows of Ivor Novello, *Bitter Sweet*, sundry Viennese imports and even George Edwardes's founding musicals. But the contemporary musical belongs to Broadway. Very occasionally the home-grown exception, like *Oliver*, *The Boyfriend* or *Salad Days*, has flourished, yet the coach-party audience continues to prefer its musical entertainment in the theatre closer to operetta or revue. Lavish production numbers and solo turns win more hearts than that intelligent American invention, cousin to *Singspiel*, the musical comedy.

So it is all the more surprising that between 1972 and 1975 five of Stephen Sondheim's eight musical comedies will have been seen in Britain. (At the time of writing *A Little Night Music*, which opened on Broadway in February 1973 and is now on tour as well, was expected to come to London in autumn 1974.) *Company* and *Gypsy* were hits with the critics and had modest runs, but didn't find their audience. *West Side Story* made a brief appearance at the Collegiate Theatre, Gordon Square. *A Funny Thing Happened on the Way to the Forum*, which ran in London for nearly two years from autumn 1963 and proved an admirable vehicle for Frankie Howerd, was revived in the wake of *Gypsy* for the purposes of a provincial tour with Phil Silvers.

Few contemporary writers in any genre have had as much exposure as this in so short a time. And Sondheim's remaining works are unlikely to be performed in Britain for particular reasons. *Anyone Can Whistle* was a failure and, despite many technical points of merit and interest and a big following among cognoscenti for the original cast recording, Sondheim now accepts that verdict. In *Do I Hear a Waltz?* Sondheim's lyrics were unhappily paired with Richard Rodgers's music, and this atypical Sondheim product was also a failure. *Follies*, a *succès d'estime* and financial near-disaster on Broadway, is probably Sondheim's most interesting work to date, but its ambience of Ziegfeld nostalgia – its Broadway particularity – makes it virtually untransferable to London. *Company* was too New York for the West End; *Follies* was too New York for New York. A ninth Sondheim musical, *Evening Primrose*, was a television special made in New York in 1967 which has never been rebroadcast. For *West Side Story* and *Gypsy*, of course, as for *Do I Hear a Waltz?* Sondheim wrote only the lyrics.

During this extended Sondheim festival in Britain, which is all the more remarkable since the musical is scarcely germane to the West End, the faith that producers and critics alike have shown in his work has not been matched by comparable audience response. This is probably because for the British he falls between two stools. For the coach-parties he is too serious; he is more theatre than musical as they understand it. For the serious audience (who take in straight theatre or opera and music) he is working in a corner of the market that has habitually been ignored. Yet this latter audience should pay attention to Sondheim, for what he is doing is of central importance to the theatrical tradition of our time.

He is indeed a theatre poet and a theatre composer rather than a predictable showbiz hack, and the elements of his art are completely integrated. It is true that the genre in which he works is a popular one, but it is sad if the popular arts are denied serious attention until they have passed out of popularity. 'B' movies, Scott Joplin rags, Stephen Foster, poster art, are all now getting recognition from the guardians of culture. Sondheim's output provides intelligent people with a chance to kick the whirligig of fashion and come to terms with a popular art while it is still alive.

Without having been born in a theatrical trunk, Sondheim is nevertheless a product of the professional American musical theatre and its slick integrated tradition. It was fortunate for him that Oscar Hammerstein II was an intimate family friend, and he early developed an interest in writing for the theatre. He describes how, when he was fifteen, he wrote a school show and decided it was good enough to offer to Hammerstein. 'I had visions,' he says, 'of being the youngest ever on Broadway, and asked him to treat it as if it were a professional work and he did not know me. Next day when I went back for the verdict he said, "It's the worst thing I ever read", and as my lower lip trembled a bit he added, "I didn't say it was untalented. I just said it's terrible, and if you want to know why I'll tell you." '

We started with the opening stage direction and went through and by the afternoon I had a complete and very concise course in writing for the musical theatre. We spoke about everything – characters, plays, scenes, songs, how to structure each.

So I daresay I knew more about song-writing at the end of that afternoon than most people know in a lifetime, because I got the distillation of his experience. I was just at the right age and I soaked it all up. He then outlined a course for me which I in fact followed quite precisely over the next four years.

This included the exercise of writing three adaptations before tackling an original musical book: first, a play Sondheim liked and thought suitable for a musical; next a play he did not think particularly suitable which would involve considerable rewriting and reshaping of the dramatic material; and then a non-dramatic work.

At the same time as pursuing this private project, Sondheim took a degree in music at Williams College where he was awarded a postgraduate arts fellowship which enabled him to study composition with Milton Babbitt for about three years before beginning work in show business. After a brief period writing television scripts he was commissioned to make a musical out of an unproduced play which was the property of the designer/producer Lemuel Ayers. Ayers unfortunately died before the project, entitled *Saturday Night*, could be staged, and it was completely scrapped. It did however provide the young composer/lyricist with polished audition material, which impressed Arthur Laurents who was writing the book for *West Side Story*. Laurents enlisted Sondheim to write the lyrics for that memorable work, thus launching a successful career. Yet *West Side Story*, as Laurents has perceptively pointed out, although imaginative, exciting, and taken as new in its day, was the end not the beginning of a kind of musical. It invented nothing; it exploited much of what the American musical had accrued of genuine theatrical value.

Traditionally (if inaccurately) the modern musical comedy was born in 1943 with Rodgers and Hammerstein's *Oklahoma*. Here for the first time critics and audience recognized a musical in which every element was directed towards telling a straightforward, credible story. Such traditional elements of the old musical show as did not fit – chorus lines, showgirls, revue-like star turns, tap-dancing – were rejected. An audience expecting the standard opening chorus of buxom beauties showing an ample expanse of attractive leg saw the curtain rise on an empty stage with a cowboy off singing 'Oh, what a beautiful mornin' '. In place of wholly irrelevant dance extravaganza, there was a fully choreographed Dream Ballet expressing the heroine's inner conflict. Not a character, not a line, not a song deviated from the object of telling the story and supporting the dramatic concept. This, in principle, was the 'integrated musical'.

Mastery of the form is what Sondheim inherited from Hammerstein and ultimately extended. The Rodgers and Hammerstein generation quickly saw that they were no longer writing musical shows but instead musical plays. Authors of the scripts recognized that in most cases a song would have to be the natural climax of a scene. The amount of time taken up by the requisite fifteen to twenty songs in a musical comedy score meant, furthermore, that there really would not be a great deal of time for dialogue. Spoken lines would have to be sparse and crisp, and at the same time move the plot along to the next musical climax. There would be no time for the leisurely exposition of character enjoyed by straight dramatists; a character would have to be presented in action at all times, leading up to that inevitable song.

The songs in a musical play have tremendous power. They provide an entirely different level of communication for the author and his character. Soliloquy and inner dialogue – dangerous and difficult in contemporary spoken drama – become plausible when sung. Song as an expression of heightened emotion, quite apart from the stage convention, is not so far from everyday experience. Therefore the theatrical expression of sentiment through song is both acceptable and credible. Passion, particularly, which would be so limited by the range of words a character might authentically speak, can be exalted through the medium of lyrics and music. Sondheim's lyrics for *West Side Story* are in this mould. Many of them stress emotional climaxes: 'Something's Coming', 'Tonight', 'Maria', and 'I Feel Pretty', all emphasize feelings that would be difficult and even possibly embarrassing in the cold sound of speech.

Also the music guides and fixes the words and their delivery by the actor in a way that is impossible in spoken drama. Maria's simple lyric explaining how she can still love a man who has killed her brother,

> I love him,
> I'm his,
> And everything he is
> I am too,

is straightforward enough to be spoken. But if spoken it could be interpreted by an actress intoning it like Portia talking about Mercy. When sung accurately, it is less open to distortion.

There were limitations, however, in the form as practised. Granted, Hammerstein's lyric for Nellie Forbush, the cockeyed optimist from Arkansas in *South Pacific*, certainly expressed 'I'm happy; I'm in love' in a superb show-stopping way typical of the 'integrated musical' with

> I'm as corny as Kansas in August . . . ,
> High as a flag on the Fourth of July . . .
> And you will note there's a lump in my throat
> When I speak of my Wonderful Guy!

But it is essentially a 'list' song, simply repeating through different clichés a signpost of an idea much like Cole Porter's 'You're the Top, / You're the Tower of Pisa, / You're the smile / on the Mona Lisa'. The difference between the two songs is that Porter's endless lyrics could be sung by any character, while Hammerstein's song – even when extracted from the context of the show – remains the statement of Nellie Forbush or another easy-going, red blooded American girl like her.

Many of Sondheim's early songs, particularly in the three lyrics-only works and in *Forum*, share this quality with Hammer-

stein and others. The lyric is thoughtfully conceived and consistent
with the character singing, but provides only an outline of the
persona and not the soul behind the mask. An instance of this in
Gypsy would be,

> Some people can be content
> Playing bingo and paying rent.
> That's peachy for some people,
> For some hum-drum people to be,
> But some people ain't me.

But the notable exception in the same show, of course, is 'Rose's
Turn', which remains one of the most electrifying moments in the
history of the American musical. This soliloquy is a full scene – not
a song, or a number – in which Rose, the real star, exposes all the
frustrations of her life which have motivated the plot. It is impossible to lift this song out of the theatre, unlike 'Everything's
Coming Up Roses' which became a hit. The latter number, however dramatically effective, is terribly old-fashioned in that the
lyric is a string of well chosen clichés which – like 'A Wonderful
Guy' – are perfect for the character and the moment:

> Clear the decks
> Light the lights,
> You've got nothing to hit but the heights,
> Starting here,
> Starting now,
> Honey, everything's coming up roses!

Hammerstein had reached middle-age before conceiving of,
developing and mastering an integrated lyric. Sondheim was already
carrying the potentialities of the musical play beyond that simple
but important level before he was out of his twenties. The disparate
elements of the musical theatre could clearly be made to fit more
tightly together. Further levels of character might be exposed. The
planes of experience already expressed through the spoken word
and the sung lyric might be subsequently developed to manipulate
time and space.

In musical comedy, unlike in opera, the words have to be heard
and are more important in carrying the drama than the music.
Musical comedy could not work except in the vernacular, whereas
opera is commonly enjoyed in its original (foreign) language. Of

course, there is virtually no native Anglo-Saxon operatic tradition, which may partly explain the development of the American musical. Furthermore opera as an international art form has moved away almost completely from spoken dialogue. And the nature of the musical language in opera and the emphasis put there upon the expressive capacity of the singer as musical instrument is quite different from the musical, where melody and lyric is not a tool for the performer, rather the reverse. The lyricist in musical comedy can hold his own with the composer. They are in fact only two persons in a joint enterprise of many, even if they are the crucial elements. For the lyricist there are all the delights of a literary challenge. He is, and is recognized as, a poet of the theatre, and it has to be remembered that in straight theatre, as in opera, the audience is no longer accustomed to taking poetic drama seriously. The lyricist is thus a nearly extinct creature in an art that has abandoned poetry.

Sondheim's fame as a lyricist preceded his success as a composer. He is certainly the unchallenged master in this field. The lyricist provides the dramatic element in the focal points of the musical theatre experience. In Sondheim's case this is often a very complex operation, however deceptively simple it appears. In his lyrics he does far more than his predecessors did. He takes upon himself the responsibility of dramatist, revealing a wide range of levels of awareness in his characters.

In a Sondheim musical the book is more like secco recitative in an opera. Sondheim's numbers in a real sense *are* the drama. They can be duets, mixtures of events presented together, ballads, self portraits, personality type analyses. Above all they are poems for the theatre. If Sondheim's skill as lyricist merits any reservation, it would be that the wit – so characteristic of his time and milieu – is indulged almost as an automatic reflex, as a defusing element, in the face of emotion nakedly and truthfully presented. Sometimes the characters reveal a puppetlike debt to the cleverness of their creator. Yet this sad, almost zany, humour with which pain is turned away, this attribute of Feste the Clown who is Sondheim's cultural ancestor, should rather be noted as a characteristic of the art than questioned. It is as much part of the game as breaking into a number at a moment of climax. Musical comedy, however deep it delves into feeling, is, after all, entertainment.

The natural lyric poetry of any age is simple, universal, and fit for singing. There has not been much natural lyric poetry in English since the seventeenth century, although there has been a literary tradition of lyric writing of which Auden is the best known contemporary exemplar. It is difficult for natural, true lyric poetry to thrive in isolation. It comes in a flood or not at all. The songs of Shakespeare's time were often affected and mawkish, however charming the passage of years has made them seem. The lyrics of the American musical theatre are a sufficient corpus to make up a real tradition. Almost the best credential they have for literary consideration in this way is their completely unpretentious utility.

Sondheim's poems, although they are much more specific in their dramatic intention than lyric poetry was historically, are among the most interesting and cleverest products of this modern tradition. They are intended to be, and work best when they are, sung. Their language is utterly contemporary, down to the self-conscious cliché employed only to be exploded. The rhymes are often brilliantly funny, seeking out improbable and inspired syllabic pairings which would have brought pleasure to Pope. The command of metre would not have been scorned by Kipling. Take 'Another Hundred People' from *Company*, one of its most authentic pieces of poetry which fixes the play's metropolitan setting. The material might have appealed to Auden.

Another hundred people just got off of the train
And came up through the ground
While another hundred people just got off of the bus
And are looking around
At another hundred people who got off of the plane
And are looking at us
Who got off of the train
And the plane and the bus
Maybe yesterday.
It's a city of strangers –
Some come to work, some to play –
A city of strangers –
Some come to stare, some to stay,
And every day
The ones who stay
Can find each other in the crowded streets and the guarded parks,
By the rusty fountains and the dusty trees with the battered barks,

And they walk together past the postered walls with the crude
  remarks,
And they meet at parties through the friends of friends who they
  never know.
Will you pick me up or do I meet you there or shall we let it go?
Did you get my message? 'Cause I looked in vain.
Can we see each other Tuesday if it doesn't rain?
Look, I'll call you in the morning or my service will explain . . .
And another hundred people just got off of the train.

By any literary criteria this is a supremely successful lyric. It works
even better when sung, and it is a whole civilization away from
'A foggy day in London town'. Not a word wasted, or out of key.
If the surface of the language is short on the verbal egotism we
have come to expect from poetry, it has to be remembered that
there is not much natural lyric poetry in the contemporary antho-
logies.

Sondheim loves word games. Another song in *Company*,
'Sorry-Grateful', is based on the meta-language of everyday inter-
course. It is almost choking, with wonderful expressive effect, on
the semi-coherent confidence of the married man in his married
state.

> You're always sorry,
> You're always grateful,
> You're always wondering what might have been.
> Then she walks in.

It continues building up the device of phrases not meaning what
they say.

> Everything's different,
> Nothing's changed,
> Only maybe slightly
> Rearranged.
> You're sorry-grateful,
> Regretful-happy.
> Why look for answers where none occur?
> You always are what you always were,
> Which has nothing to do with,
> All to do with her.

It is difficult to get outside language, particularly in a song which
seems to demand basic syntax. But Sondheim can manage this

kind of simultaneous criticism and emotion. 'Sorry-Grateful' is one of his best, if – once the premise is established – simplest achievements.

The final number of *Company*, 'Being Alive', takes big risks with words that have suffered in pop songs to the point of extinction, but with its utterly basic progress it succeeds by a narrow margin in drawing out the moral of the play without sentimentality. 'Someone to hold you too close', begins Robert, the bachelor hero, 'Someone to hurt you too deep, / Someone to sit in your chair, / To ruin your sleep . . .' After some dialogue the catalogue of functions that the missing other half would have continues: '. . . to need you too much, . . . to know you too well, . . . to pull you up short, / And put you through hell . . .' There are two more breaks in the lyric for dialogue before the daring:

> Someone to crowd you with love,
> Someone to force you to care,
> Someone to make you come through,
> Who'll always be there, as frightened as you,
> Of being alive . . .

The irony of *Company* in fact centres on the accepted meaning of such words as 'love' and 'care'. The final stanza of this song changes dramatically from statement to petition. 'Somebody hold me too close, / Somebody hurt me too deep', and so on with the spotlight suddenly focused on the central figure. It is a simple touch that skates perilously near being tacky.

> Make me confused, mock me with praise,
> Let me be used, vary my days.
> But alone is alone, not alive.
>
> Somebody crowd me with love,
> Somebody force me to care,
> Somebody let me come through.
> I'll always be there as frightened as you,
> To help us survive
> Being alive . . .

When Bernstein pays tribute to Sondheim as someone who takes risks, it must surely be this kind of very dangerous thing that he is thinking of.

Sondheim has been a prolific lyricist, and most of his lyrics are less sober than the ones quoted above. The language is always unpretentious as these examples, yet never banal. He owes part of his success to his dramatic flair, his involvement with his characters, which produces a scrupulous honesty and discretion in what he has them say. Thus Henrik in *Night Music* describes himself with 'Oh, that lawyer's son, the one who mumbles – / Short and boring. / Yes, he's hardly worth ignoring.'

On the other hand the candour of Carlotta's 'I'm Still Here' in *Follies* and Joanne's 'The Ladies Who Lunch' in *Company* is really just part of their acts which they keep playing, chins up. 'Anyone Can Whistle', the title lyric, and 'Too Many Mornings' from *Follies*, are the other kind of character-revealing song, both being presented completely straight and sincere.

> Too many mornings
> Wasted in pretending I reach for you.
> How many mornings
> Are there still to come?

Another Sondheim weapon is his extreme cleverness with images. *Evening Primrose* is about a poet who decides to desert the world and join a group of people living in a department store who only lead their lives at night when the store is closed. However, he falls for a girl who has been there longer and wants to be taken to the world again. This provides the occasion for one of Sondheim's most staggering conceits, when the girl sings of how she remembers the natural world, using for similes the familiar artificialities of the store.

> I remember sky.
> It was blue as ink,
> Or at least I think
> I remember sky. . . .
> And ice like vinyl
> On the streets,
> Cold as silver,
> White as sheets,
> Rain like strings,
> And changing things
> Like leaves.
> I remember leaves,

> Green as spearmint,
> Crisp as paper.
> I remember trees,
> Bare as coat racks,
> Spread like broken umbrellas. . . .

Finally she comes to the conclusion that her paradoxical way of living and thinking of things is all wrong.

> I remember days,
> Or at least I try,
> But as years go by,
> They're a sort of haze,
> And the bluest ink
> Isn't really sky,
> And at times I think
> I would gladly die
> For a day of sky.

In *Follies*, one of the main conceits of the show is the poetic use made of traditional revue numbers, ironically reflecting upon the personal crises of the four main characters. The big chorus-line number, 'Who's That Woman', especially, operates in this way, parodying a standard revue specialty with all the twenties cynicism of Coward's 'Poor Little Rich Girl' or 'Dance Little Lady'. The now middle-aged ex-chorines go through their old routine:

> Who's that woman? I know her well,
> All decked out head to toe.
> She lives life like a carousel:
> Beau after beau after beau.

The final line, 'Lord, Lord, Lord, that woman is me', neatly captures the disillusionment of Phyllis and Sally's lives – they, too, have pursued life and love in a frenzied self-destroying way. At this moment in the show, they have not recognized 'that woman' as themselves. But the audience, hearing the chorus 'Mirror, mirror, on the wall, / Who's the saddest gal in town?', does. It is worth remarking in passing that *Follies* shares its theme with *Old Times*, *Forget-me-not Lane*, and *All Over*, and is thus dead in line with contemporary obsessions in the legitimate theatre.

Finally there is Sondheim's amazing verbal wit, which ties in neatly and obviously with his obsessive interest in mathematical puzzles. (He used to contribute crosswords to *New York* magazine.) The puns and wordplay he manages are quite hilarious. Fredrik's song 'Now', at the beginning of *Night Music*, is a typical tour de force – a lewd meditation in lawyers' language, employing strict rhyme and no repetitions. The great Carlotta Campion number from *Follies*, a cameo bursting out of its frame, is full of jokes that in some cases already require a footnote on account of their local topicality. It's a magical history tour of America from the thirties to the sixties:

> Good times and bum times,
> I've seen them all and, my dear,
> I'm still here. . . .
> I got through *Abie's*
> *Irish Rose,*
> Five Dionne babies,
> Major Bowes. . . .
> I've gotten through Herbert and J. Edgar Hoover,
> Gee, that was fun and a half.
> When you've been through Herbert and J. Edgar
> Hoover,
> Anything else is a laugh.
>
> I've been through Reno,
> I've been through Beverly Hills,
> And I'm here.
> Reefers and vino,
> Rest cures, religion and pills,
> But I'm here.
> Been called a pinko
> Commie tool,
> Got through it stinko
> By my pool.
> I should have gone to an acting school,
> That seems clear.
> Still, someone said, 'She's sincere,'
> So I'm here. . . .
>
> First you're another
> Sloe-eyed vamp,
> Then someone's mother,
> Then you're camp. . . .

I've gotten through 'Hey, lady, aren't you whoozis?
Wow, what a looker you were.'
Or, better yet, 'Sorry, I thought you were whoozis,
Whatever happened to her?'

Carlotta's number, while, of course, it's a ball, defines for the audience more clearly than is ever actually stated, the passage of time in the lives of the protagonists of *Follies*. It is the stuff of Sondheim's subtle dramatic technique.

Madame Armfeldt's 'Liaisons' from *Night Music* is based on the merest hint in the Bergman film from which the book is adapted. She confides that she was given her château on condition she never wrote her memoirs, and Sondheim builds this number into a cornucopia of snobbery jokes. He calls *Night Music* a *schlagobers* version of *Smiles of a Summer's Night*. It is certainly double cream.

What once was a rare champagne
Is now just an amiable hock,
What once was a villa, at least,
Is 'digs'. . . .
What once was a gown with a train
Is now just a simple little frock,
What once was a sumptuous feast
Is figs.
No, not even figs – raisins.
Ah, liaisons. . . .
At the palace of the Duke of Ferrara
I acquired some position
Plus a tiny Titian . . .

Cynical *dames du monde* are Sondheim's best, or at least most entertaining, creations, and their extended nostalgia ballads are, in a way, the most memorable aspect of his brilliant lyrical talent.

When he is writing the lyrics, Sondheim is not just thinking of the words. He describes taking the lyrics of 'Maria' for the first time to Jerome Robbins, director of *West Side Story*, who was wary of the song because he did not think he would be able to stage the pauses. In a musical play, it is not generally desirable for a character just to stand there and sing. But Sondheim says, 'I not only work out very carefully what's going on tonally and subtextually, but literally how the people move on stage, where they go, etc. Then the choreographer can do anything he wants, but there's a blueprint book.' The director's ultimate solution has something fixed to work against, and this aspect of Sondheim's work is regarded by his collaborators as a particular treat seldom encountered elsewhere in the theatre.

Sondheim's attitude towards the song as scene has naturally led him to abandon conventional song structure. Realizing that musical comedy is no longer a source of popular tunes, Sondheim does not set out to write songs – popular or otherwise – unless a specific song genre is required by the project at hand, as in *Follies*. He is notorious for 'raiding the book', building a musical moment out of a line of dialogue found in the script. 'Mr Goldstone' from *Gypsy* grew in this way from a line in Arthur Laurents's dialogue, 'Have an egg roll, Mr Goldstone.'

This has resulted in complicated musical scenes in which speech and song are so rapidly and smoothly interchanged that it is impossible to ascertain where the book ends and the lyrics begin. Sondheim first developed this in several extended numbers in *Anyone Can Whistle*, and it is this inventiveness which accounts for the continuing reputation of a show that folded in less than a week. *Anyone Can Whistle* was an over-ambitious original work whose main theme was the definition of sanity. It depicted the chaos that emerges when inmates of the Cookie Jar, the local asylum, are set loose on a community festering with evil and manipulative capitalism, exemplified by the perpetration of a phony Lourdes-type miracle. It is impossible to tell the 'Cookies' and the citizens apart. An entire scene, 'Simple', in which a (bogus) psychiatrist separates the company after brief interviews into two groups, A and 1, while declining to reveal which is sane and which insane, is brilliantly effective theatre and revolutionary in the context of the musical. It lasts for an unprecedented 13 minutes, and switches rapidly from song, to chant, to speech, as the entire company is stirred into complete anarchy.

Clearly not interested in covering old ground for a second time, nor in imposing a formal concept for its own sake, Sondheim has never fully repeated this remarkable idea. And yet the intelligence and skill, which made it possible, have become hallmarks of his subsequent work. First of all his, language always moves easily from speech to song. Not only is this transition consistently fluid, but the language of his lyrics is always clear, related to everyday speech, and easy for a singer – whether a trained voice or not – to put across. Apart from *Night Music*, in fact, Sondheim musicals generally make few demands on vocal ability, which means that in casting the emphasis can uncompromisingly be on acting quality. This stands out.

Furthermore, Sondheim characters talk to each other within the music. This is not the conventional duet, but, again, the musical number as theatrical scene. In *Company*, for example, 'Barcelona' captures the spirit of a routine after-sex conversation, as the airline stewardess prepares to leave in the early morning.

Where you going?

Barcelona

... oh ...

Don't get up.

Do you have to?

Yes, I have to ...

In *Night Music* Sondheim applies his theatrical good sense to the convention of the first act closer, the jolly refrain 'A Weekend in the Country'. In less than seven minutes an incredibly complicated programme of actions and decisions important to the plot, but of minimal dramatic interest, is compressed through a series of witty dialogues involving no fewer than six characters. Each uses the same verse and refrain without at all spoiling characterization or obscuring plot detail. At the same time, the traditional structural requirement that the interval be preceded by a lively number and a provocative plot complication – completely in keeping with the slightly archaic aspect of this waltz musical – is fully satisfied.

How serious a composer is Sondheim? Given that a hallmark of his output is its seamless knit of music and poetry for the purposes of the theatrical event, it is difficult to discuss the music in isolation, without having to excuse a compositional stance which is both unfashionable and, in the eyes of the contemporary serious music world, worthless.

The American musicals of Kurt Weill, whose earlier output needs no such apology, have been largely written off by music critics. They are put down as an unworthy concession to commercial taste in the same way that Shostakovich's toeing the party line on style is regretted. Granted that Sondheim works in a popular medium with a given aesthetic, the music critic might say, but is his composition really *sui generis* and worth taking seriously as music?

This problem is further complicated by Sondheim's compositional method, of which the key is parody. That would perhaps recommend him to the enthusiastic following Walton attracted with *Façade*, one of the few popular hits by a contemporary serious composer. And Sondheim's facility in just this way is the envy of many composers. He does (as it were) five times before breakfast what even so technically adept a serious composer as Richard Rodney Bennett has declared he finds hard to do at all. Namely he can write to order in any of popular music's styles or forms.

Yet this does not mean that Sondheim is sending up his models. He is not like Bernstein a pasticheur, winking between the rests of a Latin-American rhythm so you know he does not take it seriously. (Not that Sondheim is against the humour of a musical spoof: take for one example the Delibes-like waltz of the Cookie Chase, a ballet number in *Anyone Can Whistle*, where the authorities are trying to capture the inmates of the local asylum – just as clever and literate a number as 'Glitter and be Gay' from *Candide*.)

Sondheim works through parody in the old and respectable musical sense, where the word was used to describe the borrowing by a religious composer of a secular theme. Imitation is the highest form of flattery. If Sondheim by analogy parodies it is from love not contempt. As with his lyrics, which are rooted in the received tradition, there is no element of derogation from a higher musical intention, no hint of a primary and cynical pursuit of dollars, although he works unashamedly in the commercial market. Weill's motives might be questioned, however unfairly, because the American musical was for him adopted territory. Sondheim was raised to it. This is the musical language he speaks.

And while he borrows the styles and forms he loves according to the dramatic context which he is facing, and fashions his vocal line, in rhythm and in emotional intention, according to the expressive needs of his lyric, the intervals themselves – the actual thematic material from which he works – are his own. To the casual listener the antecedents of a Sondheim number may be more apparent than the originality, just as Mahler sounds romantic, Mozart classical, and Purcell baroque. But a Sondheim number is

not like Jerome Kern, or Cole Porter, or Richard Rodgers, even
when it is the type of number they might have produced. (The
lapses and depressing character of *Do I Hear a Waltz?* are a useful
foil in appreciating Sondheim's musical personality; for example,
the precious little coda repeating the final phrase at the end of the
title number is a characteristically feeble indulgence of Rodgers's
which Sondheim would never allow himself.)

Sondheim's musical originality, which, after all, was never
intended to produce cabbages and boos from a shocked old world
audience, has an unmistakable flavour that could be attributed to
its (in the context of American popular music) modernity. It does
not sound modern in the sense that today's pop music sounds
spuriously modern, with its battery of distortive effects disguising
essentially simple and traditional material. But since musical
theatre ceased, around a quarter of a century ago, to be the source
of popular song it has not had to follow the fashions of popular
music except at its own pace. Thus, Sondheim has been able to
pursue his own musical taste in a way that was perhaps less possible
for his predecessors in the genre. He has been able to ensure that his
numbers remain trapped in their dramatic context, that his personalized arias can eschew a trite universality. And, since most of
his characters are real theatrical beings in a rather new way for
musical theatre, people with a contemporary vitality and interesting
sensibility, it is not surprising if their arias possess melody of a
questing and tonally indeterminate type.

Not that Sondheim is, in any sense, avant garde as a composer:
he knows his audience has to be able to like his music and not just
be pretend-interested in it. Of atonal music he says, 'I like some of
it, but there's something about people trying so hard. It doesn't
seem to come naturally to them.' To Sondheim it does come naturally. Yet, by an unobtrusive use of sideways chromatic shifts in his
melodies (enharmonic modulations) and the unexpected use of a
sharpened or flattened note in the line foreign to its true key, he
creates that characteristic feeling of tension and uncertainty in his
music.

It is not just a question of the well established blues note.
Sondheim employs dissconances in a way that would have been considered offensive in the theatre a few years back, though the flavour
of his music from this point of view is more governed by the context

of his matter than by any innate harmonic adventurousness. At the same time he has a fondness for close and simple pitch relationships, as in the theme of the Night Waltz from *Night Music*, which are then not underscored with the conventional harmonic progression. And his angular melodies, like 'Every Day a Little Death' from *Night Music* and 'The Road You Didn't Take' from *Follies*, are seldom obvious winners as tunes, in the sense that Gershwin designed a number as a frame for a popular melody. But Sondheim's melodies are completely original. Nobody else uses those displaced sevenths like he does. Even his songs that can be, and have been, lifted out of context – such as 'Anyone Can Whistle' and 'Send in the Clowns' – are quizzical and musically undermined: none of the familiar, sentimental, brash confidence of the oldies. Times have changed, of course, and Sondheim is different.

To start with he is a mathematics freak. He says that he would probably have majored in mathematics if he had not been sidetracked into song writing and deliberately avoided mathematics. There is a strong element of gamesmanship in his personality, and each of his works is in some sense the solution to a self-imposed problem. The starting point for *Night Music* was the problem of writing a waltz musical. Also he is classically trained, unlike most composers on Broadway, so he does all his own arrangements. He studied privately with Milton Babbitt, one of the grand old men of the American avant garde, though this did not include atonal composition.

'Milton said he wouldn't teach that to anybody who hadn't exhausted tonal resources first,' says Sondheim. 'He himself had become bored with tonal music as a composer and moved on to atonal. Now he's moved on to electronic. I liked Berg very much, but as Milton was at great pains to point out he was a tonal composer even though he used atonal techniques.' The music Sondheim listens to for his own pleasure is almost exclusively nineteenth and twentieth century and Bach. No popular music at all, and no Handel, Haydn, or Mozart. 'Bach,' he says, 'was an acquired taste for me. Mozart I don't understand. It doesn't reach me. I admire it, but I don't like it.' As a composer he admits to a very narrow enthusiasm. 'I like writing songs that take place in dramatic situations within the proscenium arch. I'm not particularly interested in art songs or pop songs that stand on their own.' He is now thinking of trying more continuous music. Although he is no opera fan, he is intrigued by the idea of making viable opera – an evening in the theatre in which everything is sung. Yet he hated *Les Parapluies de Cherbourg* passionately – not the idea, the execution.

As a composer Sondheim wears his learning lightly. Yet he is the first musical comedy composer (and proud of it) to have run three separate songs together into a single musical scene. This is the trio 'Soon-Later-Now' from *Night Music* in which different levels on the stage, as well as in the music, are woven together polyphonically with a kind of montage effect. Of course it is a particular contrivance, not to be used often. But Sondheim frequently has separate melodies or melodic material running simultaneously, or imitations and canons which produce a polyphonic texture and fluency virtually unknown in the musical before. Contradictions in the dialogue are graphically mirrored in the music. 'Every Day a Little Death' from *Night Music* and 'Getting Married Today' from *Company* are good examples of this ingenuity.

However these qualities are not to be listened for; they are just extra flavour in the pudding, whose main attribute is its lightness of touch. Perhaps it is not surprising with this liberated, almost Schoenbergian, compositional background – Sondheim certainly does not sit at his piano with a towel round his head waiting for melodic inspiration to start his compositions – that the actual tunes have to be worked at. In that respect he is just like Tippett, who says the precise pitches are the last things he fixes in a composition. Sondheim has to work at the melodic material a great deal. He says:

I think my melodic gifts are limited. On the other hand people whose melodic gifts aren't limited, like in popular theatre Kern, or in classical music Schubert, I think worked as hard over their melodies as I do. They just had greater gifts. To me music isn't only a matter of melody. It's melody plus harmony plus rhythm. I like it as music not disparate elements. And when people are talking about tunes, they are considering the element of music that happens to be the most popular, because that's what you can whistle when you go down the street.

However, it's also a subject that I'm very touchy about because, when *West Side Story* came out in New York, to a man every critic and every patron said, 'It's all very exciting but if only Bernstein could write whistleable melodies. . . .' Four years later the movie came out, and the movie company wanting to protect their investment put many thousands of dollars into the promotion. Soon as the public started to hear the songs more than once, lo and behold they could suddenly whistle them. And everybody said 'What a tuneful composer Bernstein is.' Tunes are a matter of hearing, of familiarity. You can whistle or hum anything if you hear it enough times. That's all.

In any case it is not Sondheim's object to write hit tunes. And his skill at providing a rhythm which gives his lyrics maximum dramatic effectiveness is at least as important as his melodic gifts of which, despite his diffidence, there are numerous examples. Naturally the rhythm does not exist as an independent element. Like the lyric which it points, it is dictated by the chosen musical form of the number. In *Company* for example the forms are close to what was popular in New York at the end of the sixties, including the bossa nova and similar Latin American beats. 'Liaisons' in *Night Music* is a kind of minuet. But Sondheim's actual note values are chosen to define the natural spoken rhythm of stage speech if the lyric were not being sung, and it is assumed that the numbers will swing with the characteristic performing style. In this respect Sondheim follows established convention, though with a special care for character and dramatic appropriateness. These are the tools of his craft as playwright.

One musical factor which Sondheim does not control, except indirectly, is the orchestration. This is something which the serious musical audience would find bizarre, although the personalized orchestration which they expect of composers today is a comparatively recent innovation. Italian opera composers in the seventeenth century and at the start of the nineteenth century often had only a tenuous control over orchestration, and conventions were such that probably Handel did not need to do his own.

However musical comedy is, even more than opera, a collaborative art. The writer of spoken dialogue and the lyricist are seldom the same person, and the production schedule of a musical makes it inevitable that there should be a separate orchestrator even if the composer wanted or was able to do this own orchestration.

Sondheim explains:

It's not like writing an opera where you choose your voices in advance before anybody's cast. You compose, you orchestrate according to certain key relationships, and then you present it to the opera company. And they just damn well have to find a lady who sings from D flat to high C, and if it turns out to be a 400 lb., 60-year-old playing Juliet, then that's that. It's a convention that opera audiences accept but it's not accepted on the musical stage, and you have to cast a musical for the best intentions of the script and the songs.

Which means that until you're cast and actually in rehearsal you can't set keys, and therefore can't orchestrate. So there you are, already in the five week rehearsal period, during which time in my case (because I'm always behind) I'm still writing songs. But in any case I'd have to be down in rehearsals, helping teach songs, watching run-throughs, conferring with the director and the other creative staff of the show, the actors etc. It's a full time job anyway.

As it happens, the orchestrator starts work around the end of the second week of rehearsal, and works day and night for three weeks just to get the orchestrations of those fourteen to twenty songs done in time for the out of town try-out. The composer couldn't possibly orchestrate and never has. Lenny in *West Side Story* had an idea of what he wanted the orchestra to sound like because he's a superb orchestrator, and he chose the instrumentation in terms of the make-up of the orchestra, because you're limited (again it's not like opera) to a certain number of men. There's a standard of twenty-five in New York at the most. Of course, Lenny might make some suggestions for improvement or whatever.

On top of that I don't know instrumentation; I never studied it. I studied composition and theory, and the only instrumentation I've ever done was for four instruments for background music for a play of Arthur Laurents's [*Invitation to a March*, 1960], which I did with Forsyth's handbook in one hand and a pencil in the other, and brought it piece by piece to Lenny to tell me what would sound well. But I do write very complete piano copy, because I'm classically trained, which very few Broadway composers do because they're not. One of the reasons that Jonathan Tunick, who's done the last three shows that I've written and who's the most brilliant orchestrator on Broadway, likes doing my shows is that he doesn't have to invent half as much as he has to with a composer who gives him a lead sheet, or a lead sheet with an oompah accompaniment, where he has to then add the interest himself in the instruments and in fact is a collaborator on the music. He would prefer to get the complete piano copy.

I essentially hear it for the piano because that's my instrument, that was my training. Sometimes I screw Jonathan up by giving him something that is so pianistic that it becomes very difficult to orchestrate, particularly if he hasn't allowed for a keyboard instrument in the pit.

Tunick's orchestrations have their own character which is

noticeably more original than the existing versions of the earlier Sondheim musicals. However this aspect of the collaborative musical effort is more dominated by convention and a standard level of tone than any other. It is perhaps a pity that the musical seems obliged to have a certain timbre, just as it is a pity that most performers on the musical stage today are dependent on amplification to come over the light orchestral backing. But that is show business, which is precisely where Sondheim's main loyalty lies.

Sondheim is perhaps most widely acclaimed for the depth of his characterizations and the insights he brings to them. Most of the solo numbers that he writes are intensely personal statements. In *Anyone Can Whistle*, each of the three main characters is given a song which exposes significant insecurities. Cora, the villain mayoress, protests that there cannot be 'A Parade in Town' without her. Hapgood, the hero, confesses a dependence he has never before been able to admit:

> With so little to be sure of,
> (If there's anything at all)
> If there's anything at all,
> I'm sure of here and now and us together.

And nurse Fay Apple, who has masqueraded as the sexy Mysterious Lady from Lourdes but is in fact frigid, laments her sexual problem in the title song:

> Anyone can whistle,
> That's what they say.
> Easy.
> Anyone can whistle
> Any old day.
> Easy.
> It's all so simple:
> Relax, let go, let fly.
> Well someone tell me why can't I?
> I can dance a tango,
> I can read Greek.
> Easy.
> I can slay a dragon
> Any old week.
> Easy.

What's hard is simple,
What's natural comes hard.
Maybe you could show me
How to let go,
Lower my guard
Learn to be free.
Maybe if you whistle,
Whistle for me.

These are no longer the flip 'character songs' generally associated with musical comedy. Nor are they the standard serious ballads which have been prominent in the genre. They chart for the audience the subtlety of the entire character, not merely his attitude to one event. Their sentiment can be indulged without becoming whimsical or precious.

In *Company*, the lyrics alone carry the central figure Robert from the slightly immature and unreasonable fantasy 'Someone Is Waiting' – a composite woman featuring all the surface qualities of his married female friends – to 'Being Alive', in which he recognizes that 'alone is alone, not alive', that his relationship with those friends is essentially voyeuristic and that he needs himself to experience the real pressures and pleasures of marriage.

In *Follies*, the most serious and complex of the Sondheim musicals, it is the object of the entire conception completely to expose the characters and their illusions. Each of the four main protagonists by the end of the Follies reunion has relived some of his past and come to terms with the status quo, however disappointing. In the beginning the cynical and successful Ben sees no point in questioning and perhaps regretting choices made in the past. His point of view is made perfectly clear in 'The Road You Didn't Take':

The roads you never take
Go through rocky ground,
Don't they?
The choices that you make
Aren't all that grim.
The worlds you never see
Still will be around,
Won't they?
The Ben I'll never be,
Who remembers him?

The complexity of *Follies* and the levels of self-deception which it attempts to analyse are aptly put in Sally's song, 'In Buddy's Eyes'. Taken out of context of the show, it is a simple song about a perfect marriage, but in the show it is the feeble protestation of a woman telling a man she still loves but once, rejected, that her choice of someone else was after all correct.

> In Buddy's eyes,
> I'm young, I'm beautiful.
> In Buddy's arms,
> On Buddy's shoulder,
> I won't get older.
> Nothing dies.
> And all I ever dreamed I'd be,
> The best I ever thought of me,
> Is every minute there to see
> In Buddy's eyes.

By the end of the show, each of the four is given a song in a nightmare Follies sequence which pin-points his particular problem. Although each song is compatible with the Ziegfeld Follies genre, at the same time it perfectly defines the character and his own folly. Sally sings the torch song, 'Losing My Mind', while her husband Buddy sings of the:

> 'God-why-don't-you-love-me-oh-you-do-I'll-see-you-later'
> Blues,
> That
> 'Long-as-you-ignore-me-you're-the-only-thing-that-matters'
> Feeling,
> That
> 'If-I'm-good-enough-for-you-you're-not-good-enough-
> And-thank-you-for-the-present-but-what's-wrong-with-it?' stuff,

which explains his love for Sally, in spite of his half-hearted unfaithfulness. Phyllis sings the 'Ballad of Lucy and Jessie':

> Lucy is juicy
> But terrible drab.
> Jessie is dressy
> But cold as a slab.
> Lucy wants to be dressy,
> Jessie wants to be juicy.
> Lucy wants to be Jessie
> And Jessie Lucy.

The conflict is in coming to terms with herself as she was and at the same time as she is. But it is impossible to combine the best of youth and middle-age. Her husband Ben, who has fought for and sacrificed everything to success, sings a happy-go-lucky song, 'Live, Laugh, Love' which sneers at success. As the entire show rises to nightmare pitch, he forgets his lines and cannot continue with the song.

Sondheim is one of the few successful musical comedy writers to prefer working with original stories. Most musicals have been based on well known plays, books or films and, in these, much labour is saved where story and character are concerned, since a large segment of the audience can be depended on to have a preconception of both. Since he starts from scratch, as it were, the strength of Sondheim's characterization is all the more impressive. Of the five projects which Sondheim has initiated in his own right, *Anyone Can Whistle, Company* and *Follies* have been based upon completely original scripts. *Night Music* and *Forum*, while based on Bergman and Plautus respectively, have been a lot more unorthodox in execution than the standard musical adaptation.

The composer-lyricist, of course, is not exclusively responsible for all features of the work. A team headed by producer-director Harold Prince, choreographer Michael Bennett, orchestrator Jonathan Tunick, designer Boris Aronson, and the respective authors, contributed heavily to the shape of Sondheim's three most recent musicals. The specific attitudes to marriage and middle-age found in them owe a great deal to Prince.

Sondheim's originality lies also in his pragmatic approach to developing an idea into a show. *Night Music* grew out of a desire to produce a waltz musical which long predates *Do I Hear a Waltz?* and which Sondheim has shared with Prince. They had tried unsuccessfully to obtain the rights to Anouilh's *Ring Round the Moon* way back in 1957. More recently Sondheim suggested the Bergman film, which he had seen years before. A screening was arranged and, although he liked it less than he remembered liking it, the project was adopted. Since it was to be a waltz musical, Sondheim obliged himself to compose all the numbers in triple time, or use triplets to give the impression of triple time.

As for the story detail, Sondheim had long wanted to do a Priestley-like book which distorted time and space, and he originally hoped to plot the work with Mme Armfeldt at the centre shuffling various romantic relationships like a pack of playing cards. This concept, however, proved incompatible with the naturalistic skills of Hugh Wheeler, who was writing the script, so in fact *Night Music* resembles its source far more than its composer had originally imagined.

Sondheim's most gratifying quality as the leading talent in musical comedy is the freshness of his approach. His work is never routine. He never goes back on his tracks. His sense of the proper tone, both in music and words, is unfailing. Gradually, yet securely, he has extended himself in the direction of a musical theatre in which he, as lyricist/composer, controls more and more of the dramatic side, whether or not he collaborates on the book.

If, by any chance, Sondheim is now on the look-out for a new problem to solve, and if *Night Music* establishes him more securely with the British audience, it might present a rather different kind of challenge to turn his attentions to the possibility of creating a musical comedy specifically for that audience. Perhaps, even, he might be commissioned to provide what the English National Opera is unlikely to obtain from any other source – a popular, modern, new, musical theatre piece. It would not necessarily turn out as operetta. It almost certainly would not bear much resemblance to the new operas we have been accustomed to, or to any operas. But it would be a fascinating experiment of a kind London has not seen for a long time, and a challenge worth taking.

CHECKLIST OF STEPHEN SONDHEIM'S WORKS:

West Side Story (lyrics only)
New York 1957; London 1958; film 1961 directed by Robert Wise and Jerome Robbins
Music: Leonard Bernstein. Book: Arthur Laurents. Directed and choreographed by Jerome Robbins.

Gypsy (lyrics only)
New York 1959; London 1973; film 1962 directed by Mervyn LeRoy
Music: Jule Styne. Book: Arthur Laurents, based on Gypsy Rose Lee's autobiography. Directed by Jerome Robbins.

A Funny Thing Happened on the Way to the Forum
New York 1962; London 1963; film 1966 directed by Richard Lester
Book: Burt Shevelove and Larry Gelbart after plays by Plautus. Directed by George Abbott.

Anyone Can Whistle
New York 1964
Book: Arthur Laurents (original). Directed by Arthur Laurents.

Do I Hear a Waltz? (lyrics only)
New York 1965
Music: Richard Rodgers. Book: Arthur Laurents, based on his own play *Time of the Cuckoo*. Directed by John Dexter.

Evening Primrose
Television 1966
Book: James Goldman after John Collier's *Evening Primrose*.

Company
New York 1970; London 1972
Book: George Furth (original). Directed by Harold Prince.

Follies
New York 1971
Book: James Goldman (original). Directed by Harold Prince and Michael Bennett.

A Little Night Music
New York 1973
Book: Hugh Wheeler, based on Ingmar Bergman's *Smiles of a Summer's Night*. Directed by Harold Prince.

Candide
Supplementary lyrics for New York 1974 revised production.

The Frogs
New Haven, Conn. 1974
Book: Burt Shevelove, based on Aristophanes. Directed by Burt Shevelove

That Burning Question

The author and dramatist takes a nostalgic look at four of the theatrical celebrities he interviewed.

One needs when interviewing a celebrity the courage to speak with candour rather than to ingratiate oneself, for in that way a candid response is invited, which is all to the good. Or so I was taught, very many years ago, by one who successfully practised that technique, who might almost be said to have invented it.

When I started in journalism, my teacher was Hannen Swaffer, for whom I worked as a cub reporter on joining the staff of the *Sunday Times*, and very much in awe of him I was at the time. 'Do what Swaffer tells you,' I was advised by my editor, 'and you won't go far wrong': sound enough advice to an ambitious apprentice in Fleet Street who hadn't a clue to what it was all about.

At this date (1919) Swaffer was something of a power in theatrical circles. He had earlier worked on the staffs of Northcliffe's papers, and in 1913 invented Mr Gossip, a pioneer venture that soon became an established feature of English popular journalism. Later he became the drama critic of the *Daily Express*, and when I was associated with him contributed to the *Sunday Times* a column – Plays and Players – for the advantage of appearing in which, since it included only exclusive paragraphs (Swaffer rejected the ordinary publicity handouts), theatre managers and producers went down on their knees to him. I actually saw Albert de Courville, famous for his spectacular revues at the London Hippodrome, sink to this position before a pen-and-ink sketch of Swaffer. When

13A–F REPERTORY
ROUND-UP

13a (above) One of *The Speakers*, Crucible Theatre, Sheffield

13b (right) Bob Peck in *The Popes Wedding*, Northcott Theatre, Exeter

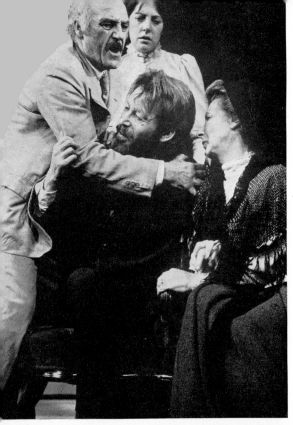

13c (left) Peter O'Toole with Norman Tyrrell, Penelope Wilton and Marie Keen in *Uncle Vanya*, Bristol Old Vic

13d (below) Paul Rogers and Gerald Harper in *Othello*, Bristol Old Vic

13e (above) Susan Penhaligon and Belinda Carroll in *Time and the Conways*, 69 Theatre Company, Manchester

13f (right) John Turner and Renee Asherson in *Long Day's Journey Into Night*, Thorndike Theatre, Leatherhead

14a (above) Robert Atkins
and his Open Air Company,
Regent's Park, 1950

14b (left) Robert Atkins
as Sir Toby Belch

15a (right) Broadway:
Carol Channing as *Lorelei*

17a (above left) Natalia Makarova and Rudolf Nureyev in *The Sleeping Beauty*, Royal Opera House, Covent Garden

17b (left) *Silver Apples of the Moon*, London Festival Ballet

18a (above right) Gathered round Stephen Sondheim, at the piano at the close of the 1973 gala, stars from his shows including Angela Lansbury, Glynis Johns and Hermione Gingold

18b (right) *A Little Night Music* (New York): the Night Waltz

19a (top left) Charles Laughton, 1928

19b (top right) W. Somerset Maugham, 1930

19c (bottom left) Dame Madge Kendall, 1924

19d (bottom right) Dame Ellen Terry, 1928

asked why, he replied: 'Because I'm damned afraid of the man!'

Swaffer had as many enemies as friends in the profession. Bitterly opposed by those who couldn't swallow his attacks, by others he was appreciated for at least having the courage of his convictions. Among the latter was Beerbohm Tree, even when himself publicly chastised, as he was on the occasion of his production of Shaw's *Pygmalion*. Swaffer ridiculed the sensation Tree expected to result from the use of the word 'bloody' on the stage. Tree thought that people generally would be deeply shocked, which would do his production no harm at the box office. But there appeared the following day on the front page of the paper Swaffer was then editing pictures of twenty famous people, among them dignitaries of the church, and all of them eminently respected citizens, whom Swaffer had observed on the first night roaring with laughter. At a costume ball at Covent Garden a few days later, a crowd gathered round to hear a heated discussion in progress between Tree (dressed as Hamlet) and Swaffer (dressed as Mr Gossip). 'Why,' asked Tree, 'did you have to spoil my sensation?' to which Swaffer replied that it was unnecessary to exploit the word 'bloody' for the sake of sensationalism. Tree reminded him that Shakespeare had said, 'Be bloody, bold, and resolute.' Swaffer's answer to that was, 'But he did not say "Be bloody bold and resolute." '

Swaffer's approach was always direct. I was with him in the office once when he glanced through some pages of copy handed him by a young girl reporter he had sent to interview an American film star who that morning had arrived on her first visit to London. Returning the girl's effort to her, he said – the cigarette he was never without twitching furiously between his lips – 'Really I don't know which of the two of you is the biggest silly cow! You ask her opinion of London. She says she loves it. What a question! What an answer! All she can have seen of London is the view from her bedroom window at Claridges.' The young girl made a tearful exit, and Swaffer thereupon lectured me on the art of the interview; the substance of which was briefly this: In order to discover what makes him tick (his phrase) you asked your interviewee at least one question calculated to arouse him – one way or the other. If you offended him he could but chuck you out. 'That's fine, you've got a story there.' (An actress he had offended – I think Frances

Doble, but certainly not Tallulah Bankhead, as has since been alleged – went up to Swaffer's table at the Savoy Grill one night and slapped his face. Here was a story after his own heart. His Christmas card that year was a photo of himself being slapped by an unknown's hand.)

Starstruck from an early age, I made a job of interviewing theatrical celebrities. It was left to me by the editors of *Good Housekeeping* and the *New York Herald-Tribune* to choose my victims, none of whom ever refused to see me; and in each case I set out determined to arouse them – in one way or another. In the event, four occasions on which I sought to follow in my master's footsteps made a lasting impression upon me.

That I would get a rise out of Dame Madge Kendal seemed a foregone conclusion. Though retired from the stage since 1908, she was still news twenty years later as the denouncer-in-chief of those evils, as she saw them, which held sway in the modern world. In her fearless and frequently expressed opinion things had come to 'a pretty pass'; and her impatience with the younger generation had reached a point at which she found forgiveness beyond her. In fact forgiveness wasn't much in her line. She preferred outright condemnation.

'I am always at home in the morning between eleven and twelve,' wrote Dame Madge in answer to my request for an interview 'Come any day this week': a surprisingly gracious invitation, I thought, from someone with such a formidable reputation. Nevertheless, I was kept waiting in the hall of 24 Portland Place quite a while before being ushered by a cap-and-aproned maid into the presence, and in the interim wondered what burning question I would finally dare to come up with.

From her seat at a desk littered with correspondence the old lady turned to observe, rather than greet, me. I could almost have believed myself face to face with Queen Victoria at a moment when she was not amused. She was short, plump, grey haired, and her head nodded very slightly, but continuously, as if she were in communication, and agreement, with someone whose voice she alone could hear. Incredible it was to think that this prim-looking woman had since her first appearance, in 1854 at the Marylebone Theatre as the child Marie in *The Struggle for Gold*, played, in addition to a wide range of Shakespeare's heroines, such dissimilar roles as Eva in *Uncle Tom's Cabin* and Paula in *The Second Mrs Tanqueray*; had in fact made stage history not only in England but also in America. That she had ever set foot on a stage seemed the height of improbability when one considered what the status of an actor was in her young days, not so far removed from that of rogues and vagabonds. As she remained silently looking me up and down, I got my little piece in first, said I didn't believe young people today were as undisciplined and heedless as I had read somewhere she considered them to be.

'You don't?' she said, 'then be good enough to tell me why young women nowadays cut their hair off. In the Bible it is written that a woman's glory is her hair. Then leave it that way. Fortunately I have servants who prepare my meals at home. But I strongly object if I do dine out at a restaurant to be waited upon by a young woman who in the first place has scarcely any hair, but combs in my presence what little she has.' She paused, her head shaking now with disapproval, and then wanted me to tell her why young women put on leather breeches and flew towards the moon.

To see if it's made of green cheese, I suppose. Old fashioned I may be, but I tell you, young man, there's nothing green about the moon. I've been watching it lately from the window of my cottage in the country. The moon hasn't changed, nothing has except man, who is always trying to be born again. He can't do it. He's born once – he dies once.

How to reply to this? Had I known it would have made no difference: I wasn't given a chance to speak. Her mention of death started Dame Madge off on another flood of eloquence: 'You young writers,' she exclaimed, 'have no business digging up the immoralities of great men. It is dreadful to think that while their bodies are being eaten by worms little people are digging into their lives instead of allowing them to rest in peace. Dickens was a great man – he reformed our workhouses; Queen Victoria was a great and moral woman – you should not make fun of her. Byron –' here she recited, quite beautifully, the poet's contempt for the littleness of man; then relapsed into thoughtful silence.

To probe her interest in the contemporary theatre I suggested that nowadays she kept in touch as a member of the audience. She gave me a look of stern disapproval. 'They tell me,' she said, 'to see a play called *Young Woodley*. Why should I? In that play, I

believe, a young schoolmaster's wife allows herself to be kissed by
one of her husband's boys. Very nice for her, I'm sure. But what an
example! Suppose she'd allowed herself to be kissed by all the boys'
– she smiled for the first, and last, time – 'Well, she'd have been a
busy woman!' She turned round to look up at a portrait of her
husband hanging on the wall (in a 1917 obituary Mr Kendal's
theatrical career was described as having been 'identical with his
wife's'). 'I lived with that man for forty years,' she said. 'I haven't
married again. To me it doesn't seem necessary to have more than
one husband.'

She returned to her criticism of the present-day woman, her
indignation with whom she now expressed with a vehemence that
hinted at what a forceful personality had once held the stage:

Why, why must they conduct this tirade against le bon Dieu by painting
their lips horrible shades, smearing blue stuff under their eyes, plucking
their eyebrows, reducing their figures, changing themselves from what
their maker intended them to be? People say sports are good for a
woman. Utter nonsense. I'd like the type of girl back again who fainted
when proposed to. Think of the fluttering of hearts that went on in those
days compared with the modern acceptance of a proposal – 'All right,
old bean!'

Deflated by this interview, I had a drink in the nearest pub, her
final oration ringing in my ears: 'You'll see, the pendulum will
swing back and women return to their rightful sphere – the home.'
Ringing in my ears, too, were the questions I had been too intimi-
dated to ask: 'How much time had a stage career left her to spend
in her "rightful sphere"? In all those years had make-up never
touched her face? And could she recall how long it had taken her
to revive after Mr Kendal had popped the question?' Oh, I had
fallen down badly on the job.

I cannot think why I avoided seeing, let alone interviewing,
Charles Laughton, until an afternoon in July 1929, when at the
Strand Theatre he played to such a pitifully small audience that
one had to feel sorry for him. At that time he had been on the stage
only four years, and was regarded by some critics as the great hope
of our theatre, and by others as the greatest exponent of overacting
then on view. Perhaps an early notice saying derisively that 'even
his toes act' kept me away; though another enthusiastically declared him capable of moving an audience 'with no more than the

lift of an eyebrow'. Anyway, he had me on his side soon after the curtain went up, and backstage a few days later. If he had over-acted in the play – it was titled *Beauty* – then I was all for over-acting, of that quality, and wished there was more of it to be seen.

From the first I sensed this to be an interview in which a straight question got a straight answer. I started off by supposing that even as a small boy Laughton had decided to become an actor, and was promptly told that no such idea had ever entered his head. His people weren't interested in the theatre, they ran a hotel, and when the time came for him to follow their example he left Scarborough to be trained at Claridges. But whatever spare time and cash he had went on gallery and pit seats, from which he got a tremendous thrill watching the actors do their stuff. I said there must have come a certain moment when it occurred to him that he too could act. It had done.

I saw Hilda Trevelyan in Barrie's *What Every Woman Knows*. At the end of the play she makes her husband laugh. It was a touch that moved the audience. It moved me, and at the same time I felt that I had the power to move an audience in just that way. I knew I could do it, and from that moment I wanted to become an actor.

Wanted, yes; but what action did you take to bring the thing about? Merely wanting can't have been enough. You were apprenticed to the catering trade.

I locked myself in my bedroom one day – and when I came out I had made up my mind to go on the stage. My people thought I was quite mad.

I put it to him that Hilda Trevelyan had, then, been the source of his inspiration, responsible for the great decision he reached while locked in his bedroom? But another, he said, had shared the responsibility, one in praise of whom his enthusiasm exceeded that of any press-agent, Gerald du Maurier. 'There's an actor for you!' he cried. 'Could any other have played the prince in *A Kiss for Cinderella* as he did? That man is our theatre, all we have to show people coming to this country from abroad. He's my idol.'

So far, so good. Laughton and I had got on splendidly together. Our parting, I felt, would be most amicable. But at the back of my mind was Swaffer's dictum, and I hesitated to risk asking him a question that, in all sincerity, I felt needed an answer: If the natural style of acting that du Maurier had brought to a fine art was his

ideal, why did he himself sometimes act with a flamboyance considered by certain critics to be 'hamming'? In the play I had seen
he was cast as a shy man unused to the sophisticated surroundings
he found himself in (a smart drawing room presided over by Isobel
Jeans at her most elegant). To say that he behaved awkwardly on
entering the room would be an understatement. He lost control of
his hands and feet, all but collided with the furniture, and when at
last seated became one big fidget. In fact he came perilously near to
clowning the part. As diplomatically as I could – not wanting to
be thrown out, however good a Swafferian story it might make – I
put the burning question which indirectly accused him of wildly
overplaying the scene.

Not in the least bit ruffled, Laughton said:

Nobody, of course, ever behaves as I do in that drawing room. But I
suspect that most of us, at some time, have felt as if they were behaving
in that way. I have done myself, and I study each part I play in relation
to myself, making the character behave as I feel I would in a similar
situation. It's the only way I can work.

How will he take it, I asked myself, if I tell him there were
moments in the play – which indeed there were – when his performance reminded me of Chaplin? He took it as a great compliment.
'Chaplin!' he cried, throwing up his hands. 'What an artist! How
wonderful he'd be in this play – playing my part.' And so ended an
interview that had been most revealing. In so many words I had
asked Laughton what made him tick – on the stage at least. And he
had told me. No hard feelings on either side.

Two interviews I had with Dame Ellen Terry were divided by
a long interval. The first was in a studio at Shepherds Bush where
she was making a film. Several of us had been invited by the film
company's press-agent 'to meet the celebrated actress on the set'.
I looked forward to asking her a particular question that I was
quite prepared for her not to answer, my conscience telling me I
had no right to ask it. It was a question the answer to which I
couldn't in any case have published, but for my own satisfaction
I wanted to confirm the truth, or otherwise, of an incident concerning her that had been told me by a close friend of hers.

A sadly frail figure clinging to her companion's arm as she
came, haltingly, down a narrow staircase from her dressing room,

was my first sight of Ellen Terry. At eleven o'clock in the morning she wore an evening dress of shimmering black sequins, and diamonds sparkled in her white hair. She paused at the foot of the staircase, and, looking vaguely about her, asked, 'What are we doing today?' Told by the director that the 'safe scene' was to be shot, she said, 'Oh, yes, I think I know the one,' and was helped to a chair on the set. Here the young actor playing her son in the film knelt at her feet in silent appeal (the talkies were yet to arrive) and presently she went with him to an imitation safe in a canvas wall, from which she took, with trembling hands, some important-looking papers.

A number of times the scene had to be repeated before the young, inexperienced actor could get it right. This was very tiring for Ellen Terry, worried by the fierce studio lights and overpowering heat. But she remained a model of patience, poor dear; and afterwards sat down absolutely exhausted. It was pathetic seeing her thus, working in a medium new to her, at the end of such a distinguished career. (Her last husband, James Carew, wrote to me shortly after her death: 'I tried to keep her from the films but she said it was sentimentality on my part. I likened her appearance on the screen so late in her life to the statue of Queen Victoria, who I have always understood to have been quite lovely in her youth, but is now to be handed down to posterity as a well fed washer-woman.')

When I found myself beside her, looking into eyes pleading for brevity on my part, I knew this wasn't the time, or the place, to ask the question I had in mind. Of the silly questions I did ask perhaps the silliest was whether she thought Shakespeare's plays should be filmed. This, after what she had just been through, was the last straw: 'Please, please don't speak to me of such a thing,' she said, covering her face with her hands. 'Why, it's unthinkable!'

I am now on my way to lunch in Queen, Elm Square with two elderly sisters – Ella and Neila Cassela – and not far from their house catch up with them returning from 'a little stroll for the good of our health'. Supported by them, one on either side, is an old lady who sometimes spends a weekend with them. Ellen Terry, wearing a flowing dress whose hem brushes the pavement, a wide-brimmed straw hat, and horn-rimmed spectacles, is carrying the largest handbag I have ever seen. But my offer to relieve her of its obvious weight is declined with a charming smile. 'I never let

anyone take it from me even for a minute,' she says, 'inside are all
my secrets.' She now looks quite a different person from the one I
saw in the studio; surprisingly alert for her age, very much on the
spot. Peering through her glasses she says, on a note of pride:
'From where I am' – and she's several feet away – 'I can read the
title of the book you're holding. What do you think of that?' She
then taps Arnold Bennett's novel with her gloved finger. 'And
what, may I ask, are you doing with a *Pretty Lady*?' The question,
for all its banality, sounds amusing on her lips; proving perhaps the
contention that if read by a really accomplished actor a telephone
directory would get the laughs.

For someone as starstruck as myself, that luncheon party was
a great occasion; its intimate nature affording me the opportunity
to assess at first hand, characteristics of the lady seated beside me.
Gazing at the carefully prepared dish placed in front of her, Ellen
Terry, referring to her hostesses, said to me in a stage-whisper that
would certainly have been heard by the galleryites at the old
Lyceum, 'It's like this every day, you know, something special
even when we're just on our own. A boiled egg, a sandwich – anything does for me. If they won't listen I shan't stay here in future,
putting them to all this trouble.' (She went out of her way always
not to be a nuisance to anyone; her sense of humour and entire lack
of affectation would have made her a welcome guest anywhere.)

Among the topics under discussion during the meal was the
furore lately caused by the modish best-seller, *The Green Hat*. 'I
met the author somewhere the other day,' Ellen Terry said, 'but
cannot recall his name . . . Oh yes, Michael Arlen. Well, to tell the
truth I'd never heard of him before, and I can't say I cared for his
book.' She wasn't, as some people were, shocked by it, but thought
the style it was written in made it rather difficult to read. Her not
objecting to it on moral grounds showed how tolerant she was for
her age, and this decided me, come what may, to get her in a corner
by herself and ask if a certain story had any foundation in fact.

It is a story I still recall whenever Ellen Terry's name is mentioned because the picture it conjures up is so deliciously amusing.
Married at seventeen to a man 24 years her senior, she soon discovered – as indeed he too must have done – what a mistake it was.
Incompatibility of temperament was rather to be expected of two
people with such a widely different outlook on life: a teenager

bubbling over with high spirits, and the sober-minded gentleman
that Mr G. F. Watts, the eminent artist, must have been in his
middle years. To other incidents which eventually caused their
marriage to come unstuck, the one alleged to have taken place that
so amused me may well have contributed. A young actress who had
worked in the theatre since she was seven cannot have got much
fun out of staying at home to play hostess to her husband's contemporaries. Very boring she must have found it, and one sympathizes
with the effort she made – or so the story went – to liven things up
a bit by bursting into the room to which Mr Watts and his cronies
had retired one evening after dinner. Their surprise may be imagined at the sight of Mrs Watts dancing round them, practically
in the nude, and throwing to each a posy snatched from the basket
on her arm!

In mentioning this possibly apocryphal story I had laid myself
open to a rebuke likely to haunt me for the rest of my days. But
from the, I thought rather mischievous, smile she gave me, I saw
that at least she wasn't offended. And her answer when it came
quite satisfied my curiosity. 'You know,' she said, 'at my age I
simply dare not trust my memory!'

Three courses are open to interviewees in their eighties: they
can answer your questions; say 'no comment'; or fall asleep.
Calling on Somerset Maugham in October 1958 (he was paying his
annual visit to London at the age of eighty-five) I wouldn't have
minded his dozing off before the interrogation was over, because
then he would not hear me obeying the editor of the *Evening
Standard*'s instruction to be sure to find out to whom the old boy
intended leaving his vast fortune – at that date a burning question
indeed. I had met Maugham on several occasions in the past, but
never in the role of a prying journalist. He was always charming to
me. But this was something else, and I doubted if his charm would
be proof against the assault upon his privacy that I was expected
to make.

We talked of this and that. He couldn't have been more con-
genial. To change this pleasant mood by asking a singularly imper-
tinent question seemed most uncalled for. I went so far, though, as
to ask what would eventually become of the Gauguins, Piccasos,
Renoirs and other pictures in his collection, hoping that if he said
he was leaving them to the National Gallery, or the Tate, I would

have an answer, of sorts, to take back to my editor. 'After my death the pictures will have to be sold,' he said simply. Which wasn't much help. An inclination to call it a day, however, conflicted with an inclination to justify my early training. After all, over the years I had never been sent packing as the result of practising the Swaffer method. And a question had occurred to me that if he were asked it might arouse Maugham's resentment sufficiently for him to order me out of the Dorchester; but at the same time, perhaps, reveal an interesting aspect of his character.

He had been a consistently successful author since the publication of his first novel. Self-discipline (three hours' writing each day, year in and year out, no matter where in the world he happened to be, or in what circumstances) had earned him an enormous fortune. He seemed never to have put a foot wrong, to have worked on a plan that eschewed any possibility of failure. But as a person he had the reputation of being an utter cynic, untouched by emotion, hard as a diamond. If I called attention to this scarcely flattering estimate of his character, would he indignantly refute it, or complacently admit to its truth?

I said: 'How gratifying it must be never to have made a mistake in your life'; to which he promptly replied: 'I have made many mistakes, but was always lucky enough to be able to convert them into copy for my stories.' I said: 'You are generally considered to be an entirely cynical person without a drop of sentiment in your make-up. Does that worry you at all?' A short pause, then: 'I flatter myself that I usually talk sense. Anyone who does that is likely to be regarded as a cynic.' I said: 'But has no book, no play, no experience in the whole of your long life ever moved you to tears?' A longer pause this time, then, a little shamefacedly: 'Whenever I hear *The Mastersingers*, and I've heard it many times, tears do come into my eyes. I don't want to cry, but I bloody well can't help it!' I hadn't done too badly. Coming from Maugham this was stop-press news.

Reference Section

The first checklist gives brief details of all commercial theatre productions in central London over a period of twelve months; it does not include lunchtime, Sunday night or club productions, nor does it take account of vaudeville seasons, ice shows or fringe ventures. Transfers are only noted when they were inter-London, and principal cast changes are in the footnotes. Separate checklists for the subsidized companies and certain seasonal theatres as well as for opera and ballet companies will be found on subsequent pages.

CHECKLISTS

London First Night Diary
Longest London Runs
The National Theatre
Royal Shakespeare Company
Chichester Festival Theatre
Opera
Ballet
Honours and Awards
Obituary

London First Night Diary

DATE	THEATRE	PLAY	AUTHOR
April 3	Cochrane	*The Owl & The Pussycat Went To Sea . . .*	David Wood
April 4	Young Vic	*Rosencrantz & Guildenstern Are Dead*	Tom Stoppard
April 12	Royal Court	*Savages*	Christopher Hampton
April 16	Theatre Upstairs	*Captain Oates' Left Sock*	John Antrobus
April 17	Duchess	*Collaborators*	John Mortimer
April 18	Mermaid	*Misalliance*	Bernard Shaw
April 26	Phoenix	*Two Gentlemen of Verona*	Shakespeare, adapt. John Guare & Mel Shapiro
May 10	Lyric	*Habeas Corpus*	Alan Bennett
May 15	Drury Lane	*No, No, Nanette*	Youmans, Harbach & Caesar
May 16	Comedy	*Dear Love*	Robert & Elizabeth Browning
May 22	Royal Court	*The Sea*	Edward Bond
May 29	Piccadilly	*Gypsy*	Laurents & Styne
May 31	Shaw	*The Me Nobody Knows*	Livingston & Schapiro
June 4	Open Air	*Twelfth Night*	William Shakespeare
June 11	Bankside Globe	*The Malcontent*	John Marston
June 19	Vaudeville	*Signs of the Times*	Jeremy Kingston
June 19	Theatre Upstairs	*Rocky Horror Show*	Richard O'Brien
June 20	Comedy (from Royal Court)	*Savages*	Christopher Hampton
June 25	Apollo	*The Banana Box*	Eric Chappell
June 25	Bankside Globe	*Twelfth Night*	William Shakespeare
June 26	New London	*Grease*	Jacobs & Casey
June 27	Fortune	*Who's Who*	Keith Waterhouse & Willis Hall
June 28	Royal Court	*Magnificence*	Howard Brenton
July 2	Mermaid	*Juno & The Paycock*	Sean O'Casey
July 3	Collegiate	*West Side Story*	Laurents, Bernstein
July 4	Criterion	*Absurd Person Singular*	Alan Ayckbourn
July 10	Westminster	*Glasstown*	Noel Robinson
July 12	Shaw	*Endgame*	Samuel Beckett

228

DIRECTOR	LEADING PLAYERS
Jan Colet	Janina Faye, Johnny Ball, Ben Aris
Bernard Goss	Nicky Henson, Andrew Robertson, Hugh Hastings
Robert Kidd Nicholas Wright	Paul Scofield, Rona Anderson, Tom Conti Nicholas Selby, Matthew Guinness, Janet Webb
Eric Thompson Alan Strachan Mel Shapiro	Glenda Jackson,[1] John Wood,[2] Joss Ackland[3] Bill Fraser, Caroline Blakiston, Jeremy Child Derek Griffiths, B. J. Arnau, Benny Lee
Ronald Eyre Burt Shevelove	Alec Guinness,[4] Margaret Courtenay, Patricia Hayes[5] Anna Neagle, Anne Rogers, Thora Hird
Peter Wood	Keith Michell, Geraldine McEwan
William Gaskill Arthur Laurents Michael Croft	Coral Browne, Ian Holm, Alan Webb Angela Lansbury,[6] Barrie Ingham, Zan Charisse[6a] Peter Straker, Pamela Obermeyer
Robert Lang Jonathan Miller Allan Davis Jim Sharman	Colin Jeavons, John Justin, Philippa Gail Derek Godfrey, Hazel Hughes, Michael Johnson Kenneth More, Liza Goddard, Dennis Ramsden Tim Curry, Richard O'Brien, Christopher Malcolm
Robert Kidd	Paul Scofield, Rona Anderson, Tom Conti
David Scase Gordon McDougall Tom Moore Robert Chetwyn	Leonard Rossiter, Paul Jones, Frances de la Tour Alfred Marks, Brian Pringle, Dudley Sutton Stacey Gregg, Richard Gere, Doug Fisher Francis Matthews, Joe Melia, Judy Cornwell
Max Stafford-Clark	Robert Eddison, Carole Hayman, Kenneth Cranham
Sean Kenny Bill Kenwright Eric Thompson Frith Banbury Braham Murray	Siobhan McKenna, Brendan Cauldwell, Eithne Dunne Peter Daly, Rosamund Shelley, Jim Smilie Sheila Hancock,[7] Richard Briers,[8] Michael Aldridge[8a] Ann Stallybrass, John Robinson, Robert Powell Wolfe Morris, Trevor Peacock, James Taylor

[1] Later replaced by Diane Cilento.
[2] Later replaced by Peter McEnery.
[3] Later replaced by John Thaw.
[4] Later replaced by Robert Hardy.
[5] Later replaced by Alan Bennett.
[6] Later replaced by Dolores Gray.
[6a] Later replaced by Jenny Lyons
[7] Later replaced by Fenella Fielding.
[8] Later replaced by Peter Blythe.
[8a] Later replaced by Paul Eddison.

229

DATE	THEATRE	PLAY	AUTHOR
July 16	Bankside Globe	*Macbett*	Eugene Ionesco
July 19	Royal Court	*The Removalists*	David Williamson
July 19	Open Air	*As You Like It*	William Shakespeare
July 24	Royalty	*The Water Babies*	Charles Kingsley
July 24	Queens	*The Card*	Waterhouse/Hall/Hatch/ Trent
July 27	Young Vic	*French Without Tears*	Terence Rattigan
July 30	Theatre Upstairs	*Sweet Talk*	Michael Abbensetts
Aug. 6	Bankside Globe	*Antony and Cleopatra*	William Shakespeare
Aug. 6	Roundhouse	*Decameron 73*	Griffiths & Sawyer
Aug. 15	Royal Court	*Cromwell*	David Storey
Aug. 16	Shaw	*Petticoat Rebellion*	D. Emyr Edwards
Aug. 27	Roundhouse	*Royal Hunt of the Sun*	Peter Shaffer
Aug. 29	Roundhouse	*Pericles*	William Shakespeare
Aug. 29	Mermaid	*An Inspector Calls*	J. B. Priestley
Aug. 30	Cambridge	*Two & Two Make Sex*	Richard Harris & Leslie Darbon
Sept. 4	Apollo	*Finishing Touches*	Jean Kerr
Sept. 5	Roundhouse	*Twelfth Night*	William Shakespeare
Sept. 6	Shaw	*Geordies March*	Peter Terson
Sept. 6	Westminster	*Relative Values*	Noël Coward
Sept. 18	Shaw	*Richard II*	William Shakespeare
Sept. 19	Albery	*The Constant Wife*	Somerset Maugham
Sept. 20	Theatre Upstairs	*Sizwe Bansi Is Dead*	Athol Fugard
Sept. 26	Royal Court	*The Farm*	David Storey
Sept. 27	Duchess	*In Praise Of Love*	Terence Rattigan
Sept. 28	Shaw	*The Bevellers*	Roddy McMillan
Oct. 3	Savoy	*At The End Of The Day*	William Douglas Home
Oct. 4	Victoria Palace	*Carry On London*	Talbot Rothwell
Oct. 9	Fortune (from Garrick)	*Sleuth*	Anthony Shaffer
Oct. 10	Adelphi	*The King & I*	Rodgers & Hammerstein
Oct. 17	Garrick	*Dandy Dick*	Arthur Pinero
Oct. 19	Young Vic	*Much Ado About Nothing*	William Shakespeare
Oct. 23	Apollo	*The Wolf*	Ferenc Molnar
Oct. 30	Her Majesty's	*Pippin*	Hirson & Schwartz
Nov. 1	Shaw	*Macbeth*	William Shakespeare
Nov. 1	Mayfair (from Royal Court)	*The Farm*	David Storey
Nov. 7	Royal Court	*The Merry Go Round*	D. H. Lawrence

DIRECTOR	LEADING PLAYERS
Charles Marowitz	Harry H. Corbett, Victor Spinetti, Terry Scott
Jim Sharman	Ed Devereaux, Mark McManus, Carole Mowlam
Richard Digby Day	Dilys Hamlett, Martin Potter, Colin Jeavons
Ross Taylor	Jessie Matthews, Richard Willis, Hope Jackman
Val May	Jim Dale, Marti Webb, Eleanor Bron[9]
Frank Dunlop	Gavin Reed, Denise Coffey, Hugh Hastings
Stephen Frears	Allister Bain, Mona Hammond
Tony Richardson	Vanessa Redgrave, Julian Glover, Dave King
Peter Coe	Mahatma, Tim Goodman, Miguel Brown
Anthony Page	Albert Finney, Brian Cox, Jarlath Conroy
Gareth Thomas	Teresa Joselyn, Nichola McAuliffe, Julia Swift
Toby Robertson & Eleanor Fazan	Rupert Frazer, Trevor Martin, Harold Innocent
Toby Robertson	Derek Jacobi, Ronnie Stevens, Marilyn Taylerson
Bernard Miles	Philip Stone, Campbell Singer, Elizabeth Tyrrell
Jan Butlin	Patrick Cargill, Diana King, Terence Alexander
Nigel Patrick	Wendy Craig, David Knight, Lionel Murton
Toby Robertson	Derek Jacobi, Marilyn Taylerson, Willoughby Goddard
Barrie Rutter	George Irving, Andy Tomlinson
Charles Hickman	Margaret Lockwood, Gwen Cherrell, Joyce Blair
Michael Croft	Francis Matthews, Alan Haliday, Shaun Austin-Olsen
John Gielgud	Ingrid Bergman, Dorothy Reynolds, John McCallum
Athol Fugard	John Kani, Winston Ntshona
Lindsay Anderson	Bernard Lee, Frank Grimes, Doreen Mantle
John Dexter	Joan Greenwood, Donald Sinden, Richard Warwick
Bill Bryden	Leonard Maguire, Roddy McMillan, Paul Young
Robert Chetwyn	John Mills, Dulcie Gray, Michael Denison
Peter Rogers	Sidney James, Kenneth Connor, Barbara Windsor
Clifford Williams	Raymond Westwell, Christopher Reich
Roger Redfarn	Sally Ann Howes,[10] Peter Wyngarde, David Morris
John Clements	Alastair Sim, Patricia Routledge
Frank Dunlop	Ian Trigger, Denise Coffey, Andrew Robertson
Frank Hauser	Judi Dench, Edward Woodward, Leo McKern
Bob Fosse	Paul Jones, Elisabeth Welch, John Turner
Peter James	Tom Baker, Sheila Allen, Barrie Rutter
Lindsay Anderson	Bernard Lee, Frank Grimes, Doreen Mantle
Peter Gill	Mary Miller, Anne Dyson, Olive Maguire

[9] Later replaced by Dinah Sheridan.   [10] Later replaced by Patricia Michael.

231

DATE	THEATRE	PLAY	AUTHOR
Nov. 8	Young Vic	*The Caretaker*	Harold Pinter
Nov. 20	Queens	*Gomes*	David Swift & Sidney Sheldon
Nov. 21	Phoenix	*Design For Living*	Noël Coward
Nov. 22	Roundhouse	*The Trial*	Kafka
Dec. 3	Queens (from Apollo)	*The Wolf*	Ferenc Molnar
Dec. 6	Westminster	*Give A Dog A Bone*	Peter Howard
Dec. 12	Vaudeville	*Cockie*	Porter, Coward, Kern, etc.
Dec. 12	Mayfair	*The Ride Across Lake Constance*	Peter Handke
Dec. 12	Shaw	*Larry The Lamb*	David Wood & Sheila Ruskin
Dec. 13	Apollo	*Why Not Stay For Breakfast?*	Gene Stone & Ray Cooney
Dec. 17	Mermaid	*Musical Adventures of Treasure Island*	Ornadel/Shaper
Dec. 18	Shaw	*Knots*	R. D. Laing/Edward Petherbridge
Dec. 18	Cochrane	*Toad of Toad Hall*	A. A. Milne
Dec. 19	Palladium	*Jack & The Beanstalk*	Phil Park
Dec. 19	Prince of Wales	*Danny La Rue Show*	Bryan Blackburn
Dec. 19	Coliseum	*Peter Pan*	J. M. Barrie
Dec. 24	Roundhouse	*Feast of Fools*	Paddy Fletcher & Peter Oliver
Dec. 26	Cambridge	*Pinocchio*	Angela Caldan
Dec. 29	Royal Court	*The Island*	Athol Fugard
Jan. 3	Comedy	*Judies*	David Fitzsimmons
Jan. 8	Royal Court	*Sizwe Bansi Is Dead*	Athol Fugard
Jan. 15	Mayfair	*Brief Lives*	John Aubrey
Jan. 22	Royal Court	*Statements After An Arrest*	Athol Fugard
Jan. 24	St Martin's	*Dead Easy*	Jack Popplewell
Jan. 29	Roundhouse	*Le Grand Magic Circus*	Jerome Savary
Jan. 30	Shaw	*Mind Your Head*	Adrian Mitchell
Feb. 6	Globe	*Chez Nous*	Peter Nichols
Feb. 11	Mermaid	*Something's Burning*	Ronald Eyre
Feb. 14	Haymarket	*Waltz Of The Toreadors*	Jean Anouilh
Feb. 18	St Martin's	*The Collector*	John Fowles
Feb. 20	Her Majesty's	*Henry IV*	Pirandello
Feb. 26	Drury Lane	*Monty Python's First Farewell Tour*	Cleese, Chapman, Palin, etc.
Mar. 4	Comedy	*Knuckle*	David Hare

DIRECTOR	LEADING PLAYERS
Philip Grout	Ian Trigger, Jeremy Irons, Paul Brooke
Peter Coe	Roy Dotrice, Rachel Kempson, Aubrey Woods
Michael Blakemore	Vanessa Redgrave, Jeremy Brett, John Stride
Steven Berkoff	Bill Stewart, Barry Stanton
Frank Hauser	Judi Dench, Edward Woodward, Leo McKern
Henry Cass & Bridget Espinosa	Gordon Reid, Donald Scott, Richard Warner
William Chappell	Avril Angers, Max Wall, Liz Charles
Michael Rudman	Alan Howard, Nicola Pagett, Faith Brook
David Wood	Melody Kaye, Geoffrey Lumsden, Norman Warwick
'Ray Cooney	Derek Nimmo, Katy Manning, Sam Sewell
Josephine Wilson	Spike Milligan, Bernard Miles, John Watts
Edward Petherbridge	Members of the Actors' Company
Peter Watson	Richard Goolden, James Cairncross, Ian Talbot
Albert J. Knight	Frankie Howerd, Dora Bryan, Alfie Bass
Freddie Carpenter	Danny La Rue, Clovissa Newcombe, Mike Goddard
Robert Helpmann	Maggie Smith, Dave Allen, Clifford Mollison
Jim Hiley	Incubus, The Hoofers, Banana Band
Richard Dale	Fiona Fullerton, Roy Callaghan, Joshua Le Touzel
Athol Fugard	John Kani, Winston Ntshona
Jonathan Hales	Pauline Collins, John Alderton, Paul Angelis
Athol Fugard	John Kani, Athol Fugard, Winston Ntshona
Patrick Garland	Roy Dotrice
Athol Fugard	Ben Kingsley, Yvonne Bryceland
John Downing	Irene Handl, Patrick Barr, Aimi Macdonald
Jerome Savary	Savary and Company
Adrian Mitchell	Nicky Henson, Barrie Rutter
Robert Chetwyn	Albert Finney, Geraldine McEwan, Denholm Elliott
Ronald Eyre & Evan Smith	Bill Fraser, Penelope Wilton, Peter Copley
Peter Dews	Trevor Howard, Coral Browne
William Redmond	Marianne Faithfull, Simon Williams
Clifford Williams	Rex Harrison, Yvonne Mitchell, James Villiers
Ian MacNaughtan, etc.	Cleese, Palin, Jones, etc.
Michael Blakemore	Edward Fox, Shelagh Fraser, Douglas Willmer

DATE	THEATRE	PLAY	AUTHOR
Mar. 7	Westminster	*Oh! Kay!*	Gershwin/Bolton/Wodehouse
Mar. 8	Shaw	*The Importance of Being Earnest*	Oscar Wilde
Mar. 11	Royal Court	*Runaway*	Peter Ransley
Mar. 13	Vaudeville	*Snap!*	Charles Laurence
Mar. 14	Piccadilly	*A Streetcar Named Desire*	Tennessee Williams
Mar. 22	Young Vic	*Roots*	Arnold Wesker
Mar. 25	Royalty	*Royalty Folies*	John Taylor, etc.

DIRECTOR	LEADING PLAYERS
William Chappell	Amanda Barrie, Robin Hunter, Thick Wilson
Peter James	Betty Marsden, Louise Purnell, Richard Kay
Alfred Lynch	Bill Owen, Cherry Morris, Susan Tracy
William Gaskill	Maggie Smith, Barrie Ingham, Elspeth March
Edwin Sherin	Claire Bloom, Joss Ackland, Martin Shaw
Bernard Goss	Tamara Ustinov, Celia Hewitt, Neil Curran
Ross Taylor	Luxor Gali-Gali, Clark Bros., etc.

The ten London productions with longest runs as at May 1st 1974 were:

The Mousetrap	8909
Pyjama Tops	1891
Sleuth	1750
Oh! Calcutta!	1531
No Sex Please – We're British	1224
Godspell	1020
The Man Most Likely To	955
Jesus Christ Superstar	719
Habeas Corpus	417
Absurd Person Singular	340

The National Theatre 1973–74

Old Vic
Directors: Sir Laurence Olivier (73 only), Peter Hall

EQUUS
Peter Shaffer
Prod: John Dexter

THE MISANTHROPE
Molière/Ad. Harrison
Prod: John Dexter

THE FRONT PAGE
Hecht & MacArthur
Prod: Michael Blakemore

THE BACCHAE
Euripides/Ad. Soyinka
Prod: Roland Joffe

SATURDAY, SUNDAY, MONDAY
Eduardo de Filippo/
   Ad. Waterhouse & Hall
Prod: Franco Zeffirelli

MEASURE FOR MEASURE
Shakespeare
Prod: Jonathan Miller

EDEN END
J. B. Priestley
Prod: Laurence Olivier

SPRING AWAKENING
Wedekind/Ad. Bond
Prod: Bill Bryden

THE CHERRY ORCHARD
Chekhov/Ad. Hingley
Prod: Michael Blakemore

MACBETH
Shakespeare
Prod: Michael Blakemore

JUMPERS
Tom Stoppard
Prod: Peter Wood

LONG DAY'S JOURNEY INTO NIGHT
O'Neill
Prod: Michael Blakemore

THE PARTY
Trevor Griffiths
Prod: John Dexter

THE TEMPEST
Shakespeare
Prod: Peter Hall

NEXT OF KIN
John Hopkins
Prod: Harold Pinter

The Company included: Jenny Agutter, Sarah Atkinson, Gillian Barge, Dai Bradley, Anna Carteret, Nicholas Clay, Julie Covington, Paul Curran, Cyril Cusack, Rachel Davies, Gabrielle Daye, Carol Drinkwater, Michael Feast, Frank Finlay, David Firth, Peter Firth, Rupert Frazer, John Gielgud, Dana Gillespie, Gawn Grainger, Paul Gregory, Mary Griffiths, Christopher Guard, David Healy, Ram John Holder, Michael Hordern, Michael Jayston, Gemma Jones, Viola Keats, David Kincaid, Michael Kitchen, James Laurenson, Harry Lomax, Patti Love, Arthur Lowe, Kenneth Mackintosh, Alan MacNaughton, Alec McCowen, Desmond McNamara, David Markham, Alex McCrindle, Joseph O'Conor, Laurence Olivier, Julian Orchard, Geoffrey Palmer, Judith Paris, Antonia Pemberton, Ronald Pickup, Jennifer Piercey, Joan Plowright, Louise Purnell, Denis Quilley, Veronica Quilligan, Louie Ramsay, Beryl Reid, Malcolm Reid, Diana Rigg, Maggie Riley, Peter Rocca, David Ryall, Leslie Sands, Martin Shaw, John Shrapnel, Keith Skinner, William Squire, Daniel Thorndike, Jennifer Tudor, Harry Waters, Jeanne Watts, Benjamin Whitrow, Stephen Williams.

Royal Shakespeare Company 1973–74

Director: Trevor Nunn

Stratford 1974:

KING JOHN   RICHARD II   CYMBELINE

Production team for the three plays:
Director: John Barton
with Barry Kyle (KING JOHN and CYMBELINE)
and Clifford Williams (CYMBELINE)
Designer: John Napier
with Martyn Bainbridge & Ann Curtis

The Company included: Sheila Allen, Robert Ashby, Hilda Braid, Janet Chappell, Tony Church, Jeffery Dench, Michael Ensign, Susan Fleetwood, Jean Gilpin, Denis Holmes, Emrys James, Louise Jameson, Charles Keating, Clement McCallin, Richard Mayes, Richard Pasco, Ian Richardson, Sebastian Shaw, Leon Tanner, Albert Welling, Janet Whiteside.

Aldwych 1973–74:

THE ROMANS
(CORIOLANUS, JULIUS CAESAR, ANTONY AND CLEOPATRA, TITUS ANDRONICUS)

Production team for the four plays:
Director: Trevor Nunn
assisted by Euan Smith
Designer: Christopher Morley
with Ann Curtis

LANDSCAPE & A SLIGHT ACHE
Harold Pinter
Prod: Peter James & Peter Hall

DUCK SONG
David Mercer
Prod: David Jones

SHERLOCK HOLMES
Conan Doyle/Ad. Gillette
Prod: Frank Dunlop

SECTION NINE
Philip Magdalany
Prod: Charles Marowitz

The Company included: Darren Angadi, Peggy Ashcroft, Colin Blakely, Joseph Charles, Brian Croucher, Mark Dignam, Michael Egan, Edwina Ford, Paul Gaymon, Peter Geddis, Judy Geeson, Patrick Godfrey, Carole Hayman, Alan Howard, Gareth Hunt, Geoffrey Hutchings, Richard Johnson, Malcolm Kaye, Jonathan Kent, Dilys Laye, Barbara Leigh-Hunt, Sidney Livingstone, Philip Locke, Rosemary McHale, Joe Melia, Robert Oates, Trevor Peacock, Tim Pigott-Smith, Corin Redgrave,

Norman Rossington, Mary Rutherford, Peter Schofield, Nicholas Selby, Mark Sheridan, Elizabeth Spriggs, Barry Stanton, Patrick Stewart, Janet Suzman, Keith Taylor, Harry Towb, Margaret Tyzack, David Waller, Margaret Whiting, Nicol Williamson, John Wood.

The Place 1973:

SECTION NINE
Philip Magdalany
Prod: Charles Marowitz

A LESSON IN BLOOD AND ROSES
John Wiles
Prod: Clifford Williams

CRIES FROM CASEMENT
David Rudkin
Prod: Terry Hands

SYLVIA PLATH
Prod: Barry Kyle

HELLO AND GOODBYE
Athol Fugard
Prod: Peter Stevenson

The Company included: Darren Angadi, Colin Blakely, Phil Brown, Brenda Bruce, Loftus Burton, Judy Geeson, Patrick Godfrey, Gareth Hunt, Geoffrey Hutchings, Louise Jameson, Malcolm Kaye, Jonathan Kent, Ben Kingsley, Estelle Kohler, Rosemary McHale, Stephen Moore, Gerard Murphy, Peter Schofield, Nicholas Selby, Morgan Sheppard, Janet Suzman, Garry Towb, David Waller, Margaret Whiting, John Wood.

Chichester Festival Theatre

Director: Keith Michell

1974

TONIGHT WE IMPROVISE
Luigi Pirandello
Prod: Peter Coe

THE CONFEDERACY
John Vanbrugh
Prod: Wendy Toye

OIDIPUS TYRANNUS
Sophocles/Ad. Rademacher
Prod: Hovhanness Pilikian

A MONTH IN THE COUNTRY
Turgenev/Ad. Nicolaeff
Prod: Toby Robertson

The Company included: Rosalind Atkinson, Kay Barlow, Keith Baxter, Dora Bryan, Patsy Byrne, Nicholas Clay, Patience Collier, Gemma Craven, Diana Dors, Peter Gilmore, Richard Greene, Noel Howlett, Derek Jacobi, Miriam Karlin, David King, Howard Lang, Alfred Marks, Keith Michell, Frank Middlemass, Peggy Mount, June Ritchie, Annie Ross, Jeannette Sterke, Tony Sympson, John Turner, Dorothy Tutin, Richard Wattis, Timothy West.

Opera 1973–74

Royal Opera House, Covent Garden:
DON GIOVANNI: Mozart/Colin Davis/John Copley
ARABELLA: R. Strauss/Silvio Varviso
OWEN WINGRAVE: Britten/Steuart Bedford
FIDELIO: Beethoven/Josef Krips/Davis
IL BARBIERE DI SIVIGLIA: Rossini/Aldo Ceccato
WOZZECK: Berg/John Matheson
CARMEN: Bizet/Solti/Michael Geliot
TANNHÄUSER: Wagner/Colin Davis/Nicholas Braithwaite/Vaclav Kašlík
TURANDOT: Puccini/Gaetano Delogu
DEATH IN VENICE: Britten/Bedford/Colin Graham
TOSCA: Puccini/Leif Segerstam
SIMON BOCCANEGRA: Verdi/John Matheson
ELEKTRA: Strauss/Rudolf Kempe
IPHIGÉNIE EN TAURIDE: Gluck/John Eliot Gardiner
LA FORZA DEL DESTINO: Verdi/Giuseppe Patané
A MIDSUMMER NIGHT'S DREAM: Britten/Charles Mackerras
AÏDA: Verdi/David Atherton
DON PASQUALE: Donizetti/John Pritchard
LA BOHÈME: Puccini/Silvio Varviso/Robin Stapleton/Copley
RIGOLETTO: Verdi/Edward Downes
BORIS GODUNOV: Mussorgsky/Downes/David Lloyd-Jones
LA TRAVIATA: Verdi/Pritchard
SALOME: R. Strauss/Christoph von Dohnányi
LA CLEMENZA DI TITO: Mozart/Davis, David Shaw/Anthony Besch

Sadler's Wells Opera, Coliseum:
THE RHINEGOLD: Wagner/Goodall/Koltai
LA TRAVIATA: Verdi/Nicholas Braithwaite/Mackerras/Copley
COSÌ FAN TUTTE: Mozart/Bryan Balkwill
THE MERRY WIDOW: Lehár/David Lloyd-Jones/Wilks/Clive Timms
SIEGFRIED: Wagner/Goodall/Koltai
IOLANTHE: Tchaikovsky/Mackerras, Hazel Vivienne
TWILIGHT OF THE GODS: Wagner/Goodall/Koltai
KATYA KABANOVA: Janáček/Mackerras/John Blatchley
IL TROVATORE: Verdi/Roderick Bryden
MINES OF SULPHUR: Richard Rodney Bennett/David Lloyd-Jones
LA BOHÈME: Puccini/Bryden
THE BARBER OF SEVILLE: Rossini/John Wilks
THE DEVILS OF LOUDUN: Penderecki/Braithwaite/John Dexter
THE CORONATION OF POPPEA: Monteverdi/Vivienne
A MASKED BALL: Verdi/Braithwaite
DIE FLEDERMAUS: J. Strauss/Balkwill/Mackerras
MARY STUART: Donizetti/Mackerras/Copley
THE VALKYRIE: Wagner/Goodall/Koltai

ORPHEUS IN THE UNDERWORLD: Offenbach/Noel Davies
MANON: Massenet/Mackerras/Graham
WAR AND PEACE: Prokofiev/Lloyd-Jones
CARMEN: Bizet/Alexander Gibson/Noel Davies
MADAM BUTTERFLY: Puccini/Lloyd-Jones/Colin Graham
THE STORY OF VASCO: Gordon Crosse/Charles Groves/Michael Elliot

Glyndebourne Festival:
DIE ZAUBERFLÖTE: Mozart/Haitink/Pritchard/John Cox
THE VISIT OF THE OLD LADY: Von Einem/John Pritchard/Cox
IL RITORNO D'ULISSE IN PATRIA: Monteverdi/Raymond Leppard
LE NOZZE DI FIGARO: Mozart/Pritchard/Peter Hall
CAPRICCIO: R. Strauss/Pritchard/Cox

Welsh National Opera:
DON CARLOS: Verdi/Richard Armstrong/Geliot
TURANDOT: Puccini/Armstrong
MADAM BUTTERFLY: Puccini/James Lockhart/Malcolm Fraser
BILLY BUDD: Britten/Armstrong
THE MAGIC FLUTE: Mozart/Georg Fischer/Armstrong
IDOMENEO: Mozart/Armstrong/Geliot
DIE FLEDERMAUS: J. Strauss/Alan Suttie
THE BEACH OF FALESÁ: Hoddinott/Armstrong/Geliot
LA BOHÈME: Puccini/Armstrong/Fraser

Scottish Opera Company:
TRISTAN UND ISOLDE: Wagner/Alexander Gibson/Michael Geliot
PELLÉAS ET MÉLISANDE: Debussy/Gibson
MADAMA BUTTERFLY: Puccini/David Frame
THE MERRY WIDOW: Lehár/Frame/Gibson
LA TRAVIATA: Verdi/James Loughran
THE MAGIC FLUTE: Mozart/Christopher Seaman
THE CATILINE CONSPIRACY: Iain Hamilton/Gibson/Anthony Besch
FIDELIO: Beethoven/Alexander Gibson
BORIS GODUNOV: Mussorgsky/Gary Bertini

New Opera Company:
THE NOSE: Shostakovich/Leon Lovett/Anthony Besch
TIME OFF? NOT A CHOST OF A CHANCE!: Lutyens/Lovett
INFEDELIO: Lutyens/Lovett
ARDEN MUST DIE: Goehr/Meredith Davies/Jonathan Miller

London Opera Centre:
LA PÉRICHOLE: Offenbach/James Robertson
L'ORMINDO: Cavalli/Raymond Leppard
LOUISE: Charpentier/Robertson/Malcolm Fraser

English Opera Group:
IDOMENEO: Mozart/Steuart Bedford
THE TURN OF THE SCREW: Britten/Montgomery/Colin Graham
IOLANTHE: Tchaikovsky/Steuart Bedford/Colin Graham
TRIAL BY JURY: Sullivan/Bedford/Graham

Ballet 1973–74

The Royal Ballet (large company)

New Productions:
SLEEPING BEAUTY (Kenneth MacMillan/Tchaikovsky/Peter Farmer)
IN THE NIGHT (Jerome Robbins/Chopin/Anthony Dowell)
THE SEVEN DEADLY SINS /Kenneth Macmillan/Kurt Weill/Ian
Spurling)
PIANO CONCERTO NO. 2 (Balanchine/Tchaikovsky/Terence Emery)
MANON (MacMillan/Massenet/Nicholas Georgiadis)
Also in repertory during the year:
THE FIREBIRD (Fokine/Stravinsky), GROSSE FUGE (Hans van Manen/
Beethoven), DANCES AT A GATHERING (Robbins/Chopin), ANASTASIA
(MacMillan/Tchaikovsky, Martinů), THE DREAM (Ashton/Mendelssohn),
AFTERNOON OF A FAUN (Robbins/Debussy), RAYMONDA Act 3
(Nureyev/Glazunov), PAVANE (MacMillan/Fauré), ENIGMA VARIATIONS
(Ashton/Elgar), TRIAD (MacMillan/Prokofiev), DAPHNIS AND CHLOE
(Ashton/Ravel), LA BAYADÈRE (Petipa prod. Nureyev/Minkus),
ROMEO AND JULIET (MacMillan/Tchaikovsky), THE WALK TO THE
PARADISE GARDENS (Ashton/Delius), THAÏS (Ashton/Massenet),
SIDESHOW (MacMillan/Stravinsky), SCÈNES DE BALLET (Ashton/
Stravinsky), MARGUERITE AND ARMAND (Ashton/Liszt), SYMPHONIC
VARIATIONS (Ashton/Franck), GISELLE (Petipa, Wright/Adam), AGON
(Balanchine/Stravinsky), LA FILLE MAL GARDÉE (Ashton/Hérold arr.
Lanchberry), SWAN LAKE (Petipa, Ivanov/Tchaikovsky), SERENADE
(Balanchine/Tchaikovsky), SONG OF THE EARTH (Macmillan/Mahler),
THE NUTCRACKER (Nureyev/Tchaikovsky), CONCERTO (MacMillan/
Shostakovich), THE RITE OF SPRING (MacMillan/Stravinsky), LES
NOCES (Nijinska/Stravinsky), REQUIEM CANTICLES (Robbins/Stravinsky)

The Royal Ballet (new group)

New productions:
SACRED CIRCLES (David Drew/Shostakovich/Terence Emery)
TWILIGHT (Hans van Manen/John Cage/Jean-Paul Vroom)
TILT (Van Manen/Stravinsky/Jean-Paul Vroom)
CARD GAME (John Cranko/Stravinsky/Dorothee Zippel)
THE SWORD OF ALSACE (Drew/Joachim Raff/Terence Emery)
SEPTET EXTRA (Van Manen/Saint-Saëns/Vroom)
Also in repertory during the year:
FLOWER FESTIVAL AT GENZANO (Bournonville/Helsted), PINEAPPLE
POLL (Cranko/Sullivan arr. Mackerras), LES PATINEURS (Ashton/
Meyerbeer arr. Lambert), THE LADY AND THE FOOL (Cranko/Verdi arr.
Mackerras), TRIAD (MacMillan/Prokofiev), SCÈNE D'AMOUR (Ashton/
Glazunov), GROSSE FUGE (Van Manen/Beethoven), IN A SUMMER
GARDEN (Ronald Hynd/Delius), ROMEO AND JULIET (MacMillan/
Prokofiev), THE RAKE'S PROGRESS (De Valois/Stravinsky), THE

MAIDS (Ross/Milhaud), THE POLTROON (MacMillan/Rudolf Maros), SOLITAIRE (MacMillan/Arnold), LES SYLPHIDES (Fokine/Chopin), FAÇADE (Ashton/Walton), LA FÊTE ÉTRANGE (Andrée Howard/ Fauré/Ronald Crichton), LAS HERMANAS (MacMillan/Martin), THE GRAND TOUR (Joe Layton/Noël Coward)

Ballet Rambert

New productions:
THERE WAS A TIME (Christopher Bruce/Brian Hodgson/Nadine Baylis)
INTERIMS 1 & 2 (Nanette Hassau/Anna Lockwood)
INTERIM 3 (Hassau/Scott Joplin)
CANTATE (Graham Jones/Michael Gibbs)
LES SALTIMBANQUES (Joseph Scoglio/Edward Cowie/Picasso)
YESTERDAY AND YESTERDAY (Julia Blaikie/Richard Crosby)
MAGIC THEATRE – NOT FOR EVERYONE (Leigh Warren/Nicola LeFanu)
THE EMPTY SUIT (Louis Falco/Salzedo)
BLIND SIGHT (Bruce/Bob Downes)
PIERROT LUNAIRE (Norman Morrice/Schoenberg)
LISTEN TO THE MUSIC (Falco/Anthony Hymas)
TUTTI-FRUTTI (Falco/Burt Alcantara/William Katz)
DUETS (Bruce/Brian Hodgson/Baylis)
ISOLDE (Morrice/John Lewis/Baylis)
Also in repertory during the year:
THE WHOLE IS MADE UP OF SINGLE UNITS (Mary Prestidge/John Metcalf), 4 PIECES FOR 6 DANCERS (Pietje Law/various), PATTERN FOR AN ESCALATOR (Chesworth/Jonathan Harvey & George Newson), SOLO (Morrice/Downes), CONSIDERING THE LILIES (Lar Lubovitch/Bach), STOP-OVER (Scoglio/Takemitsu), LADIES LADIES! (Norman Morrice/ Anthony Hymas), FOR THESE WHO DIE AS CATTLE (Bruce/no music), TIC-TACK (Chesworth/Kreisler), ZIGGURAT (Tetley/Stockhausen), OPUS '65 (Sololow/Macero), AD HOC (Chesworth/various), THAT IS THE SHOW (Morrice/Berio), RAG DANCES (Tetley/Hymas), 'TIS GOODLY SPORT (J. Taylor/16th century court music), RICERCARE (Tetley/ Seter), WINGS (Bruce/Downes)

Festival Ballet

New productions:
CINDERELLA (Ben Stevenson/Prokofiev/Peter Farmer)
THREE CORNERED HAT (Massine/Manuel de Falla/Heikki)
CONSERVATOIRE (Bournonville/prod. Mona Vangsaa/Paulli/Michael Stennett)
TCHAIKOVSKY PAS DE DEUX (Balanchine/Tchaikovsky)
IN NOMINE (Barry Moreland/Peter Maxwell Davies/Nadine Baylis)

LA SOURCE (Balanchine/Delibes)
DARK VOYAGE (Moreland/Satie)
WEBERN OP. 5 (Béjart/Webern)
GAÎTÉ PARISIENNE (Massine/Offenbach)
ECHOING OF TRUMPETS (Anthony Tudor/Martinů/Birger Bergling)
THREE PRELUDES (Stevenson/Rachmaninov)
SILVER APPLES OF THE MOON (Timothy Spain/Morton Sabotnick/
Derek Jarman)
PARADE (Massine/Diaghilev, Satie/Picasso)
Also in repertory during the year:
PETRUSHKA (Fokine/Stravinsky), LE BEAU DANUBE (Massine/Strauss),
SUMMER SOLSTICE (Moreland/John Field), ROMEO AND JULIET (Ashton/
Prokofiev), LA PÉRI (Peter Darrell/Dukas/John Fraser), NOIR ET
BLANC (Lifar/Lalo), MOZARTIANA (Ronald Hynd/Tchaikovsky/Peter
Docherty), MENDELSSOHN SYMPHONY (Denis Nahat/Mendelssohn),
SWAN LAKE (Petipa/Ivanov prod. Beryl Grey/Tchaikovsky), GISELLE
(Petipa prod. Mary Skeaping/Adam), THE SLEEPING BEAUTY (Petipa
prod. Stevenson/Tchaikovsky), COPPÉLIA (J. Carter/Delibes), DVOŘÁK
VARIATIONS (Hynd/Dvořák), THE NUTCRACKER (J. Carter/Tchaikovsky)

London Contemporary Dance Theatre

New productions:
WISEACRE (Flora Cushman/various)
MOONSTONE NIGHT (Tammy McLorg/Pink Floyd)
MASS (Robert Cohan/Vladimir Rodzianko)
MAD RIVER (Remy Charlip/Massenet/Bill Gibb)
STEPS OF SILENCE (Anna Sokolow/Anatol Vieru/John Read)
DRESSED TO KILL (Robert North/Denis Smith, Harry Miller/Peter
Farmer)
PILOT (Siobhan Davies/Iggy Welthy)
LAY-OUT (Richard Alston/Anna Lockwood)
Also in repertory during the year:
RAGA SHANKARA (Cushman/Alford & Sathe), SCALENE SEQUENCE
(Cushman/Berio), CANTABILE (Lapzeson Finnissy), HUNTER OF ANGELS
(Cohan/Maderna), TIGER BALM (Alston/Lockwood), DANCE ENERGIES
(May O'Donnell/Ray Green), PEOPLE (Cohan/Downes), GAMMA
GARDEN (Cushman/Shusha & Ignatius Temba), RELAY (Siobhan
Davies/Colin Wood & Bernard Watson), ECLIPSE (Cohan/Lester),
STAGES (Cohan/Downes), COLD (Alston/Adolphe Adam), BLUE
SCHUBERT FRAGMENTS (Alston/Schubert)

Scottish Theatre Ballet

New productions:
LE CARNAVAL (Fokine/Schumann/Bakst)

GISELLE (Peter Darrell/Adam/Cazalet)
THE NUTCRACKER (Darrell/Tchaikovsky)
WAYS OF SAYING BYE-BYE (Poptie/Purcell)
EMBERS OF GLENCOE (Walter Gore/Tom Wilson/George Devlin)
LA SYLPHIDE (August Bournonville/Herman von Lövenskjold/
Adolphe Nourrit)
Also in repertory during the year:
THREE DANCES TO JAPANESE MUSIC (Jack Carter/Kisahisa Katada/
Norman McDowell), FLOWER FESTIVAL AT GENZANO (Bournonville/
Helsted), SONATE Á TROIS (Béjart/Bartók), SOIRÉE MUSICALE (Tudor/
Rossini/Hugh Stevenson), SCORPIUS (Darrell/Thea Musgrave)

Northern Dance Theatre

New productions:
BRANDENBURG THREE (Charles Czarny/Bach/Stockvis)
FLOWER FESTIVAL AT GENZANO DIVERTISSEMENT (Bournonville/
Helsted/Piers Beaumont)
PART EXCHANGE (Jonathan Thorpe/no music)
IN CONCERT (Simon Mottram/Shostakovich)
LE CARNAVAL (Fokine/Schumann/Vijay Batra)
THE GREEN TABLE (Jooss/Simon Mottram)
THE TEACHINGS OF DON JUAN (Hywel/John McCabe/Tom O'Neill)
THE SOLDIER'S TALE (Meyer/Stravinsky)
Also in repertory during the year:
THE WANDERER AND HIS SHADOW (Jonathan Thorpe/Brahms),
TCHAIKOVSKY SUITE (Simon Mottram/Tchaikovsky), HOOPS (Walter
Gore/Poulenc), QUARTET (Thorpe/Beethoven), PETER AND THE WOLF
(Staff/Prokofiev), CINDERELLA (Meyer/Robert Stewart/Michael Holt),
VALSE TRISTE (Meyer/Sibelius), GAMES FOR FIVE PLAYERS (Chesworth/
Takemitsu)

Visiting companies:
*Alvin Ailey American Dance Theatre; Georgian State Dance Company;
Ballet Gulbenkian (Lisbon); Ballet Folklorico de Mexico; Bayanihan
Dance Company of the Philippines; Umewaka Noh Troupe; Chinese
Acrobatic Theatre; Australian Ballet; International Ballet Caravan;
Hungarian State Ballet in* SPARTACUS *(Budapest); Black Theatre of
Prague; Pilobolus Dance Theatre (Vermont); Ballet-Théâtre Contemporain
(Anger); Dutch National Ballet; Royal Danish Ballet; Ramon Villar
Spanish Dance Theatre; Paul Taylor Dance Company; Jeux et masques;
Ballet Gallego; Nigerian Dance Troupe; Bulgarian State Dance Company;
Netherlands Dance Theatre.*

Theatre Honours and Awards 1973–74

Birthday Honours 1973:
KNIGHTHOOD: Peter Daubeny
CBE: Anthony Dowell, Ivor Newton, Antoinette Sibley, Rudolph Schwartz
MBE: John Chilvers, Otakar Kraus

New Year Honours 1974:
KNIGHTHOOD: Emile Littler
CBE: Stuart Burge, Constance Cummings, John Dankworth, Myers Foggin, Charles Mackerras, Dilys Powell

Plays & Players *1973 London Drama Critics' Awards:*
Best Play: SAVAGES/SIZWE BANSI IS DEAD; *Best Musical:* THE ROCKY HORROR SHOW; *Best Actor:* Nicol Williamson (CORIOLANUS); *Best Actress:* Angela Lansbury (GYPSY); *Best Supporting Actor:* Frank Grimes (THE FARM); *Best Supporting Actress:* Frances de la Tour (SMALL CRAFT WARNINGS); *Most Promising Actor:* Peter Firth (EQUUS); *Most Promising Actress:* Mary Sheen (THE MOTHER); *Best Director:* John Dexter (THE MISANTHROPE); *Best Designer:* Tanya Moiseiwitsch (THE MISANTHROPE).

Evening Standard 1973 Drama Awards:
Best Play: SATURDAY SUNDAY MONDAY; *Best Musical:* THE ROCKY HORROR SHOW; *Best Actor:* Alec McCowen; *Best Actress:* Janet Suzman; *Best Comedy:* ABSURD PERSON SINGULAR; *Most Promising Playwright:* David Williamson; *Opera Award:* Reginald Goodall; *Ballet Award:* Christopher Bruce; *Special Award:* Laurence Olivier.

Variety Club Stage Awards:
Best Actor: Alastair Sim (DANDY DICK); *Best Actress:* Wendy Hiller (CROWN MATRIMONIAL); *Best Playwright:* William Douglas Home; *Special Award:* Evelyn Laye.

1973 Shakespeare Prize: Peter Brook.

USA:
Tony Awards 1973:
Best Play: THAT CHAMPIONSHIP SEASON; *Best Musical:* A LITTLE NIGHT MUSIC; *Best Director/Choreographer:* Bob Fosse; *Special Award:* John Lindsay.

Time Magazine Top Ten 1973:
THE RIVER NIGER; EL GRANDE DE COCA-COLA; MEDEA; WELCOME TO ANDROMEDA; A LITTLE NIGHT MUSIC; UNCLE VANYA; NICOL WILLIAMSON'S LATE SHOW; THE CONTRACTOR; BOOM BOOM ROOM; GOOD EVENING.

Norman Allin, *Bass* (88)
John Armstrong, *Designer* (79)
Stuart Bacon, *General Manager,*
  Sydney Opera House (67)
Rodney Barrie, *Actor* (78)
James Beck, *Actor*
Guy Beckett, *Actor* (78)
S. N. Behrman, *Playwright* (80)
Robert Bernal, *Actor* (49)
Sidney Blackmer, *Actor* (78)
Gordon Blyth, *Actor* (85)
Fanny Bradshaw, *Teacher* (76)
Owen Brannigan, *Bass* (65)
Joe E. Brown, *Comedian* (81)
Barbara Bruce, *Actress*
Charles Buckmaster, *Actor/*
  Manager (83)
Ken Calder, *Designer* (44)
Vivienne Chatterton, *Actress*
Jimmy Clitheroe, *Comedian*
Elsie Codner, *Wardrobe Mistress*
  (75)
Peter Collins, *Musical Director*
Melville Cooper, *Actor* (76)
John Cranko, *Choreographer* (45)
George Cudden, *Playwright* (69)
Gareth Davies, *Musical Director*
  (41)
Stringer Davis, *Actor* (75)
Roger Delgado, *Actor* (55)
Astra Desmond, *Contralto* (80)
Joe Dockery, *Stage Doorkeeper, St*
  Martin's (98)
Wallace Evennett, *Actor* (84)
Lance Fairfax, *Actor* (73)
Betty Field, *Actress* (55)
Iris Fraser Foss, *Actress* (80)
David Franklin, *Broadcaster* (65)
Rollo Gamble, *Actor/Director* (63)
George Geddes, *Chairman, Dundee*
  Rep. (68)
James Gibson, *Actor* (79)
Betty Grable, *Actress* (56)
Herbert Graf, *Producer*

Gladys Henson, *Actress* (89)
George Harding, *Stage Doorkeeper,*
  Strand
Laurence Harvey, *Actor* (46)
Elisabeth Hauptmann (75)
Jack Hawkins, *Actor* (62)
Sessue Hayakawa, *Actor*
John Healy, *Wardrobe Master*
William Inge, *Playwright* (60)
Ronald Jeans, *Lyricist* (86)
Ursula Jeans, *Actress* (66)
Sean Kenny, *Designer* (40)
Harold de Kinton, *Actor* (98)
John Kirby, *Actor* (41)
Veronica Lake, *Actress* (53)
Benn Levy, *Playwright*
Muriel Lillie, *Revue Writer*
Prince Littler, *Impresario* (72)
Victor Lorraine, *Actor* (86)
Polly Luce, *Actress* (68)
Anna Magnani, *Actress* (65)
Gilbert Martin, *Tenor* (73)
Dorothy Mather, *Agent*
Bert Mayers, *Costumier*
Tony Mercer, *Singer*
Mary Merrall, *Actress* (80)
Guy Middleton, *Actor* (65)
Nancy Mitford, *Adaptor/Novelist*
  (68)
Ursula Moreton, *Ballerina* (70)
Nora Nicholson, *Actress* (83)
Lord Nugent, *Comptroller, Lord*
  Chamberlain's Dept. (77)
William Parker, *Playwright* (60)
Carl Paulsen, *Manager* (47)
Donald Peers, *Singer*
Dennis Price, *Actor* (58)
John Pritchett, *Musical Director*
Henzie Raeburn, *Actress* (72)
Gabrielle Ray, *Actress* (90)
James Verner Reed, *Founder,*
  Stratford Connecticut (71)
Barry Richardson, *Chief*
  Electrician

François Rosay, *Actress* (82)
Percy Rowland, *Actor* (78)
Robert Ryan, *Actor* (59)
Clothilde Sakharoff, *Dancer* (80)
Lucien Samett, *Producer* (82)
Diana Sands, *Actress* (39)
Dora Scott, *Actress* (95)
Carlos Selvagem, *Playwright* (60)
Jean-Marie Serreau, *Director* (58)
James Sherwood, *Manager* (79)
Dorinea Shirley, *Actress* (74)
Lydia Sokolova, *Ballerina* (77)
Jim Stack, *Actor*
G. B. Stern, *Playwright*

Nancye Stewart, *Actress* (80)
Walter Swash, *Actor* (77)
Alla Tarasova, *Actress* (75)
Cissie Thornton, *Wardrobe Mistress*
Ernest Truex, *Actor* (83)
Alan Tucker, *Publicist* (55)
Binda Tuke, *Ballerina*
Eric Warren, *Actor* (64)
Kenneth J. Warren, *Actor* (43)
Jimmy Wheeler, *Comedian*
Meadows White, *Actor* (72)
Paul Whitsun Jones, *Actor*
George Woodbridge, *Actor* (66)

Index

Compiled by F. D. Buck

Numbers and letters in italics refer to illustrations